JEWISH LITERATURE AND CULTURE

Series editor, Alvin H. Rosenfeld

AHARON APPELFELD
The Holocaust and Beyond

Gila Ramras-Rauch

Indiana University Press

Bloomington and Indianapolis

Stephen Mitchell's translation of Dan Pagis's "Written in the
Sealed Railway-Car" is from Dan Pagis, *Points of Departure* (Philadelphia:
Jewish Publication Society of America, 1981) and appears here by
permission of the publisher.

© 1994 by Gila Ramras-Rauch

The paper used in this publication meets the minimum requirements of
American National Standard for Information Sciences—Permanence of
Paper for Printed Library Materials, ANSI Z39.48-1984.

Manufactured in the United States of America
⊗™

Library of Congress Cataloging–in-Publication Data

Ramraz-Ra'ukh, Gilah.
Aharon Appelfeld : the Holocaust and beyond / Gila Ramras-Rauch.
p. cm. — (Jewish literature and culture)
Includes bibliographical references and index.
ISBN 0–253–34831–5
1. Appelfeld, Aron—Criticism and interpretation. 2. Holocaust, Jewish
(1939–1945), in literature. I. Title. II. Series.
PJ5054.A755Z84   1994

892. 4'36—dc20   93–5016

1 2 3 4 5 99 98 97 96 95 94

Written in Pencil
in the Sealed Railway-Car

here in this carload
i am eve
with abel my son
if you see my other son
cain son of man
tell him that i

Dan Pagis

CONTENTS

Contents

PREFACE

I MET AHARON APPELFELD in the early 1980s at a midwestern university where I was teaching. He had come to give a lecture. Walking through the campus, we struck up a conversation about Bukovina. I told him my mother was born not far from Czernowitz. When he asked for the name of the town, I replied, "Jadova." He stopped and exclaimed, "I was born there!"

The Hebrew poet Saul Tchernichovsky once remarked that a person is the image of the landscape of his or her childhood. In addition, we are the continuation and permutations of our parents. My parents emigrated to Israel as young pioneers. Most of my father's family perished in the Holocaust, as did part of my mother's family. My curiosity and pain never ceased—the loss of family, memories erased, stories left untold and unheard, homes unvisited. My entrance into the world of my mother and father came by way of literature, the repository of a world that no longer exists. For this reason my hunger for a story never ceases. Miraculously, through the verbal path paved by one individual, we connect with past reality through fiction.

This book is about Aharon Appelfeld's fiction, from his first collection of stories, *Ashan* (Smoke, 1962), to the novel *Mesilat Barzel* (The railway, 1991). I consider his complete body of work, both his novels and his five collections of short stories, most of the latter not translated into English. (Some stories from the early collections have appeared in various English-language periodicals.)

From thematic, aesthetic, and developmental points of view, it was of vital importance to take into account the complete body of Appelfeld's fiction, not just the novels that are available in English. Although I had been tempted to write a comparative study of the literature of the Holocaust, I chose instead to focus on one writer, his narrative technique, and the ethical and existential problems that emerge from his texts.

Aharon Appelfeld himself was generous with his time; our conversations contributed greatly to the book. The Jewish Memorial Fund and the Lucius Littauer Fund were generous in their grants; I am grateful to both these sources. My thanks go also to the Genazim Institute in Tel Aviv, to Mr. Dov Ben Ya'akov, its director, and to Dvora Stavi. The Hebrew College Library was extremely helpful, as always; my special thanks go to Dr. Murray Tuchman and to Harvey Sukenik.

My son Michael Rauch acted as my literary adviser and gave sound suggestions for the structure of the text; my son Daniel Rauch lent his spiritual support. To my husband, Professor Leo Rauch, who was there at the inception of the book and saw it to its completion, my love and my thanks.

I.

APPELFELD, HIS TIME
AND ART

I

BIOGRAPHY

Bukovina lies between the East Carpathian Mountains and the upper Dniester River. The region was part of Ottoman Moldavia until 1775, then passed to the Austro-Hungarian Empire, which ruled it until 1918. The capital of Bukovina is Chernovtsy (German, Czernowitz; Romanian, Cernauti). Jews settled in Bukovina from the fourteenth century on. In 1408 they were granted freedom of movement along the Moldavian trade routes. In the course of the fifteenth century, Sephardic as well as Ashkenazi Jews settled in the capital and surrounding communities.

Over the years the Jewish population of Bukovina increased. Jews were mostly involved in transit trade and the purveying of alcoholic beverages. Into the mid–nineteenth century, Bukovina Jewry included a Sephardic element. The Ashkenazi character of the community asserted itself with the growth of a Polish-Jewish population at the end of the seventeenth century. Yiddish became the language of Bukovina Jewry. Early in the nineteenth century, Hassidism was established in Bukovina by two major dynasties: the Ruzhin dynasty, which settled in Sadigora, and the Kossow dynasty, which settled in Vizhnitsa. Simultaneously, Bukovina Jews were part of the Hebrew Enlightenment movement (Haskala), seeking secular education and a Westernized way of life.

The works of Aharon Appelfeld reflect the multicultural nature of Bukovina, his homeland, and especially of Czernowitz, where intellectual life comprised a unique mixture of East and West. The German, Austrian, Ruthenian, Ukrainian, Romanian, and Jewish populations made Czernowitz a commercial and intellectual center. Judaism itself was represented in Bukovina by assimilated Jews, Zionists, observant Jews, and the Hassidim. This ethnic variety fascinated Appelfeld, who has drawn on it in many of his narratives. Beyond the prevalent Jewish themes, Appelfeld depicts the life of the typical Ruthenian village. Also figuring in his work is the cultural German influence in Buko-

3

vina, especially in Czernowitz. Czernowitz was the birthplace of important writers in Hebrew, Yiddish, and German, among them Itzik Manger, Rosa Auslander, and two poets who are close to Appelfeld in mood and tone, Paul Celan (born Paul Anchel, 1920–1970) and Dan Pagis (1930–1986).

The relatively tolerant rule of the Emperor Franz Joseph (1848–1918) was welcomed by the Jews of the Empire, especially by those of Bukovina. By 1890 there were approximately ninety thousand Jews in the region. In 1918 Bukovina was incorporated into Romania, together with the provinces of Bessarabia, Dobrogea, and Transylvania. A prewar nation-state, Romania became a multinational and multicultural country. Anti-Semitism had been a deep-rooted phenomenon in Romania since the nineteenth century and probably earlier. The historian Ezra Mendelsohn states:

> opposition to foreign domination of Romanian life, real or imagined, played a large role in the growth of Romanian nationalism, and since the Jews were almost invariably identified as foreigners, no matter how long they had lived in the country, Romanian nationalism was almost automatically anti-Semitic.[1]

Culturally, Czernowitz was a Germanized city, even though Germans did not constitute an ethnic majority in the province of Bukovina. Four German-language daily newspapers were published in Czernowitz during the 1930s. The city's popular cafés were named after Viennese cafés: Astoria, Europa. One of the city's large parks was named Schiller. At the University of Czernowitz courses were conducted in German well into the 1930s, with few exceptions. The Jews of Bukovina by and large did not adopt Romanian culture; rather, middle-class Jews identified with German culture and language.

In the 1930s two major complaints were voiced by anti-Semitic elements in Romania. The first was that in the nineteenth century the country had been invaded by Jews from Galicia. The second was that these Jews were pro-Soviet. Jews in Romania were considered "foreigners." As Mendelsohn stated in his book *The Jews of East Central Europe between the World Wars,*

> In Romania . . . as in Poland, the Jews were hated by the peasants for being symbols of wicked capitalist exploitation, and by the representatives of the "native" bourgeoisie for being obstacles to the formation of a Romanian commercial class. This hatred of the Jews fit well with the general hatred of foreigners so deeply embedded in Romanian consciousness.[2]

The Romanian nationalist idea of "through ourselves alone" excluded Germans, Hungarians, and Jews. And the notion that the Galician Jews "invaded" Romania in the nineteenth century and were pro-Soviet in the interwar period galvanized the deeply rooted anti-Semitism. Toward the end of the 1930s, Romanian Jews were being thought of as members of a separate race rather than of a religion, and on this false belief the possibility of their assimilation into Romanian life and culture was rejected; both practicing and baptized Jews suffered. Mendelsohn quotes a statement made by Corneliu Codreanu, a Romanian fascist leader, in an interview in 1938:

> The Jews, the Jews are our curse. They poison our state, our life, our people. They demoralize our nation. They destroy our youth. They are the archenemies. You talk of the Jewish problem; you are right. The Jews are our greatest problem, the most important, the most urgent, the most pressing problem of Romania. The Jews scheme and plot and plan to ruin our national life. We shall not allow this to happen. We, the Iron Guard, will stand in the way of such delivery. We shall destroy the Jews before they can destroy us. There are influences, important influences on the side of the Jews. We shall destroy them, too.[3]

Decrees in the 1930s forbade Jews to own property in Romanian villages. Jews also were ousted from the army and forbidden to publish newspapers. A *numerus clausus* limiting the number of Jewish students allowed in universities was imposed, along with other civil, political, and economic restrictions. Attempts were also made to suppress German culture.

It was into this environment that Appelfeld was born, in Jadova, Bukovina, on February 16, 1932, an only child. His semiassimilated family was residing permanently in Czernowitz. Both his grandfathers were Hassidic Jews; one was a Sadigora Hassid, the other a Vishnitzer. His first language was German, but he heard Yiddish spoken at the home of his grandparents and later in the camps.

In the summer of 1941 Appelfeld went to visit his maternal grandmother in the village of Drogobycz, where his father, who sold machinery for mills, owned property. Appelfeld recalls that while at his grandmother's house he became ill with the mumps. One day, as his parents and grandmother were sitting in the garden, a shot rang out; the Germans, accompanied by Romanian collaborators, had begun the destruction of the Jewish population in Bukovina and Bessarabia. His mother and grandmother were killed in the garden; his father managed to escape to a nearby cornfield, where Aharon, then known as Irwin, joined him. Later that year, father and son were separated and did not see each other again until they were reunited in Israel after the end of the Second World War.

As a result of a Russian ultimatum in 1940, Romania had been forced to return Bessarabia to Russia. Before the beginning of the war in the East on June 21, 1941, Jews had been evacuated from villages and hamlets between the rivers Prut and Siret. Bukovina had been attacked and conquered by German and Romanian armies on June 3. In the following days, Jews who supposedly supported the Soviet regime were massacred; Jadova's Jews were killed on July 4, 5, and 6. Czernowitz was taken over by combined German and Romanian forces. On July 10 the province of Bukovina was annexed to Romania. A special department for "Romanization" was, in effect, appropriating all Jewish property. Synagogues were closed; all gatherings for the purpose of prayer were forbidden, and from the 30th of July, Jews were required to wear the yellow star. On August 4 the first attempt was made to expel the Jews of Bukovina to Trans-Dniestria, a part of Soviet Ukraine conquered by Romania during the war.

A ghetto was set up in Czernowitz on October 11, and forty thousand Jews were deported from there; another thirty-five thousand were sent to death camps in Trans-Dniestria. Appelfeld and his father were expelled to Trans-Dniestria. From there the next stop was concentration and labor camps. In all, 400,000 Jews were killed in Romania by Germans, Hungarians, and Romanians.

Appelfeld wrote about the wartime experience for the first time in his 1991 novel, *Mesilat Barzel*. He recalls the trek of the Jews who were rounded up and sent on their way to Ukraine. They walked from town to town, from village to village, all of which were deserted. Many of the houses, clearly Jewish homes, were without doors or windows, and Hebrew books were scattered about on the floors. The walk lasted for months. The captors would make the Jews run; those who fell from exhaustion were left to die by the wayside. Others died of hunger and illness. When Appelfeld and his father reached Ukraine, it was winter. In Mogilev Podolski, men and women were separated, and the men were taken to labor camps. It was there that Appelfeld and his father were parted.

A short blond boy, Appelfeld was hardly noticed. His looks helped, as did the fact that he spoke Ukrainian, the language of the maids in his home. According to him, a combination of luck, chance, and will contributed to his survival. He began wandering alone from village to village. Typically, the richest peasants lived in the center of the villages; they were not about to take in a strange boy, let alone a Jewish one. On the village outskirts, however, lived marginal populations of prostitutes and horse thieves, and some of them needed servants. His rule was not to stay in any one place for very long. He saw the deep-rooted anti-Semitism, and he was careful.

In 1944 the Russian army entered Ukrainian villages, and Appelfeld joined the soldiers as a kitchen aide. He stayed with the mobile army for a year. As the unit advanced toward Bukovina and Romania, Appelfeld and eight other boys attached to the Russian units decided to escape. They made their way to Yugoslavia, where they subsisted by stealing. From there they proceeded to Italy. Near Naples they encountered a monk, who took them in. For the first time in years they had sufficient food and rest. They were taught Italian and French. Appelfeld is certain that an attempt was made to convert the boys to Catholicism. Strangely, despite the calm and rest, this experience too became a nightmare. Near the monastery the boys met a soldier from the Palestine Jewish Brigade. In Naples they encountered throngs of displaced persons.

On the Italian shores Appelfeld and other survivors of the wartime atrocities were given both space and time, seemingly allowing for a new process of individuation. But, as Appelfeld points out in *Massot Be'guf Rishon* (Essays in first person, 1979), it was time for a great escape. That meant a variety of things to the survivors: some went readily into commerce; some were involved in shady deals; some embraced middle-class ways of life. There were prophets and soothsayers; there were persons who hoarded food. One group refused to settle down in the huts provided by the allies but embraced a life of retreat and abstinence, moving from place to place, doing seasonal manual work in the villages and silently meditating.

In 1946, aboard the ship *Hagana*, Appelfeld reached Palestine, where British authorities imprisoned illegal refugees in a camp in Atlit, near Haifa. Appelfeld spent a winter there. Members of an underground group called Hagana taught him Hebrew. Nevertheless, this experience was a continuation of life in a camp. At the end of 1946 Appelfeld and other boys were taken to an experimental agricultural school in Jerusalem, Havat Ha'Limmud al yad Armon Hanaziv, run by Rachel

Ya'na'it, one of the founding mothers of early settlement in Palestine and the wife of Yitzhak Ben-Tzvi, the second president of Israel. Life there was a combination of study and labor. Hebrew was taught for two hours daily, and there was agricultural work for four to five hours. Appelfeld tells of his love for reading. Since he had not had a formal education, he would sneak out to the Hebrew University on Mount Scopus and read whatever he could find there. Despite his limited knowledge of Hebrew, German, and Yiddish, he attributes his intellectual coming-of-age to his intense reading. Appelfeld remained in this educational settlement until 1948. During the 1948 war the students were temporarily moved to the western part of Jerusalem, Ein Kerem, and later to Mikve Yisrael, the first agricultural school in Palestine.

After holding numerous odd jobs, Appelfeld was conscripted into the Israeli army in 1950. During his two years in the army he was assigned to various support services, since he had little military experience. During these years of mass immigration following the establishment of Israel, many young newcomers did not fit easily into Israeli life and were relegated to service jobs.

Appelfeld has related what he calls his Cinderella story. One day the camp commander and his deputy were playing chess in the dining hall while Appelfeld was cleaning the tables. He had been a good chess player since childhood, and his father had been chess champion in Vienna. The deputy was called away for duty. Appelfeld offered to continue the game, and eventually he managed to beat all contenders. That aroused the interest of the commander, who called him in and asked about his background. Appelfeld expressed a desire to study and to receive a high school diploma, and his wish was granted. For Appelfeld this was a hard, tense period. The final examinations required difficult intellectual efforts in English, Bible, Biblical interpretation, Talmud, physics, and math.[4]

Appelfeld tells of the sense of uprootedness that young boys and girls experienced upon arrival in Israel. The process of replanting oneself in a new place, he notes, always includes an element of artificiality, and the pain of the severed roots forever accompanies the uprooted person. He questions the validity of the term *acclimatization*. According to Appelfeld, various factors were at work when his group arrived in Israel. The country then had a population of 650,000; only a few years later, it was filled to overflowing with refugees from all parts of the world who brought their harsh experiences with them. Thus the country consisted of a sparse local population and people who came from "there." (As Appelfeld sees it, the fusion of the two populations has not yet been completed.) Individual fates were both strange and difficult, involving in most cases a load of private guilt. Most refugees acquired some basic Hebrew, although many, Appelfeld feels, were unable to express their inner life. Although it seems that a great deal of "expressing" goes on in Israel, he says, there is much emotion that has not yet found an outlet. His novel *Michvat Ha'or* (The searing light, 1980) reflects the anguish of the newcomers.

Appelfeld refers to the multiplicity of cultures that gathered in Israel. Some émigrés came from a culture of civilized talk, some from a culture where shouting was the prevailing mode of expression; some came from a tradition where every child is expected to complete his or her university studies, others from a culture that did not send its children to school. The relationship of Israeli Jews to their Judaism is dialectical, Appelfeld believes; they wish both to be connected to their past and to sever their connections to the past.

To Appelfeld the child, Judaism was merely a biological fact. As an adult he adopted the spiritual dimension of Judaism and its intellectual rigor. The time he relates to is Jewish time, and Jewish time is occasionally depicted as synoptic time, in which the Jewish experience is revealed through historical archetypes. Appelfeld claims that he does not write about the Holocaust but deals in people, especially in writing about himself. Through his writing he tries to make contact with what might be called the personal and national unconscious, to achieve through the prism of language a fictional self-exposure.

Appelfeld speaks of his deliberate decison to enter the Hebrew University to study Yiddish literature, which he regarded as a special vehicle into his past and himself. He also decided to reside in the Orthodox quarter of Jerusalem, Mea Shearim. For eight years he pursued his studies at the university as a way of overcoming his cultural disorientation. It was a period of deep personal crisis, his "dark days," during which he apparently repressed much of what he had undergone in the Holocaust years.[5]

At the university he met a group of Jewish intellectuals from Germany and central Europe, including Martin Buber, Max Brod, Gershom Scholem, and Dov Sadan. In various interviews he speaks of having studied under Buber and Scholem—his first real schooling. A number of these intellectuals had been personal friends of Franz Kafka

—Brod was also his biographer—and in time Kafka and his writings exerted a major influence on Appelfeld. As for Buber's influence, Appelfeld states:

> What Buber did for the German Jews he also did for the Israelis. He gave us a new perspective for today. Coming, as I did, from a very assimilated home, my early view of Judaism reflected all the old antagonisms. But suddenly Buber and Scholem opened new gates for me. It was a new life. All the good things we had been led to believe existed only in Socialism and in Marxism . . . we found to exist in our own tradition and at a more refined, civilized level. I came to realize that Judaism was not an archaic, primitive religion but a living religion of the highest level. It brought me back to myself and to my people.[6]

The works of the Hebrew writers he studied at the university, such as Bialik, Brenner, and Agnon, also left their mark on Appelfeld. So did the Yiddishist Leib Rochman, who was a close friend and mentor.

Appelfeld managed to combine the influence of Hebrew and Yiddish, Bible and Kabbala; all contributed to shaping his perception, style, role and point of view. As he told me, he had neither a native language nor a native soil at that time; he did not know who he was. He was introduced to himself through writing; writing "made" him. He compared himself to a man digging a tunnel who, through the process of digging, reveals interesting finds. The process of self-revelation was combined with the emergence of a personal voice. His deep realization is that despite a desire to forget, he is somehow "compelled" to remember a childhood he had not experienced on the banks of the Prut. A dialectical tension continues between the desire to remember and the desire to forget, as well as between the desire to reveal and the desire to conceal.

In the early 1950s Appelfeld published poetry in the periodical *Ba-Ma'ale*. He admits that he wrote his "adolescent" poetry when he was in his early twenties. As for his fiction, he has suggested that the fact that his early stories were not centered on a specific time or place reflects his own state.

Since the early 1970s his fiction has been more centered on places and more defined by time. Moreover, his transition from the short story form to the novella and novel marks his further capacity to focus on time and place. Questioned about his sense of belonging, he replied that he is a Jew, an Israeli patriot, an apolitical man for whom everything Jewish is close to his heart; from the Lubavich Hassid to the ardent Communist Jew, he embraces the totality of Jewish existence.

In 1989 in Jerusalem, he told me that a writer needs a homeland, and "homeland" for him means the first formative experience in life: the first trees one observes, the first snow. For him the microcosmic homeland is Jadova and Czernowitz. He admits that he found another "homeland" after many years in Israel and in his writing. It was a great challenge for him to find a language for his characters—people who did not speak Hebrew.

In interview after interview, Appelfeld has reiterated the enormous importance of writing to his very being. In a talk with Philip Roth, Appelfeld said:

> At first I tried to run away from myself and from my memories, to live a life that was not my own. But a hidden feeling told me that I was not allowed to flee from myself, and that if I denied the experience of my childhood in the Holocaust, I would be spiritually deformed. Only when I reached the age of thirty did I feel the freedom to deal as an artist with those experiences.[7]

Appelfeld belongs to the Statehood Generation in Israeli literature, the generation that came of age in the second decade of statehood, in the 1960s. Nonetheless, he has made a conscious attempt to be a Jewish writer rather than a strictly Israeli writer. His need to identify with the world of the lost Jewish past is uppermost. Yet his reconstruction of the past is not based on personal memories; he is set on creating nothing less than a Jewish imaginative universe.

He has chosen a personal, ahistorical route. In the absence of "pure" memory, he reconstructs a map of charted and uncharted Jewish "terrain." His map of Europe is a Jewish map whose boundaries are not clearly defined, since it is a thematic rather than a demographic map. He tests and challenges the various options Judaism had in the nineteenth and twentieth centuries: communism, socialism, Zionism, the Bund, the ideology of assimilation, enlightenment, and conversion. He believes that assimilation, as a phenomenon, has been the most persistent feature of modern Jewish existence, having produced figures such as Freud, Kafka, and Einstein. For him, universalism and Judaism are closely connected. As he states in "After the Holocaust,"

> The survivors' testimony is first of all a search for relief: and as with any burden, the one who bears it seeks also to rid himself of it as

hastily as possible. . . . Agonies of guilt, sometimes alternating with reproaches against the heavens, show up in almost all the testimony, but they are only marginal signs and not the essence of the writing, which is, as I said, in relief.

To avoid misunderstanding, I shall immediately add that the literature of testimony is undoubtedly the authentic literature of the Holocaust. It is an enormous reservoir of Jewish chronology, but it embodies too many inner constraints to become literature as that concept has taken shape over the generations.[8]

Jadova, Czernowitz, and Jerusalem are departure points for many of Appelfeld's literary excursions. They appear in a variety of guises, as Badenheim and other places. Appelfeld's house of fiction is uniquely his. Painstakingly, he continues to build various parts of this edifice. His modest intention in the 1960s probably was to exorcise the haunting ghosts of the past. In the 1980s he declared his desire to reconstruct a hundred years of Jewish suffering and isolation. His work is almost archaeological; carefully he pieces together a verbal entity. He submerges himself into it and then reemerges. His narratives are short and do not aspire to depict a totality of experience. Occasionally the distinction between novella and novel is blurred. Yet together his fictions form an extended saga, a Jewish map. Tragically, his Jewish map often depicts alienated Jews outside the Jewish calendar. His stories are parables of a disrupted life. He does not write systematically. He moves freely from one period to another, from one milieu to another, from one style to another. One systematic element is the gradual process of his own opening up, of trying, against strong inhibitions, to give voice to his personal experiences. Until the 1990s he consciously avoided his personal story.

Appelfeld has lived in or near Jerusalem since his arrival in Israel. He is the father of three children; his wife, a teacher, was born in Argentina. Israel remains a laboratory, and Appelfeld continues to "observe" in it. His house is close to a center for new émigrés, and he talks about his conversations with the newcomers, to whom he feels a close affinity. He also has a subdued fascination with the usual metamorphosis to be observed. Most of these people will never feature in his fiction, yet his role as observer—a Jewish writer who lives in Israel and writes in Hebrew—is justified by Jewish history and Jewish geography.

2

AESTHETICS AND NARRATIVE

The restoration of memory through language allows for a modicum of re-creation. Hebrew literature has always been rich in accounts of catastrophe and lamentation—going back to the fifth century B.C.E. and continuing through the twentieth century, from the mourning of David over the death of Saul and Jonathan to H. N. Bialik's "On the Slaughter" and Uri Zvi Greenberg's "The Amputated Wing." Sacred texts—from the Bible through the Talmud and Midrash—form a continuous literature that has canonized the verbal memory of the people. It is a national code, a history rife with persecution and destruction reinforced by repetitious historical patterns, that has created a literature of *Hurban* (destruction). The collective memory is intertwined with the personal. This concept, both historical and ahistorical, was emphasized when (according to Jewish tradition) both the First and the Second Temples were destroyed. Events moored in history entered a metahistorical heritage of a continuous presence of past events. Jewish history is studded with words and names serving as markers and signs that continue to carry meaning despite elapsed time: Amalek, Babylonia, Massada, Chmielnitzky, Auschwitz. Thus the collective memory and personal response coalesce into a totality, making the past not a cold historical fact but a vital, ever-present experience.

This synoptic view creates what Harold Fisch calls historical archetypes. All this assumes a collective cultural consciousness that can be evoked by a text or by the word *zachor* (remember). Among the Hebrew writers who relate to catastrophe and the Holocaust in the twentieth century, Aharon Appelfeld is one of the few who does not join (either through allusion or style) the millennia-old literature of destruction. Perennial reverberative themes such as the Akeda (the binding of Isaac) and Kiddush Ha'Shem (the sanctification of the holy name by self-inflicted death in preference to committing transgression) are not found in his fiction.

As a young man, Appelfeld was preoccupied with his search for language and the process of reindividuation; Israel and the Hebrew language were presences with which he had to grapple. (To this day he remains a cautious person. None of the typical Israeli bravura, so prominent among others of his age group when he came to Israel, stuck to him.) He went through a reconstruction of the self in which acquisition of a new language was the greatest challenge. He has often noted that many of the people with whom he shared his deepest experiences and who also found refuge in Israel acquired their capacity to read Hebrew from the daily newspaper and cannot read his fiction; this linguistic handicap barred them from coming to terms with their own being and their own past. Appelfeld consciously individuated himself through writing, through a struggle to find a voice. One must bear in mind that this is not a phenomenon unique to Israel. Many of the writers of the Statehood Generation were not born in Palestine or Israel but went there after the war. Nonetheless, they adopted the Israeli experience in one way or another and became strictly "Israeli writers."

Appelfeld did not adopt a literary style that was rife with Biblical, Mishnaic, or Aggadic allusions. The great masters of modern Hebrew literature—Abramovitz (whose pen name is Mendele Mocher Sforim), Bialik, Agnon—created a style that eventually became the infrastructure of modern Hebrew fiction and poetry. It is important to note that modern Hebrew literature developed in Europe with no spoken vernacular to support it; its growth from a pseudo-euphemistic style in the mid–nineteenth century (for example, Abraham Mapu's *Ahavat Zion* [The love of Zion], 1853) to a distinctly modern style has made Hebrew a vehicle for expressing contemporary experience. The infrastructure for Hebrew and Yiddish literature was established between the 1880s and the second decade of the twentieth century. Thus the idiom of the period, the ethos and the Zeitgeist, were expressed in Hebrew. Modern sensibility in fiction and poetry was made possible by a handful of men and women who advanced the Hebrew language from a religious function to one of contemporary secular expression. The personal idiom and the personal signature returned to secular Hebrew literature through the molding of rabbinic, Biblical, and contemporary layers of language. The establishment of the verbal-literary convention was challenged by modern writers such as Gnessin and Vogel, who in turn influenced Appelfeld. Within less than a century an incomparable transition occurred in the Hebrew language, turning it from a lame instrument ill suited for modern expression into a vehicle of great sophistication. To writers it has been a task and a challenge to fashion their world in Hebrew.

This task is difficult for native Hebrew writers because of the richness opened to them; from the Bible to medieval Hebrew poetry, the language is comprehensible and accessible, resisting the temptation to use a higher level of expression that challenges the modern writer. Appelfeld too has resisted this temptation—to enrich his language with canonic allusions. He does not rely on intertextuality or on the creation of new words. In a conversation in Jerusalem he told me that he prefers the short Biblical sentence, a functional sentence without allusions. To him, the most beautiful thing in the Bible is the silence between the verses. He believes that language is not a value unto itself but a functional instrument. He talked about the writer's vocabulary and mentioned a few words that he would never use.

As for the general tenor of his fiction, Appelfeld has stated:

> My stories are not sensational. Many of them lack a plot. I tend to minimize and reduce rather than exaggerate things. I cannot offer anything titillating, shocking, or extravagant. Art usually attempts to accentuate and dramatize the facts of life as much as possible. I go in the opposite direction.[1]

A master stylist, Appelfeld aspires to clarity of expression through an attempt to reach a musical balance. While every contemporary Hebrew writer is trying to find a style, an idiom, Appelfeld's decision to create a world that exists only in the imaginative mind and to present this timeless world in the Hebrew language took great daring. The absence of dialogue in his early stories is one indication of the struggle he went through. He opted for a metaphoric language, using impressionistic techniques rather than the classical model of narrative. Philip Roth has reflected on the unique nature of Appelfeld's fiction:

> His literary subject is not the Holocaust . . . or even Jewish persecution. Nor, to my mind, is what he writes simply Jewish fiction or, for that matter, Israeli fiction. Nor, since he is a Jewish citizen of a Jewish state composed largely of immigrants, is his an exile's fiction. And despite the European locale of many of his novels and the echoes of Kafka, these books written in the Hebrew language certainly are not. Indeed, all that Appelfeld is not adds up to what he is, and that is a dislocated writer, a deported writer, a dispossessed and uprooted writer.[2]

Appelfeld spoke to Roth about his credo as a creative writer. It is linked to his novel *Tzili*, a description of the life of a young female survivor whose existence among European peasants was not dissimilar to Appelfeld's own experience. Appelfeld stated:

> I tried several times to write "the story of my life" in the woods after I ran away from the camp. But all my efforts were in vain. I wanted to be faithful to the reality and to what really happened. But the chronicle that emerged proved to be a weak scaffolding. The result was rather meager, an unconvincing imaginary tale. The things that are most true are easily falsified. The reality of the Holocaust surpassed any imagination. Had I remained true to the facts, no one would have believed me. But the moment I chose a girl a little older than I was at that time, I removed "the story of my life" from the mighty grip of memory and gave it over to the creative laboratory. There memory is not the only proprietor. There one needs a causal explanation, a thread to tie things together. . . . I had to remove those parts which were unbelievable from "the story of my life" and present a more credible version.[3]

Appelfeld's seemingly nonautobiographical fiction was his hallmark from the very beginning. His tales are psychological parables without being emotive; he does not bring the reader to tears. He does not infuse his stories with colloquialisms. He is close in style and sensibility to Uri Nissan Gnessin (1879–1913), one of the masters of modernism in Hebrew literature. Gnessin had preceded European writers in introducing internal monologue and stream of consciousness. But Appelfeld's fiction does not dwell in the inner landscapes of his characters. Gnessin was a master of the "arrested mood." Movement, a moment, were arrested and captured in an impressionistic style.

For both Gnessin and Appelfeld, space is no mere backdrop. It engulfs the characters and frequently presses against their physical and mental being. The mature Gnessin was a model for Appelfeld: a highly selective fashioning both of exteriors and interiors. The attempt to find a verbal objective correlative to a split moment, one aim of Appelfeld's fiction, is entirely Gnessinian in nature. Like Gnessin, Appelfeld retells the life he lived (and did not live) in a mosaic of movement and arrested moments. And like Gnessin, Appelfeld is preoccupied with mood, atmosphere, and an attempt to seize the moment as a concrete entity. As Sidra Ezrahi writes,

> There is the quality of a primal struggle in Appelfeld's prose, a chiseling and shaping of language by a writer who encounters Hebrew unencumbered by layers of classical association; this struggle with the linguistic medium, which resists transposition into another idiom. . . . Some of the chisel-marks which show through the Hebrew

text, like Michelangelo's "Captive" sculptures, just barely emerging from, yet still imprisoned in the unhewn rock, have been polished over in the English version . . . [4]

Ezrahi points to writers who have clung either to a language (Celan, Nelly Sachs) or to a place. It is valuable to realize that most of the writers who emigrated to Palestine or Israel embraced Hebrew as a "new" language. Yet, as Ezrahi comments,

> Appelfeld stands out as one survivor writer for whom the Hebrew language seems to provide neither a bridge nor a window onto the past. In the land which was envisioned by prophets, poets, and philosophers as a haven for the dislocated soul of Israel, Appelfeld remains, in a fundamental, linguistic sense, in exile.[5]

One would think that Appelfeld, having been torn from both homeland and language, would have little chance of articulating his experiences through fiction. But, furnished with a fund of broken languages, Appelfeld was meant to be a writer. He now knows that silence can signify not only acquiescence but also strength. And if verbal expression reflects order, then silence might entail chaos. For his verbally impaired characters he creates a narrative space in which silence gains significance. Their fragmented relationship to objects and people is often shrouded in silence.

As noted, Appelfeld's search has been for both a language and an idiom—relinquishing the strictly descriptive mode, avoiding a mimetic treatment of past events, and obviating the need for an autobiographical persona. In seeking these ends there were difficulties. The first, of course, was to acquire a language, a goal that goes far beyond the mere need to break one's estrangement. The second was to find a personal voice but also to create a fictional universe to combat the tendency to talk about the known and the familiar. Alan Mintz has written:

> For Appelfeld as survivor, the Holocaust was the founding event of the self. It is the event which forms him, creating a world with its own conditions and its own laws. The survivor lives inside it. There is no distance to be overcome, and also no possibility of leaving. It was necessary to reach outside for something which the world of catastrophe lacked entirely: a language and a poetics.[6]

Appelfeld is one of the few writers centering on the Holocaust years who has a clear aesthetic credo. It has allowed him to expand his geographical and historical domain. He now speaks of his project of writing about "one hundred years of Jewish solitude." Presumably, such a fiction would show time and space as interconvertible; thus the intense horror of the Holocaust experience often warped the perceptions of time and space for those who suffered it. Without the familiar dimensions of objective and subjective time and space or of those dimensions as modified by the Holocaust experience, we may well ask what it is that denotes the "Holocaust writer." Appelfeld challenges the label:

> Mainly, I write Jewish stories, but I don't accept the label Holocaust writer. My themes are the uprooted, orphans, the war. I write about the Holocaust because I grew up in that time. Of my twenty books, perhaps one-third are on the Holocaust period, one-third on Israel and one-third on Jewish life in general. One of my interests is the Jewish intelligentsia, the Jews who lost their culture in Eastern Europe and became vulgarized. I am not a politically oriented writer. I have my say in fiction and I think I say a lot. I find that fiction is more permanent than other forms of writing. Literature is endangered when it becomes only a trumpet.[7]

Though Hebrew for Appelfeld is an acquired language, he is one of the foremost stylists among contemporary Hebrew writers. He also belongs to the line of Central European Jewish writers—Kafka, Bruno Schulz, and earlier writers of the Austro-Hungarian monarchy such as Svevo, Schnitzler, and Wassermann—but like Canetti and Wiesel, Appelfeld writes in a language other than that of his birthplace.

Appelfeld's fiction touches on two seemingly incompatible spheres. While historically he is in the tradition of the Central European Jewish writers, he also belongs to the postmodern, post–Second World War fiction generation as well as the Statehood Generation in Israeli literature.

In his postmodern fables he creates a limited and restricted universe for his characters to inhabit. Whether we find them ensconced in elegant resort towns or wandering over unidentifiable vistas as persecuted refugees, they move in a world that gains its raison d'être from their presence, their movement, their experience. His characters are fragmented and dislocated, though his fiction is not. He does not violate the rules of traditional syntax. Terms such as *meaninglessness*, *abyss*, and *void*, often used by postmodern writers, become the daily, often unexpressed experience of his characters. The unarticulated self bears an unspoken sense of horror. It is the very absence of the direct depiction of the Holocaust experience and its omnipresence that conveys the sense of horror. The human being as a "torn fabric" is depicted in highly metaphorical language, and that gives his fiction its power. The frequent omission of causal relationships between events, the technique of juxtaposition rather than comprehensible continuity, and the depiction of an almost "flat" character devoid of particular characterizations tie him to postmodern techniques.

That assertion must be treated carefully, however. Appelfeld's early characters consciously or unconsciously have severed their ties with their past and their memories. For these traumatized individuals there has occurred a basic dislocation of the self, the "I." Accordingly, the reader cannot at will paint the character with data unattached to the Holocaust. It is the stark drama of the suppression of memory and the prior self that allows a mode of survival and a limited mode of functioning in a post-Holocaust world. And thus the reader's task of filling in the gaps is extremely difficult for one who was not "there."

Appelfeld weaves highly sensitive tales about individuals in the pre- and post-Holocaust worlds. His characters have been affected by the Holocaust in a fundamental way: they are fragmented human beings, depleted and mute, roaming through his tangential and fantastic narratives in a state of quest. Appelfeld consciously suspends the framework of both the historical and the endured time of the Holocaust experience, to raise it to the plane of mythic narrative. Thus the Holocaust is for him an apocalyptic rupture in the very fabric of being. With the suspension of the temporal frame of reference there emerges the theme of a new Fall of Man. It is a fall wherein humanity has been stripped not only of its usual categories of understanding but even more profoundly of its accustomed self-image as human; the individual is thrust back into an elemental, precognitive state.

In Appelfeld's early narratives, the traumatized individual is rendered naked, as someone devoid of memory and desire. As both these faculties involve temporal and spatial parameters, the individual is deprived of all attachments to a past or a future, to a history or a continuous social structure. As a further result, time is divorced from selfhood itself—a connection of the most intimate sort under normal circumstances. Driven inward by the hostility of the external world, the individual would at least have had the temporal dimension of memory as the basis for self-identification; but even that is now suppressed.

This elemental individual defies historical time. Conventionally, he or she related to the seasons, to the changes in nature whose cyclical quality echoes his or her aversion to change, to novelty, or to any cumulative memory. On the other hand, the suffering itself—repeated and intensified as daily experience—does occur in a definite span of time. The clash, therefore, between time denied and time manifested has the effect of placing individuals in a (temporally) permanent situation wherein they themselves become "durations of uncertainty." Time and self have been severed by the unnamed horror of the outer world, and thus the individual retreats to an insular existence: to oblivion, inaccessibility, silence—all within an opaque and tenuous existence. All this, of course, has the makings of the fantastic in literature. In speaking of the fantastic as a literary category, the literary theorist Tzvetan Todorov has written:

> In a world which is indeed our world, the one we know, . . . there occurs an event which cannot be explained by the laws of this same familiar world. The person who experiences the event must opt for one of two possible solutions: either he is the victim of an illusion of the senses, or a product of the imagination—and the laws of the world then remain what they are; or else the event has indeed taken place, it is an integral part of reality—but then this reality is controlled by laws unknown to us. Either the devil is an illusion, an imaginary being; or else he really exists, precisely like other living beings. . . . the fantastic occupies the duration of this uncertainty.[8]

But how are today's readers to come to terms with Appelfeld's unique form of narrative? Can they achieve a similar "distance"? Here another question presents itself: can the literature of the Holocaust retreat into the fantastic? In regard to the literature of the fantastic, the suspension of disbelief is a matter of volition. In regard to the Holocaust, there is nothing volitional; just as we cannot suspend believing that its horrors happened, so no fictive suspension is applicable. Nothing here happened "once upon a time." Everything happened at a definite time and at a definite place. Nor is there a fictive refuge for the characters; the reality allowed no escape. Yet the writer of Holocaust literature can make use of the fantastic by transcending the flow of narrative and inserting a different reality within it, thereby suspending realistic time and placing within it a character of an insular type. Yet Appelfeld cannot ask for a suspension of disbelief directed at the impossible. On the contrary, the actualization of the inconceivable serves to dispel our hesitation between the real and the imaginary, in Todorov's terms.

In Appelfeld's fiction the fantastic is a quality of the individual, of the torn psyche. For this reason the fantastic is not a realm of myth for his characters; it does not belong to the imagination or the supernatural. Instead, the impossible has actually become possible. The "duration of uncertainty"—in the sense of having to choose disjunctively between the real and the imaginary (as the explanation of an event)—cannot be applied to the Holocaust. It is all too real, yet it cannot be explained by the laws pertaining to the familiar world. It is real but incomprehensible. The effect of this is shattering, and it is internalized by Appelfeld's characters. They therefore become "durations of uncertainty"—but in a new sense. There is an element of certainty here, inevitable as death, in connection with the impossible that has become a reality, an entire engulfing world. That world is a betrayal of the former one—and with the realization of that betrayal, the self turns back upon itself as an insular entity.

With the suspension of the consecutive unfolding of time, space gains a central importance in Appelfeld's fiction. The depiction of outwardly and inwardly passive individuals is enhanced by trying to encapsulate the solipsistic individual within an airless bubble.

Appelfeld's early characters do not regularly occupy a habitable space. As in a fairy tale, their "space" has been carved out for them, and it ceases to exist once we leave the purview of their house of fiction. As noted, Appelfeld has recognized that silence can signify not only acquiescence but also strength. And if verbal expression reflects an order, then silence would involve chaos. Thus he creates for his verbally impaired characters a narrative "space" where silence gains significance in light of the impending disaster. And from this we conclude that their relation to objects and people is also fragmented and partial, so that no character is given a complete or reconstructible past. The "space" of the past is related to the way one constructs—or reconstructs—objects and persons.

Often one of Appelfeld's characters relates to objects in such a way that the relation or object gives the character his or her tangible existence. Bertha, a character in an early short story, constantly knits, then unravels what she has knit, not wishing to introduce anything new into her existence: change prompts self-appraisal and the questioning of the present in such a way as to admit the full scope of horror.

In Appelfeld's world, clearly, there is no common space for reader and characters to share. The "space" in which the characters move is stylized. There is little or nothing of the familiar that might decrease the distance between narrator and reader. Instead, Appelfeld's aim is to "defamiliarize" and thus to expand the distance between reader and text. This defamiliarization is both a thematic and a rhetorical element of Appelfeld's, so that there is ambivalence in the reader's relation to the text. Aesthetic "distance" is a characteristic feature of the epic or saga, in which pathos and emotionality are kept to a minimum.

Appelfeld's fiction has evolved in its treatment of characters. His early stories feature three or four characters but no protagonist at the center of the unfolding tale. It is the typical and not the unique that occupies him, so that his protagonist, if there is one, might be called a collective protagonist. In Appelfeld's post-Holocaust world, we often do not know his characters' feelings about the world. They are cognizant of their situation but rarely verbalize it. Their dialogue is sparse and laconic, dealing with the minutiae of existence. There is rarely a "why?" or a "why me?" The reader has a limited view of their existence, and they in turn do not conceptualize the world they live in.

Though Appelfeld's stories and novels create a unique world in the age of the Holocaust, they do so without depicting its direct horrors. Appelfeld conducts an ongoing dialogue with the Holocaust, yet he does not place it at the center. Instead he is concerned with the fate of people before and after. Dialogue and language itself are of diminished importance. He avoids using German, Russian, Ukrainian, or Yiddish words, but on rare occasions he uses a word such as *Rucksack* and makes it evoke a world of memories, sights, sounds, and smells. Yet he does not relate to the Holocaust itself in mimetic fashion, and he refrains from touching on its historical dimension. Instead he relates to the Holocaust as an ontological explosion that cannot be confined within the boundaries of descriptive language.

It is, for him, a mythic experience beyond time and place, although it is all too definitely moored in specific times and places. The ontological explosion marks a fall—not from divine grace but into an elemental vulnerability. The historical cycle is suspended, to be replaced by a mythic timelessness, an endless winter with no chance for spring or revival.

In this framework of timelessness, Appelfeld's fiction depicts two movements: a narrative of assimilated Jewish society before the war, with its excessive cultivation and intellectualism brought to the point of atrophy, and a narrative of the hollow survivor, reduced to an elemental state of nature with suspended memories and no desires. In the depiction of prewar Jewish urbanism, the decline of the family is matched by a Chekhovian rootlessness, while the non-Jewish peasant is shown as still connected to the land, to nature and its temporal cycles. Yet any attempt of the Jew to leave the conventional urban world and join that of elemental nature proves inevitably tragic.

Since the 1970s, Appelfeld had centered his fiction on a rounded character. In his earlier writing, characters reflect off one another in an inarticulate situation. But throughout, it is rare to find self-search, confession, self-laceration. Instead, his typical character is caught up in a process that cannot be evaded, however much it portends change. There is no private time for his characters, and in the post-Holocaust narratives there is no anger, revenge, spitefulness or self-consciousness. All this gives his fiction its spatial rather than temporal quality.

Frequently the actions of his characters can be interpreted as immoral. But that is because Appelfeld has placed his characters beyond the range of accepted morality—as reflected in the truncated dialogue and inane words his characters use, as though Appelfeld were deliberately avoiding the presentation of a complete individual. In some short stories, it is possible to take a character from one narrative and place him or her in another without upsetting the plot. This possibility reflects an epic dimension, but it also widens the gap between real time and the *durée* Appelfeld achieves. It enables him to depict hollow men and women in various stages of vulnerability and in a world beyond the ordinary division of good and evil, so that the reader is asked to suspend ethical judgment.

As a writer in the (qualifiedly) fantastic mode, Appelfeld transcends the here and now of the Holocaust experience in order to extend it to universality. The breach with the "normal," the separation from the normative ethical categories, is reflected in the emblems he uses. Yet language is no longer the conventional thoroughfare of communication with others. Many of his characters have blocked that thoroughfare for themselves and opted for an existence with limited verbal expression. The meager existence suffices where projections for the future are no longer a part of the characters' makeup.

His drama is made up of seemingly unheroic people, although all contribute to creating a mythlike tale. Appelfeld moves his narratives by means of pictoriality, occasionally even by means of a pointillist play of light and shade, with undefined essences flowing through the shimmering air. His narrative is in no hurry to disclose "plot" or depict "characters." A passage from his story "Bertha" reflects this unique quality:

> The street gradually filled with rich colors. The shadows, dumb and cautious, passed across. Dark circles whirled at its end. When he turned his head back, he saw the thick redness strangled by damp powerful arms. . . . Now, he was already in the realm of forms. Reality, as it were, shed its skin; all he felt was a kind of familiarity, as if he were being drawn—he did not know toward what; to the blue color, to the trees or to the stray dog that chanced to be there. He did not see Bertha. . . . "[9]

The intricate pictoriality and the detailed depiction of mood and atmosphere in an almost impressionistic mode—together with the diminution of dialogue—contribute to shaping a highly stylized fable. Yet Appelfeld does not employ a stream-of-consciousness technique; that fact and the deemphasizing of dramatic dialogue add up to his reluctance to create highly individualized characters, standing in full portrait. Concern with inner motivations and intentions is not a part of his method, especially in his early narratives. The stream-of-consciousness technique, had he employed it, would have given his characters a rich inner life based on memory and internal "time." Yet Appelfeld's typical character is "flawed" in precisely this category. "Kitty," an early story, tells of an eleven-year-old girl who finds herself in a French convent toward the end of the war. She is devoid both of language and memory at the beginning of the tale. For her, memory is inaccessible. She emerges from her insulated, autistic state through a series of revelations. She discovers her life through her senses, and this synesthetic "conversion" lifts her from an elemental, subverbal creature to someone who relates to the world through her body. In her growth she opens to touch and to sight. A surging and expansive sense of life fills her, but while opening up she continues to weave her unique and enclosed self.

Appelfeld's sensitive, nonconfessional narratives admit little room for questions of *ars poetica*—namely, questions of an objective correlative between the Holocaust and artistic expression—although he did address the problem in his essays.[10]

In another early story, "Cold Heights," a narrator does appear qua narrator.[11] Here we are in the Appelfeldian realm of the indeterminate and indefinable, an atmosphere redolent of an unspoken past. It is a world of convalescent refugees in the stark height of an old tower, which is a replica of the survivors themselves. Appelfeld often uses passive verbs in Hebrew, thereby adding to the indefiniteness. The unique character is a "writer" who is there in the tower, although the story is told in the third person. Whose voice, then, do we hear? Is it that of the omnipresent narrator, or is it that of the writer?

> What was needed was a writer to come and record people's stories as well as his own, since he might possess the kind of detachment which makes observation possible. Let us hope that he is not hurt, for if he may speak for himself, he has none of the gentile's equanimity. And if his gaze seemed cool, it was not because he was serene. (P. 87)

The irony continues:

> If the writer had been calm and patient as a gentile, surely he would have seen more. As it was, he watched death retreat, folding its wings and slinking to the corner as a beast of prey withdraws, only to lurk there forever. Cool light filtered in, tracing its shadows on the floor. What does a man see in his hallucinations? Death certainly sees all, staring down from the ceiling beams. Sometimes during a sleepless night it takes on a certain feeling. One could not call it pity, or cruelty, or by any other of the usual names. It was more like passive attentiveness. (P. 88)

There is an indeterminacy in the narrator's own definition of his role and in the mode of his portrayal. On one hand he is a separate being, and on the other he merges with the subjects, or potential subjects, of his tale:

> Gradually, generalizations slipped through the writer's fingers. Disease and sleep took on a variety of forms in words and gestures, which tried to say something when hung together. A pale hand gestured greetings in an attempt to announce rebirth, to embrace one's kin, or neighbor still unable to sit up. How miraculous were these first beginnings like the groping of a newborn child. (P. 91)

That opens the door to further ambiguity, with the supremacy of gesture over words: " 'What for?' was the question behind their every word. And the usual answer was an explicit gesture. Perforce they responded with that familiar blank expression, as though sharing an unmentionable secret" (p. 97). In due course, the ambiguity turns back upon the narrator himself: "And the message? After all, that was what he had in mind as he sat facing the fading pages, trying to lend the moment a glimmer of festivity" (p. 100). How shall he account for the gap between the narrated moment and the moment of narration?

> The writer gave up writing, as though letting events follow their course. The laws of drowning and floating would again become valid and he would not try to stop them. Perhaps he did well by giving up writing in good time, thus fully admitting the existence of other forces which control us and rule by irrevocable decree. Let it not be considered sinful if he too sat on the veranda and tried to listen to his innermost feelings, because he was waiting all the while for a miracle to descend and enlighten him. (P. 117)

The others disperse and he alone carries their story—and he is forgotten. There is, of course, an element of paradox in this, as in his realization that actions have supplanted words, that his is an existence on a tightrope between the two extremes of utter catatonia and unbridled violence in a theater of the absurd. If Appelfeld can be said to depict the "Jewish archetype" before and after the war, he is also concerned with the fragmentation of that archetype. His novel *Badenheim 1939* (English version, 1980), reflects a slow process in the cultural stripping down of the Central European assimilated Jew, his deterioration and disintegration, before the Holocaust. This holds true for later novels as well. The assimilated Jew moved in a cultural milieu that was perishable because of its rootlessness. *Badenheim 1939* can serve as a model for later novels that center on the assimilated Jew. The process of change and disclosure affects the town of Badenheim itself: from an exclusive spa and resort, it gradually becomes a detention camp. A feeling of ethereal weightlessness leads the assimilated Jew in his last spring in Badenheim to search for his Polish-Jewish roots. Yet the air is now saturated with a cultural malaise. The almost mythical drama now bears the seeds of the impending catastrophe. Again, the Holocaust per se is not mentioned. As in previous works, Appelfeld achieves esthetic distance: the third-person narrative could only suggest the experience, never disclose its inner source.

Tor Ha'pelaot (The age of wonders, 1978) marks a radical departure for Appelfeld, primarily in the use of a nonautobiographical first-person narrative. The image of the afflicted family begins to figure centrally in his fiction. *Be'et Uve'ona Ahat* (1985; English version called "The Healer"), *For Every Sin* (1989), and *The Retreat* (1984) portray the family's inner collapse. The dysfunctional individual in a disintegrating family is central or marginal in many of the novels after the 1970s.

One must be careful to distinguish here between the aestheticization of the horror and the inability of language to depict the scope of the experience. Appelfeld's characters in his early fiction are flat, and yet we do not have a flat multiplication of the same. Seemingly they are postmodern because no depth is accorded to their portrayal. Despite the flat depiction, however, readers of Appelfeld's texts know they are exposed to only one archaeological layer of the personality of the character. Other layers may have been destroyed, erased, suppressed, or denied.

A sense of alienation permeates the Appelfeldian fictional milieu. Almost all his characters are physically or psychologically in a state of deep dislocation from their surroundings, deprived of a sense of referentiality and familiarity. Thus, through the suspension of the familiar and the identifiable, many of his early narratives correspond to the psychological state of his characters. Even his later, fully developed characters, having gained a past, a memory, and a better sense of the self, are disenfranchised, uprooted, and in a state of acceptance or rejection of the self. The absence of unified personality marks their inability to structure a three-dimensional differentiated persona that evolves in time and place. The characters display discord and discontinuity in their existence. None can claim a life that evolved gradually in continuous time and place. It is in this sense, then, that the modes of depiction correspond to the state of the protagonists. That is why, moreover, Appelfeld's earlier short stories are closer to the postmodern mode of narration. That is, his writings since the 1970s are closer to the modern mode; an attempt is made to create more complex and unique characters with a deeper sense of self.

The effect of Appelfeld's encounter with the fiction of Kafka has been recounted frequently by Appelfeld himself, most clearly in his conversation with Philip Roth:

> I discovered Kafka here in Israel during the 1950s, and as a writer he was close to me from my first contact. He spoke to me in my mother tongue, German, not the German of the Germans, but the German of the Hapsburg Empire, of Vienna, Prague and Chernovtsy, with its special tone, which, by the way, the Jews worked hard to create. To my surprise he spoke to me not only in my mother tongue but also in another language which I knew intimately, the language of the absurd. I knew what he was talking about. It wasn't a secret language for me and I didn't need any explications. I had come from the camps and the forests, from a world that embodied the absurd, and nothing in that world was foreign to me. What was surprising was this: How

could a man who had never been there know so much, in precise detail, about that world? Other surprising discoveries followed. Behind the mask of placelessness and homelessness in his work stood a Jewish man, like me, from a half-assimilated family, whose Jewish values had lost their content, and whose inner space was barren and haunted. The marvelous thing is that the barrenness brought him not to self-denial or self-hatred but rather to a kind of tense curiosity about every Jewish phenomenon, especially the Jews of Eastern Europe, the Yiddish language, the Yiddish theater, Hassidism, Zionism and even the idea of moving to Mandate Palestine. This is the Kafka of his *Journals*, which are no less gripping than his works. Kafka emerges from an inner world and tries to get some grip on reality, and I came from a world of detailed, empirical reality, the camps and the forests. My real world was far beyond the power of imagination, and my task as an artist was not to develop my imagination but to restrain it, and even then it seemed impossible to me, because everything was so unbelievable that one seemed oneself to be fictional.[12]

Appelfeld's art of the narrative is not consistent. At times he uses a laconic, "thin" style; at other times his language is redolent with metaphors creating atmosphere and mood. In his short fiction of the 1960s, style, mood, and tight expression are all in accord. Dialogue, as stated earlier, is sparse and symbolic. Nature and humanity are not in accord. A realistic narrative quite often puts the full load of a novel on the shoulders of the characters who advance the movement of the narrative; traditional nineteenth-century novels are a case in point. In modern texts, where the characters at best evoke enigmas, it is movement, unpredictable change, or incomprehensible occurrences that create the narrative line.

In Appelfeld's fiction up to the 1970s, most characters are drawn with only a few outlines. The technique, as the Israeli critic Yigal Schwartz points out, is structured along the line of separation of entities. The telling voice is a noninterfering authority emotionally uninvolved in the depicted world, and the characters are such that their whole power of speech, expression, and observation is limited. The telling voice or narrating voice is in charge of words and insights, whereas the characters are in charge of the physical expression. Schwartz correctly points to 1972 as a turning point, when Appelfeld published his first family novella, *Ke'Ishon Ha'ayin* (The pupil of the eye). The point of view, entrusted to an all-observant voice in the short stories, is now shifted to a character. Schwartz's observation certainly applies to *The Age of Wonders* and later novels. The first-person narrator in the early stories did not provide a clearly focused point of view;

in *The Age of Wonders*, a first-person *Bildungsroman*, the young narrator, as the central character of the novel, orchestrates and reports the events.

The sense of cultural dislocation is reinforced in Appelfeld's fiction. For example, his characters clearly do not speak Hebrew, even though they reside in Israel. That creates an atmosphere of defamiliarization and estrangement. But beyond that, the language of speech identifies the character and his or her relationship to both past and present. It is a common aspiration of Appelfeld's characters, for instance, to acquire German as a sign of both emancipation and enlightenment. Language bespeaks familiarity. Toni, in *To The Land of the Cattails* (1986), is delighted to speak the local dialect of Ukrainian spoken by Ruthenian peasants. And in a reverse direction, Jewish writers (such as the father in *The Age of Wonders*) are conceived as people who contaminate the German language. In *For Every Sin* (1989) the total demise of the character Theo is related to the fact that his German was contaminated by the Yiddish of his fellow survivors. Thus what defines the characters is the presence or absence of language. Beyond all its signs, language is an act of choice. The assimilated Jew preferred the German language; Katerina, the gentile housekeeper, finds a refuge in Yiddish. The process of transformation is tightly connected to language and what it stands for. The move from one domain to the other often creates a need for a different linguistic identification. Beyond physical movement, Appelfeld's characters move geographically, culturally, religiously—and all these moves entail a change in language affiliation.

A binary relationship exists between the centrality of a character and the controlling presence of an uninvolved telling voice. In the earlier fiction there was a gap between the two. With a more sophisticated character, the gap between the two shrinks. The observing/telling voice was central in the early stories. The austere depiction of the survivors did not involve introspection. What is more, the telling voice supplied neither a past nor a background for the character. This objective tone of the omnipresent teller or narrator, by its distancing and remoteness, was concerned with setting a mood or introducing doubt rather than providing information. In any event, it provided certain basic markers, such as the change of seasons, so prevalent in Appelfeld's world. This is connected in earlier narratives with the presence of "authorities"; decisive metapersonal powers, either divine or psychological, erode all possibilities of free will. In his later fiction, Appelfeld abandoned this factor, since it was clearly influenced by his reading of Kafka. It did, however, contribute to the ambiguity and the poetic quality of the narration. The later focusing on one character defused the more evasively elliptic quality of the early narratives and brought the narrative toward the mainstream. Some of his early stories are more modern, i.e., very often there are no psychological or ethical questions in the text, but their very absence evokes questions as to parallel psychological and ethical elements in the characters. Characters that appear marginally in earlier stories appear fully drawn in the later novels.

Paradoxically, Appelfeld's fiction does not evoke collective historical memories. Rather, it raises basic questions about choice versus predestination. To what extent was the Holocaust avoidable? Were not the Jews (as in many of his novels) acting as if the text had been prescribed and preordained? Appelfeld does not try to come to terms with the Holocaust in a confrontational manner. He does not pose the question of where the Jewish God was when his people were being massacred, and yet the very absence of the direct question points to the problem of phrasing it. Appelfeld chose not to write stories of lamentation and supplication, which most often assume the existence of an addressor and an addressee. He deletes two major factors in the traditional literature of destruction: the divine presence and the enemy. That allows Appelfeld to particularize the state of the Jew through a universalizing of it. He speaks of Everyman and Everywoman and at the same time tries to tell the Jewish story. Appelfeld has written realistic stories, metarealistic stories, neo-Hassidic stories, and fantastic stories. His characters are varied: intellectuals, cab drivers, butchers, journalists; the naive and the sophisticated; the mobile and the stationary. Through his narrative art he catalogues the complete historical inventory of the Jews of Eastern and Central Europe in the past hundred years.

The fantastic in literature bears spatial qualities, in contrast to the premodern novel, which can generally be perceived as having a temporal orientation. The nineteenth-century concept of the teleological nature of fiction (and its representational function) no longer holds true for twentieth-century modern and postmodern novels. The idea of verisimilitude, of the proximity of the text to the societal structure and its conventions, no longer holds the central interest of the novelist. In nineteenth-century Europe, the novelist was either a commentator on society or an observer of it. Toward the end of the century a more analytical approach appeared. And yet the assumption persisted that there is a tie between novelist and society. The fantastic mode can be either utopian or escapist, but the texts considered in this study do not fall into this category. Appelfeld's literature is a literature of angst, of doubt and indeterminacy, a literature in which the elements of the elliptic and the ambiguous unite and separate the reader and the protagonist.

Appelfeld's protagonist no longer walks in a forest of symbols, since the correspondence between symbol and its referent has become ambiguous. Irony, paradox, metonymy—so prevalent in modern literature —no longer allow for a simple bond between signifier and signified. Modern and postmodern fiction no longer is enslaved to the unities of time, place, and plot. Accordingly, once the continuous, the causal, the comprehensible, and the probable no longer are seen to be necessary or sufficient conditions for acceptable narrative, a place can be made for the fantastic, and it can be ushered in—in the midst of what continues to be modern and postmodern narrative. A traditional approach to the function of the narrative sees it as holistic in nature, employing elements of denouement and resolution. An atomistic approach, on the other hand, is reflected in modern and postmodern fiction, where the fabula is often open-ended. The holistic approach draws reader and protagonist together; the atomistic approach, with its uncertainties and indeterminacies, separates author and protagonist, reader and protagonist, protagonist and protagonist. Appelfeld's fiction poses a problem to the implied reader who is sympathetic to the plight of the characters but often is at odds with their actions or decisions.

The decentralized and spatial quality of the modern tale has produced a different type of protagonist, one who cannot be said to accumulate qualities or dimensions in the course of time. This protagonist often is beyond good and evil; moral issues are not faced, norms are not challenged, because often the social background is eliminated or is detached from any depiction of the protagonist, so that the background does not figure centrally in the life of the protagonist or in the total structure of the narrative.

The deletion of time and place paves the way for a modern expression in Appelfeld's fiction. And the tendency to divest the character of qualities—or to leave qualities unidentified and unnamed—lends the narrative a spatiality it never had before. Thus we find the protagonist or character detached from the backdrop that had made up so much of the substance of the realistic novel. Because the spatially oriented characters in modern and postmodern narrative are noncumulative, they do not develop or evolve according to the rules of probability.

If we list characteristics of the protagonist in modern and postmodern literature, we can see that Appelfeld's characters share many of them: a character (as noted) who is noncumulative in the course of the narrative, moves in a world that does not conform to "logical" expectations of probability, is often devoid of self-perception or self-observation, is unable to learn from the accumulated experience of others, is often devoid of a comprehensible past, is no part of a societal framework involving family ties or love, is therefore opaque and remains so, since both character and reader are barred from inner consciousness or inner voice, and exhibits the depersonalized qualities of a displaced or dislocated individual.

One cannot ignore the temporal dimension of Appelfeld's text. Once Appelfeld places his characters in one location (as in *The Retreat*, *The Immortal Bartfuss*, and other novels), the movement is more limited; the protagonist gains a past and becomes more introspective in trying to understand his or her existence in light of the past. The question that arises is the extent one can talk about a poetics of the Holocaust—a poetics whose ground rules are established by its subject matter, the Holocaust itself.

The role of the reader (one assumes it is a sympathetic, informed reader) is important in Holocaust literature. In the case of missing historical data, the reader supplies the information or frame of reference. The reader finds himself or herself between a realistic historical event and a nonrealistic literary depiction. Appelfeld's fiction presents the vacuum in which his characters move. This unique "not-of-this-world" vacuum surrounds many of the characters, even after their liberation and their coming to Israel. They move, react, think, and function in a different manner. That raises the question of irony. In literature the reader knows the power of irony and knows what is real and what merely seems to be real. In a fundamental way, through the process of reading the reader dissolves the contradictions in the story. This feat is based on familiarity with the genre (fairy tales rarely are ironic), with the normative system of society, and with the vagaries of human nature. But in a universe whose ground rules are not known to the characters, a universe that has betrayed their basic trust in systems of human nature, only nihilistic irony can exist. In such a universe the reader acknowledges the absence of a reigning normative system that distinguishes good from bad, what is allowed from what is forbidden.

The Holocaust as a basic experience can serve as an anchor to the reader. And yet we may ask whether the experience of the individual ought to be the sole focus of fictional Holocaust literature. In a facile way, the reader can supply information to fill in the missing gaps in the narrative of many of Appelfeld's characters, labeling their behavior with tags from the world of social science, medicine, and other fields. The point is that the inaccessible and opaque nature of the depiction points exactly to the effects of the most traumatic of experiences. Thus the sympathetic reader, in the case of Appelfeld's fiction, is not drawn into the scenes. There is an ever-present tension between the artistic aim to transcend the experience and the experience itself in its ineffability. In Appelfeld's earlier stories, the characters often are marionette figures whose actions and reactions are few, limited, and mechanical. They are beyond indignation, rage, anger, or revenge.

Appelfeld's early characters are simple people, often middle class or lower. Their predicament as survivors and people branded by horrific experience is met by the sensitivity of Appelfeld's style. The implied and not the explicit, the suggestive rather than the expressive, gives a certain aura to their existence. They continue to live in a world that has long since gone astray, but they move in a universe uniquely theirs. The absurd, according to Camus, is exactly the unfamiliarity one senses in the world. One's feeling as a stranger is the ultimate expression of the absurd. Survival has created a gap between the survivors and the rest of the world. The world as a concentration camp is their experience.

As critics such as Dan Miron and Gershon Shaked have noted, Appelfeld created a prose style with a unique rhythm and plasticity. Carefully crafted and with an exact pace, it presents the reader with highly terse yet richly embellished sentences. The clean style and the controlled expression bring to the narrative added dimensions. The voice—the observant voice described earlier—notes the change in the seasons, the quality of light and air. Certain symbols run through Appelfeld's fiction: water, light, smoke, the digestive system, fatigue, sleep, pipes, a backpack, the train. These symbols do not allude to earlier texts. Appelfeld has created his own symbols, some of which he shares with other Holocaust writers. These symbols give his fiction its signature, its idiom; they chart his territory.

Appelfeld's fiction is structured on details, on concrete images that reflect the psychological changes in the characters. Abstract terminology is not widely prevalent in his stories; the paucity of plot contributes to the sense of an anaerobic existence. Men and women are not introduced as rational individuals who can make themselves objects of self-introspection. The dislocated individual does not exercise this cognitive privilege. The sense of a world without providence is enhanced by creating characters devoid of a defined, individuated self with a clear, individual voice. As stated earlier, the vocabulary of many of his characters is limited and repetitious, and it reappears in various stories. Juxtaposition is characteristic of his narrative style; his characters too are created by the technique of juxtaposition; no clear inner causal relationship exists between the various components of their personalities.

For Appelfeld, "pure memory" does not exist. He reconstructs remnants of memory and tries to work in two directions: to expand the scope of his fiction beyond personal remembrance and to create a gallery of characters not directly or indirectly reflecting himself.

Appelfeld's personal and aesthetic credo is expressed in his slim volume of talks, essays, observations, and memories, *Essays in First Person*. It is Appelfeld's attempt to come to terms with his life, his art, and the state of the artist as a survivor. He pays his respects to people who helped him expand his intellectual sphere, people who ushered him into Hebrew, Yiddish, and world literature. His reflections on the post-Holocaust period, especially on the shores of Italy, are closely connected to his aesthetic meditation on artistic expression in the light of the Holocaust. The title points to the approach he will reach: art and not history, art and not theology, is the key to the particularization of experience. Both history and theology somehow deface the personal effects of the horror; only expression in drama and literature can capture the unique personal-spiritual dimension of the Holocaust.

In the first essay of that collection, "Testimony,"[13] Appelfeld declares his credo: "In spite of everything, I still believe in the essentially personal cast of every truly spiritual experience" (p. 91). He speaks of events and visions that shaped and molded his generation, of the assimilated Jew in Central Europe, for whom assimilation was no longer a debatable choice but rather a fixed way of life, with Judaism marginal: "fragments of an attenuated Judaism still hung on." To the assimilated Jew who had great hopes for his children, Judaism was mainly "an embarrassing anachronism to be consigned to a remote corner of one's life" (p. 92). What is more, the assimilation of his generation was already an inherited one, and no one bothered either to justify it or to reject it.

The Holocaust put an end to the heterogeneous nature of European Jewish society. Nothing was left but the piercing nakedness of being a Jew. Appelfeld talks about the young children of the Holocaust who absorbed the unexpressed agonies of their parents. Children, bereft and culturally deprived, absorbed the atavistic knowledge of the tribe, its suffering and pain. Once on the shores of Italy, the children tried to become what their parents had been: communists, Orthodox Jews, whatever. The desires of sons and daughters recur in the fiction. In *For Every Sin* it reaches frightening proportions. The sense that there was an innate duty to follow the parent's path took on a certain intensity, even in the open-ended existence in Italy. The words of the fathers returned to the children who were searching for roots.

Appelfeld's attraction to the interwar generation, seen in his fiction, extends to his essays. He is especially concerned to understand and explain the Jewish intelligentsia. Its passion for politics, literature, and music was combined with a sense of the universal and the humanistic, not with the national or the religious. Appelfeld talks about Jewish children whose Judaism did not have a social basis or a Jewish frame of reference. Accordingly, those Jews who exiled their Judaism to the remote corners of their existence were the direct victims of their Jewishness. Their children, in order to survive in a hostile environment, had to hide being Jewish. After liberation, many of the surviving children sought to relocate their Jewish ties. As Appelfeld states in "Testimony,"

> So we searched for a path towards literature—first to Jewish writing. That was a hard encounter, for we found out that we no longer had the ability to accept the normal as a norm. We had consciously and unconsciously another norm, that of apocalypse. Ordinary artistic expression, however subtle, appeared to us only to brush the surface of life. (P. 94)

For Appelfeld and for other survivors, literature was a way out of the prison of utter silence. Silence carried its own weight, that of guilt. Faith, belief in progress or indeed in any human endeavor, could no longer serve as the basis for speech. Doubt and skepticism made it impossible to endorse any general truth. As a writer, Appelfeld talks about the very possibility of using language, of the rebirth of a language in the attempt to find models one could emulate. For him, Kafka was the answer.

The fiction of Kafka made possible the verbal expression of the inexpressible. The nonrealistic nature of Kafka's fiction, the protagonist as a person devoid of name, family, or cumulative memory, suited Appelfeld's attempt to depict the horror: not to replicate his experiences in a descriptive manner but rather to project a metaphoric depiction of the state of the psyche. Reading Kafka gave Appelfeld the sense that Kafka (who had died in 1921) was "there" but also the sense of a possible outlet for expression that would create a fictional world with its own ground rules. That was necessary because every other basis for writing was gone. As he says, "Any attempt to understand things, to express and give form to feelings, seemed not only hopeless but also ridiculously pretentious" (p. 94).

It is interesting to note the similarity between the factual account of "Testimony" and Appelfeld's fiction. In both, a direct description of the Holocaust is absent; in both, the main concern is with the life of the assimilated Jew before the war. In his factual account Appelfeld uses a very literary, metaphoric language, and by doing so he avoids the merely memoiristic mode of expression. He talks about himself and his contemporaries, but he does not use "I," even for personal experiences. He offers the reader the factual subject matter of subsequent fiction as well as the problems involved in the delivery of the horrible experience. In his words, the search was for "new words and new melody." The solution to the problem is given in his fiction: painstakingly creating his own universe, a world uniquely his, in an attempt to find a verbal structure to capture a complex and truncated reality.

Appelfeld challenges every possible depiction of the Holocaust experience for its very possibility. Many of the testimonies were given in a state devoid of introspection. The externalization of the experience seems superficial, but it was one of the ways of both avoiding and coming to terms with the experience. He clearly realizes that many of the testimonies are in essence suppressions and not introspection, attempts to pour the experience into a chronological sequence in the vain hope of bestowing some semblance of order onto it. Mere survival was problematic in the extreme—the survivor existing in a state of being unparalleled by any other; one had to explain oneself to oneself and at the same time to try to contact the outer world, which could never reach the essence of the horror.

The decision to become a writer meant, first and foremost, a confrontation with language and order. There was no way of choosing between silence and the cry, between suppression and expression. Appelfeld created a space, a climate and environment, for his characters. In this private fictional universe there is an inner order in constant dialogue with the chaos to which it refers. Within this space there is ambiguity, uncertainty, opaqueness. Yet a mode of expression becomes possible. The title of the collection refers to the "first person," suggesting personal disclosure, even though many of the essays involve exercises in concealment as well as revelation. Here, as in his fiction, Appelfeld uses scaffoldings and other devices to serve his attempts at expression.

The essay "On One Continuing and Leading Sensation" speaks about self-forgetfulness as a hidden form of protest, i.e., a protest against being Jewish. From this point the lowest stage was reached: that of the victim justifying the malicious intentions of the victimizer. Appelfeld talks about self-hate as an adoption of negative stereotypes by the victim. Thus the survivors created for themselves a penal colony whose motto was to forget, to uproot all memory. But this attempt at suppression meant a total denial of the past, while the process of awakening meant reclaiming one's past, adopting one's childhood memories and the faces of one's parents.

In parallel fashion, this process takes place in Appelfeld's fiction. From a presentation of the elemental person devoid of a personal history, his fiction after the 1970s strives for a more complete portrayal of his characters. These characters (as in *The Immortal Bartfuss* and *For Every Sin*) have gained a past, or a semblance of a past, that demands their attention. Appelfeld uses his basic metaphor to depict the process of reclaiming the past. He talks about a train that charges inward, that collects the years and the faces; and the more inward it charges, the more familiar is everything in its road.

Basic questions are raised by writers and thinkers, questions that create sonorous titles: The Holocaust and History, The Holocaust and Theology, The Holocaust and Theodicy. Appelfeld's problem is more immediate: The Holocaust and Its Expression. In coming to terms with the problem, he tries to recall, in his essay "Beyond the Tragic," the first buds of artistic effort. The desire to verbalize was pertinent during the war. After the war, with the new situation, one found it impossible to relate to those who were not "there," and silence was preferable. Thus the two primordial urges, to speak and to keep silent, were crisscrossing the expression of the survivors. Entertainment groups appeared in the displaced persons' camps. These groups consisted of old actors and various other people who sang, recited poems, told jokes. In the return to normality, to a regular life of eating, drinking, sleeping, there was a grotesque element. Those wandering entertainers pointed to this and to another sphere. Some people saw elements of desecration in the cheap performances. There was no realization that the survivors were deprived of the sense of the tragic. The survivors were beyond the tragic. Attempts were made in the camps to revive the classical theatrical Jewish repertoire, but they failed. That was even more ridiculous than the entertainment troupes. The grotesque was expressed in the strange combination of cheap entertainment and a religious sense. This combination presented a new grotesque devoid of an ethical dimension.

The normative world and its verities no longer held true for the survivors. The old treasure of Jewish artistic expression could no longer serve. The new form was introduced by the children in the camps. With faces shaped in monasteries and forests, the children sang, combining Jewish folk songs and Christian liturgy. There was something awkward, sad, and grotesque in their voices. But it was new. The children, as singers, acrobats, sound imitators, roamed from camp to camp. They were devoid of a concrete memory, however; the horror and the terror were absorbed by their very being. Their cells were afflicted by the nameless horror. Thus the children were the ones to forge the new poetics of suffering.

The question of the approach to Holocaust literature, as noted earlier, is still an issue of discussion and disagreement. Critics who would endorse an open-ended reading of texts insist on a particular approach and understanding of our relationship to the event and its depiction. David Roskies takes a clear, unequivocal approach:

> It now seems to me that to approach the abyss as closely as possible and to reach back over it in search of meaning, language, and song is a much more promising endeavor than to profess blind faith or apocalyptic despair. The alternative, to focus solely on the Event itself, succeeds only in robbing the dead of the fullness of their lives and in inviting the abstraction of survivor into Everyman, the Holocaust into Everything.[14]

The key to Appelfeld's aesthetic is that as a creative artist he searches for a way beyond both the general and the particular. Both are unsatisfactory; the first defaces the personal experience, while the latter leaves it in the domain of the autobiographical. For Appelfeld, neither the generalized nor the autobiographical voice is a suitable form of expression; it is the personal vision itself and not the retold personal account that allows the particular and the universal to dwell in one text. His answer is to place the individual in a world Appelfeld created for him, in the selective domain of fictional narrative. Appelfeld's essays are unique: he relates to the days when, without a solid language and without a living family and its background that would serve him as a basis, he began to chart his future as a writer committed to his past.

Borges claims that among the four devices shared by all fantastic literature there is "the contamination of reality by dream." If we take his words in a literal sense, reality is contaminated by horrors undreamt of. Appelfeld's fiction is a very personal attempt to superimpose a map of possible comprehensibility on unfathomable physical and psychological occurrences. In this light, Appelfeld aims at broadening the scope beyond the Holocaust period.

II.

EARLY SHORT FICTION

3

SMOKE

Appelfeld's first collection of short stories, published in 1962, is *Ashan* (literally "Smoke," although it is sometimes referred to as "Ashes"). It includes some mature stories characteristic of the Appelfeldian tale. Some commentators have claimed that Appelfeld is at his best in this collection; there are realistic as well as metarealistic stories, but the difference is often tenuous. In none of the stories is an attempt made to reach the "totality" of experience. The influences of Kafka and Agnon can be clearly seen.

The stories vary in the extent and intensity of disclosure of the characters' past. In "Three," time and place are not given, and we learn little about the characters, who emerge from the woods after an escape, only to stagger into the open vistas as the story ends. But even in his most barren stories, Appelfeld does not aspire to a Beckettian sparsity or a total deletion of framework. The change of seasons is one reliable element in these narratives; nature in its constancy is the basis both of familiarity and the absence of familiarity, carrying a variety of meanings. It is a time marker in a world where civilization has betrayed human beings. A breach in the ability to predict is a basic trauma felt by those who experienced the Holocaust; their capacity to conjure up a feasible future has been destroyed. Nature serves as a hiding place in the flight to the fields or the forests, providing a temporary relief.

Smoke (I will use the English title, though the full collection has not been published in English) also marks the geographical location of Appelfeld's fiction: Europe and Israel (the Israel of the European survivors). One rarely encounters the Zabar, the native-born Israeli. Appelfeld presents Holocaust survivors who live in Israel, who are part of the Israeli population—voiceless though most are. Without a language they are nevertheless Israelis.

Smoke sets the mood for Appelfeld's subsequent fiction. Like a musical key that sets the tone for the entire piece, his early characters, some oblique, some unexpressive, seem to listen to voices that speak to them and them alone. Their limited verbal and emotional vocabulary gives these characters a unique quality. They are moored in an inner world that reacts to the outside world selectively. Even in the new place, Israel, they continue their survivalist existence. They make no attempt to adjust themselves to the new reality or to answer its implicit expectations; it is as if they are tuned to sounds and flows that are muffled against the noise of the surrounding "actuality."

The stories are marked by visceral reactions of the characters to weather, to cold and heat. The neck is a sensitive area, expressing both the vulnerability of the characters and their exposure to the elements. The skin seems to be the meeting point between the self and the outer world pressing against it. Physical endurance is the real test. Basic realities afflict the characters; nothing in their past can undo their present, and that is combined with an aversion to change of any kind. Characters are bodies in space. Thus a great emphasis is put on bodily proportions: Berl in "Cold Spring" gains so much weight he can hardly move; Bertha's growth in "Bertha" is stunted. This emphasis on bodies in space expresses a psychological plight reminiscent of Kafka's "Hunger Artist." A similar consideration often applies to the characters' use of language. Discovering new fields of experience through speech challenges the individual who prefers to use clichés rather than give in to free verbal expression. In "Slowly," the main character repeatedly utters the phrase "the trees grow slowly," as though wishing to move at the same pace. He is offered lucrative real estate deals but refuses to act upon them. These protagonist-survivors try to be in accord with their interpretation of the familiar.

Appelfeld is not interested at this stage in intellectualizing his characters or in lending them an inner articulated voice. His characters are merchants, peddlers, cab drivers. We are exposed to the everyday reality of cooking, knitting, stomach ailments, excessive smoking—the humdrum lives of the survivors in Israel. And yet there is a deep sense of displacement on the part of people whose lives have been truncated. German as well as East European Jews appear in these stories. The German Jews are depicted as living a comfortable middle-class existence; they seem to be financially more secure than the Jews from Eastern Europe.

A prevalent theme is the idea of partnership based on a bonding between two individuals unrelated to one another. This partnership creates a type of a surrogate family: strangers bonded in the forests and the bunkers, becoming like families; young girls bonded with adult males who saved them in the forests, as in "Bertha" and "Along the Shore." In the title story, "Smoke," Max and Reb Arye are partners in a butcher shop in Jerusalem, a partnership formed in the forest of Smelinka, in Poland. Max was saved by Reb Arye, who carried him on his back. In "Bertha," Max is like a cell, Bertha his mutant extension. Such connections are even stronger than family ties. In the partnerships between men, the illness of one portends the illness of the other; the dissolution of the bond destroys both parties. Change is detrimental to these characters; any attempt at escape from the extended unit ends unhappily. The past is inscribed upon the survivors like the verdict in Kafka's "Penal Colony." The lack of an introspective dimension in many of these early characters contributes to a fatalistic factor that governs their lives, with little chance of change.

The first story in the collection, "Three," suggests a sense of guilt —guilt at having survived. (The sentiment will be echoed in the novel *For Every Sin.* There, guilt over survival is implied but not openly expressed.) But even beyond that, the characters are broken, disenfranchised, dislocated individuals, surviving and preoccupied with their survivorship.

The opening of "Three" could serve as an artistic credo for all of Appelfeld's fiction:

> Three were left. Can we say by chance or do we err through lapse of memory, or suppression of memory, in our anxiety to befog the sequence of events which ultimately tossed them, these three, into this forsaken spot? At any rate, no more than three were left. The fields glistened in the distance, surrounded by the forest. Awakening memory insisted upon explanation, justification, something which was impossible at that moment, as it was to remain impossible in the days to come. They assumed they had escaped, had run for it, slipped out of the way, that it was the thick forest which had hidden them. Was that in fact what happened? Was it not something else that had happened? something similar? The riddle began to revolve about them, like a palpable thing in motion, impelled even faster, till nothing could stop its spinning.[1]

I have pointed to Appelfeld's way of going against the ethos of his time by constructing his own well-wrought world. His characters do not express anger, nor is there a sense of accusation. The subtext tells a different story. "Three" is told in the third person, creating a distance between the narrator and the characters. This opening paragraph addresses the reader with an editorial "we," yet the third-person narration persists throughout the story. This technique is used again and again in Appelfeld's early collections.

The opening paragraph refers both to the horrific experience and to the mode of transmitting it. Forgetfulness suggests the hidden desire of the author, the storyteller, and the characters to escape memory. There is a sense of indeterminacy. This too is typical of Appelfeld's subsequent fiction; explanation and justification are rarely found there. Uncertainty, marked by rhetorical questions, challenges the veracity of events.

Another sentiment is intimated here: the very act of telling the story is called into question. That calls to mind Appelfeld's novel *Tzili*, published twenty year later. Its opening sentence reads: "Perhaps it would be better to leave the story of Tzili Kraus's life untold. Her fate was a cruel and inglorious one, and but for the fact that it actually happened we would never have been able to tell the story."[2] This opening is clearly a rhetorical device, an attempt to cover autobiographical footprints. Similarly in "Three," a certain dichotomy is presented: "Did it matter how they had got away? Could this supposition, or that, alter the fact of their existence?" (p. 6). Characters, like the author, have suspended any attempt at viewing the situation from a clear vantage point. The only certainty is that there are three and that they had managed to escape. The mode of escape is unclear. A sense of doom surrounds the three and their actions after the escape. They muffled the cries of a boy who awakened when they broke into a warehouse in search of food: "He was silenced in a way which cannot be re-told. He was assuredly strangled. If he survived, it was by mere chance" (p. 7).

The unspecific nature of time and place, the collective nature of the three in the beginning of the story, and the indeterminacy alluded to earlier give this short tale its postmodern, truncated aspect. Movement is the lifeline of the characters: I move, ergo I exist. Furthermore, excessive eating leads to "nauseous surfeit." But inside they feel chaotic turmoil, confusion of feelings, darkness of thought. They have managed to escape, to survive, to hoard stolen food, and to kill. One of the three suggests creating a bunker, but his suggestion is rejected in favor of moving on.

The voice of the omnipresent narrator does not clarify the tale. It intimates uncertainty: "There was a feeling of the opening of gushing pipes. What did the skies portend?" Dialogue is reduced to a minimum; frequently one character reiterates the words of another without further comment. We know the characters by their bodily reactions, which reflect a chaotic inner existence. The dichotomy continues as the narrator tells us that an intense spirituality began to possess them. The reality is that they are afraid to return to the forest; they are afraid to stay in the fields because it means being handed over to the peasants or the Germans. There is an inherent futility in their actions, in the obsession with food, as with their letting food rot on the ground without touching it. The youngest observes the peasants planting potatoes.

> A little brook streamed at their feet, its water crystal-clear, like something experienced once before, not far from here, or perhaps experienced only in a dream. At that moment they came very close to reconciliation, very close to making their peace. The face of the big boy began to change, as though he were preparing himself to meet the great hour. Who could this be? Was it death, or perhaps Death's harbinger? Was there not some arcane meaning to this escape? We couldn't have escaped ourselves. From this place our salvation must come. (Pp. 14–15)

Who are these three, an adult and two youngsters? What are the authoritative, hidden powers that seem to govern their lives? There is little but ambiguity. "A man and a boy were seen approaching, axes in their hands. Were these messengers?" (p. 15). The peasants are bludgeoned to death. Violence, raw strength, animal instincts move the three; movement had been a solution of sorts. Putting on the dead peasants' clothes, holding the axes, they continue to move. There is a decisive determination on their part, signaled by their decision to put on the peasants' clothes; yet an equal and opposite certainty emerges, to the effect that they will never escape, that one day they will be caught. They decide to escape into the forest. The red sky above them has a scorching effect.

The overvoice of the omnipresent, omniobservant, omnispeculative narrator interrupts the flow of events by the questions posed, questions about the nature of certainty. The story gains its structure from the interchange between movements and actions of the three, and the intervening voice of the narrator. The narrator introduces uncertainty by using such words as "it appears," "it seems." The dialogue is sparse, and the unnamed characters open up only at the end of the tale. The narrator's voice carries mystical speculation, not relating openly to the ethical questions that might bother the reader.

The adult among the three was wounded in the altercation with the peasants. His condition slows down their movement. He is badly hurt and sends the two youngsters ahead to bring food. Immobile, they stay in the forest. Movement does not allow for introspection; it is flight from danger and often a flight from the self. At this point their voices are heard for the first time, referring to their past. They admit they have escaped and left others behind. A deep sense hits them that they will never be forgiven. (The theme of betrayal will also appear in Appelfeld's subsequent works.) They feel deeply that they have not done what they could have done. The reader surmises that they have escaped from a concentration camp to save their lives, maybe at the expense of the lives of others.

The characters go from hunger to surfeit, from surfeit to hunger. Everything changes and everything stays the same. At the end we find them in a position similar to the one they were in at the beginning. Wearing the lambskin clothes of the peasants they have killed, the two younger men try to escape an almost inevitable fate. The theme of cover is reiterated in the changes in the forest around them, from the naked to the covered, and this applies to the characters, too. Their ethical reckoning is awakened by remembering events that happened to them before the escape; they betrayed their brothers by saving their own lives. In their new existence, the ethical apparatus is changed. They are haunted by the past, yet for the present a different set of rules applies. Survival as an ultimate value requires a suspension of ethical considerations. As Appelfeld said in an interview, "My first life scenes showed me murder, violence, hostility, ruthlessness. My childhood memories are an ongoing series of horror pictures—sadism on one hand, and helplessness on the other."[3]

The forest is the geographical terrain inhabited by many of Appelfeld's early characters. Some have never left their "forest," even after arriving in Israel. Similarly, the bunker has been a place of hiding, and the place from which surrogate families emerged. In "Cold Spring," the disintegration of such a family occurs upon liberation. The characters, with the exception of one, do not search immediately for their lost family; nor do they express a desire to return to their birthplace. The sentiment is to stretch the distance between themselves, their past, and their memories. A fierce realization encompasses many of the characters in the postliberation period: the realization that they have no home. (Only in the novel For Every Sin does the protagonist, Theo, express a desire to return to his hometown following liberation.) The characters in "Cold Spring," without saying so, project themselves toward an undefined future. They are on the move. The gap between them and the world around them is expressed by an observation of a peasant woman, who tells her daughter as they watch the refugees: "Look, Jews, they are going in search of their families." This natural sentiment cannot be attributed to the refugees in this story with the exception of Reb Itzhak, the father figure in the group. Tzeitl, the mother figure, is devastated by the disintegration of her adopted family. But the young boys, Berl, Herschel, and the unnamed narrator, are looking for another life.

The church is an important presence in "Cold Spring," as it has been in Appelfeld's other writings. Sometimes it has been a silent presence, sometimes an active one. It may serve as background or as the place where the plot occurs. Church and monastery have appeared in his stories about liberated refugees following the war and in his novels about the assimilated Jewish middle class in the prewar era. In "Cold Spring" the members of the "family" come to a monastery on the road and are turned back because the place is full to capacity with refugees. Berl, climbing the walls, cries: "I'm a Christian!" This son of Nachman Katz will eventually find his place in the bed of a peasant woman, and his "loss" depresses Tzeitl, who mourns him. The "good old days" of the bunker are gone, and for those days she is ready "to walk from one end of the world to another." The underground bunker in the forest sustained the family; spring and liberation shut off its existence. Their subterranean existence could not survive once it was touched by freedom and the outer world. There was an existence of an extended winter, of cover and hibernation. Spring meant exposure, nakedness, vulnerability. Their abnormal existence under dire circumstances gave the group strength and solidarity. Liberation came as a test. As Mintz writes, "With the liberation comes the return to speech and consciousness."[4] Despite its fragmentary exposition, the story is moored in reality. We are given names, places, hometowns.

One characteristic of the Christian world in these stories is stability. That is especially true of the peasants in the villages. It is to the Christian holy man that the group goes in search of answers. He reaffirms the demise of their past. They have been orphaned. Here the sense of being an orphan, without protection and without people one knew as a child, is a devastating factor, as it is in much of Appelfeld's fiction. Beyond the confines of the immediate family, being an orphan refers to an existence suffused with a great sense of irredeemable loss and loneliness.

The story ends with no clear resolution. The few members of the family left are preparing for another night under the skies. They huddle together as Tzeitl wishes for life in the bunker. As Appelfeld has noted,

> Paradoxically, the survivors are seeking something they had in the war and which now seems to be lost forever—the feeling of solidarity and mutual responsibility. When the external pressure let up, friendships dissolved, groups broke up, and brotherhood was exposed as a mere illusion. So that the end of the war brought about yet another, albeit paradoxical, disappointment.[5]

Here as elsewhere, Appelfeld presents us with a story that has no clear beginning, middle, or end. This story is devoid of a climax or a point of reversal and change. It is episodic, and mostly "middle." The text comes to an end, but the characters' stories will continue, with variations, in Appelfeld's other writings.

The Holocaust experience cannot be explained by the rules of the familiar world. Rather, it is transmuted in fiction into the symbolic and the fantastic. Bertha's existence, in the story bearing her name, is totally insular, connected to no social structure. To the outer world, she is a young retarded child, a victim of the Holocaust. To her protector, Max, she is a mysterious being who exercises a magic hold on him. Max and Bertha are bound together by the Holocaust. Max saved the young girl, and she in turn became a part of him. Bertha refuses to be put into an institution in Jerusalem; this refusal is her only expressed wish.

One can read "Bertha" realistically as a story about a strange bond between an adult man and an autistic girl. An additional reading sees Bertha as a metonym for Max's psyche. She is the embodiment of his life, frozen to a certain point, not to be changed. Their connection is deeper than mere dependency; Bertha tries to complete her hold on Max, and Max tries to break the union. He professes a desire to break away and enter a relationship with a mature woman. Max's friends at work, all survivors with deep affinity to one another, decide he needs a wife, and they find one for him. Max craves sleep, forgetfulness, and a nonconfrontational life.

The dichotomy between change and nonchange is a false premise in the story. During the fifteen years Bertha has been with Max, she has not changed; she remains small and dwarfish. Then Max does not see Bertha for months. He goes through physical changes: he becomes more wrinkled, his hair turns white, he has stomach problems and a harsh cough—all signs of physical and mental deterioration, of aging and inner restlessness. Bertha retains her perpetually childish behavior, her constant knitting and unraveling—an analogy to her state of being.

We know about conversations taking place between Max and Bertha, but we do not know the content of the conversations. Minimal, repetitious dialogue is another hallmark of Appelfeld's fiction; he prefers to use indirect speech and to present an uninvolved narrator or voice. This technique adds an element of mystery to "Bertha." At times the relationship between Max and Bertha resembles the intimate ties between a man and a woman. Bertha *is* a grown woman, though she still has the body of a child. Max tries to discuss her future: "she would burst into tears. This weeping was deep and bitter. It wasn't she that wept; some sleeping animal wept inside her. Sometimes it was a high pitched wail."[6]

Bertha, with her limited vocabulary, bases her strength upon her unchangeability: "Closed, encased in a hard shell, she dragged after him like a dead weight, and sometimes like a mirror wherein his life was reflected" (p. 147). Like a spider she tries to knit a web in the form of a sweater, a shawl, in order to capture Max; her deep fear of change, however, makes her unravel it. Bertha's childishness secures Max's care for her; maturity may bring change and separation. Her growing maturity is connected to her way of posing questions to Max.

> They were not the sort of questions that one person asks another, but a sort of eruption, not entirely irrational, that would claim his complete attention. These questions drove him out of his mind; at those moments he was ready to throw her out, to hand her over to the welfare authorities, to denounce her, even to beat her, something that he, incidentally, never did. At these moments, he felt the whole weight of this human burden that had been thrust upon him. (P. 147)

Somehow both Max and Bertha desire both change and nonchange. They both exercise self-denial on the verge of self-deceit.

A question one might ask is this: from whose point of view is Bertha being perceived?

> Her memory froze at a certain point. You couldn't make her disclose anything from the past, nor was she capable of absorbing anything new. "Some pipe is stopped up." This feeling, oversimplified as it might be, remained a sort of certainty that he could not doubt, feeling as he did that something was clogged up in him, too. (P. 148)

Bertha appears as herself but also as a reflection of Max's psyche. She tries the impossible: to remain a child and become a woman. She is in a tragic predicament: he rejects her as a woman and accepts her as a child. She senses the impending separation and decides to unclog the pipes, to allow herself to play a new role. This woman arrested in a childish shell feels that she is losing her hold on him. Max is urged by Mitzi, his intended fiancée, who suspects a sexual connection between the two, to make up his mind: Bertha will be put in an institution, and Max and Mitzi will be married.

On his last trip to Jerusalem Max is about to commit Bertha. On the road, "the chill wrapped itself around his neck. He was exposed to the cutting air." A dual vulnerability occurs—the exposure to inclement weather will eventually undo Bertha. Max does not explain his early return. He brings Bertha new clothes and they go for a walk. During Max's last absence, Bertha has matured and acquired some gestures of a woman. A theme frequently found in Appelfeld's fiction concerns fear of sexuality and of coming of age, associated with penetration of the private domain of the body. Young girls, traumatized by the loss of family, of the familiar and the known, suffer stunted growth and arrested femininity. Their misshapen form is a reflection of innate fears of sexuality and responsibility.

> Their walk continued for some time. It was solemn as a ceremony, as a farewell, as a simple never-to-be forgotten occasion. You are not in control of yourself, other powers dominate you, lead you as in a procession. Oaths are broken, but another oath, greater than all, takes their place. Your eyes glisten with tears. The lights begin to dance. Now he was already in the realm of mystery. A smile lit up on Bertha's face, and there was something sharp in her eyes like an inanimate object unexpectedly changing its form. . . . When they returned home, her face was very flushed—a fire burned in her. Her eyes were open, but you could see nothing in them. (P. 155)

Death comes to the young woman when she is on the verge of maturity, of gaining a sense of her own self. The feverish Bertha is brought to a hospital: "She was as light and as small as on the day when he had received her; the years have added no weight" (p. 156). While she is in the hospital Max deceives himself into believing that his load is lighter. His heart falters, however, and inside his skull he senses the floating of heavy liquid. He takes on some characteristics of Bertha; the description of his condition resembles hers: "There was no connection between one thought and another. It was as if they had frozen in one of the arteries" (p. 156). Bertha's physical demise is paralleled by Max's mental demise. When Bertha is in the hospital he becomes undone; he cannot remember or connect one thread of thought to another. He cannot tear himself from the hospital, from the magic circle that draws him there. The enigma called Bertha is not solved.

> Was it Bertha, or only a vision? Again details rose up, denying it. The shoes, the beads, the knitting needles, the blue wool—was this Bertha? again you went out to search for her the way you searched for her in the forest, the way you searched for yourself in the street. You just found details; you couldn't see her, just as you couldn't see yourself. . . . Suddenly he saw that Bertha's clothes lay in his hands. He didn't dare to open them—or perhaps these were no longer his hands, but iron rings . . . " (Pp. 158–159)

"Bertha" presents various reading possibilities. A realistic reading emphasizes an image of a retarded, literally "held back" girl. A more psychological reading allows us to observe her as a girl who willed her stunted growth. As long as she is a young, helpless child, Max will take care of her and protect her. One can extend this reading and claim that Max too was suppressing his sexuality: he stays for months outside his home. The status quo suits him, too. Bertha in turn stunts her growth in order not to challenge the established relationship or Max's sexuality. Only when she senses the existence of an unknown rival, Mitzi, does she decide to become a woman, to grow up. However, Bertha is not protected against the outer world, be it the elements or people. The first wind that swirls around her neck sounds her death knell. Conversely, Max was content with the dwarfed Bertha; she did not challenge his masculinity, and her dependence on him gave him a certain power.

Symbolically we can perceive Bertha as Max's own unchanged psyche. Max, like many of Appelfeld's characters, ingested the Holocaust in its entirety. Outwardly he goes through changes: he ages, suffers ailments. Like other survivors he takes the Holocaust with him wherever he goes. Bertha is a metonym of Max's experience. At times she is almost an inanimate object that Max feeds and clothes; at times she is his conscience. With her death, Max has, in an inverted manner, ingested the embodiment of the Holocaust.

All marriages and partnerships in the *Smoke* collection end with the death of one of the partners. Regardless of whether the story takes place after liberation, in a displaced persons camp, in Tel Aviv, or Jerusalem—neither time nor place can cure the characters' malaise. Appelfeld often suspends the attempt to create a comprehensible psychological inner system for his characters. This in turn gives added meaning to objects, to sickness, to excessive and obsessive or repetitious behavior. It is the body that is the site of the impaired and suffering psyche.

Smoke is one of the basic symbols of the Holocaust. Appelfeld, in the story entitled "Smoke," focuses on the obsessive cigarette smoking of the protagonist. This story is related through the daily activities of one character and tells a different, deeper story about another. As the story draws to its end, we learn that the first character's partner and rescuer is seriously ill. The protagonist's excessive smoking and his unexplained pains are a reflection of his partner's imminent death, and consequently his own. Max, the protagonist, who has never opened the rucksack he brought from Europe, decides to look into his past. The rucksack contains the broken remnants of his family, his parents and his sister Jeanie: a silver salt shaker, two silver spoons, some cracked plates, and tattered clothes. His attempt to rearrange the backpack is as futile as his attempt to rearrange his life on the verge of its impending end.

What is the significance of the cigarette obsession? We do not know. Max is left without cigarettes and decides to go to Reb Arye's home to get some. The hour is late and he is short of breath. Sitting down, he feels dizzy while breathing the dry night air of Jerusalem. He decides to rest a bit and then return home, and the story ends.

Thus this story too lacks a clear end or a resolution. In an implied manner, however, we see the loneliness of the two men and the deep affection between them, as well as their impending death. The backpack evokes a past and at the same time points to an end. In a way, a clear ending would have detracted from the power of the story. All the signs are indications of the future without spelling it out.

Here as elsewhere, Appelfeld's universe is made up of survivors. Other Israelis play little part. The survivors all share a secret language that does not need articulation. Whenever Israelis appear, they represent harsh, demanding authorities.

Characters in *Smoke* are afflicted by certain ailments, physical or mental, often mysterious ailments that cannot be explained. For an explanation we must look to psychology. A magazine article entitled "They Cried until They Could Not See," for example, tells about Cambodian women who lost their sight after seeing family members killed in front of them. It was believed that physically there was nothing wrong with their eyes. The article quotes psychologist Eve B. Carlson:

Dissociation is that lack of integration with what's happening. In an extremely traumatic state you eventually begin to depersonalize things around you and detach from the world. Reality is distorted. . . . Researchers now believe that some personalities caught in this altered state of awareness are somehow primed for psychosomatic illness. In order to advance the escape from the trauma a physical sacrifice is then made. In 1910, Freud called this sacrifice "conversion disorder." He speculated that unresolved conflict is transferred to an "offending body part. . . . Freud believed that these conflicts were always sexual, but more recently psychologists and psychiatrists have come to accept other types of conflict to account for conversion disorder. . . . No one is certain why one area of the body becomes the focal point of the conflict and not another. (Psychosomatic loss of hearing and speech have been observed—and memory loss was common in Holocaust victims, among whom dissociation was also prevalent.)[7]

In Appelfeld's fiction, "conversion disorder" is always associated with young women or girls like Bertha, and is frequently connected with the transition from girlhood to womanhood.

Survivors in Israel are depicted in Appelfeld's fiction as the "other." They do not define themselves in relation to Israeli society. Their discourse, voiceless and inaudible, is with a past engraved in their psyches. Marginality was a form of self-imposed or socially imposed protection.

4

IN THE FERTILE VALLEY

Aᴘᴘᴇʟꜰᴇʟᴅ's ᴅᴇᴇᴘ study of Jewish motifs begins in his second collection of short stories, *Ba'guy Ha'poreh* (*In the fertile valley*, 1963). Appelfeld sometimes uses the first-person narrator in these stories of the 1960s; but when he does, the effect is not markedly different from his third-person narration. The reader is not introduced to the inner life of the character; nor is a single point of view maintained. Thus no special certainties are in store for the reader when a first-person narrator is introduced. On the contrary, the first-person voice often introduces doubt and uncertainty. Statements are often rhetorical, speculative, even poetic, but they do not supply any special information related to that voice. The omnipresent voice of the narrator, in conjunction with the first-person mode, does not introduce information; rather, it may allude to "hidden intentions" whose source is unknown. At times the oblique statements are reminiscent of the "authorities" that pervade Kafka's text; occasionally those hidden intentions have an affinity to Hassidic lore, in which metapersonal powers intervene in mysterious ways. Moreover, there is a subtle connection between such unnamed powers and the manifestations of the human psyche.

The image of the monastery, alluded to in *Smoke*, features centrally in this second collection. The stories "The Last Refuge," "Kitty," and "Enrico's Journey" view the monastery from within. "The Last Refuge" depicts a Jew who has found refuge in a monastery. After being baptized, he is involved in the production of a mysterious potion extracted from a plant that grows around the monastery. The atmosphere in the monastery is unperturbed by the events outside. The war, the arrest of the Jews, their deportation to the camps—none of these affect the monastery. It thrives financially, and that allows for renovations and new purchases. Working on the production of the potion allows the body to cleanse itself of thought and memory through excruciating pain. The protagonist, renamed Ivan after the local saint, sinks slowly; the potion is absorbed by his system, transmitting pain to his very being. The ambiguous end suggests a fatal metamorphosis—death or madness. On the eve of St. Ivan's Day, two women seek refuge in the monastery, but two monks hurl them outside the gates.

The nonincriminating tone of the story adds to the silent horror it evokes. The story's strength lies in its simplicity and opaqueness. One can suggest an allegorical reading as to the symbolic nature of the potion, its effects and purpose. (What comes to mind is Agnon's short story "The Lady and the Peddler," about the allure of Christianity.) The theme of change is alluded to. Sin and expiation are inverted when perceived against the background of the Holocaust. Mode of escape is a major theme in Appelfeld's fiction.

The intricate pictoriality, the detailed depiction of mood and atmosphere in an almost impressionistic technique, and the diminution of dialogue contribute to shaping a highly stylized fable in "Kitty." Yet Appelfeld does not employ a stream-of-consciousness technique; that and the deemphasizing of dramatic dialogue add up to a reluctance to create highly individualized characters. Concern with inner motivations and intentions was not part of Appelfeld's methodology during this period. The stream-of-consciousness technique, had he employed it, would have given his characters an inner life based on memory associations and personalized time. Appelfeld's typical character is flawed in precisely this faculty.

"Kitty" tells of an eleven-year-old girl who finds herself in a French convent toward the end of the war, devoid of both language and memory. She emerges from her insulated, autistic state through a series of revelations, discovering her life through her senses. This synesthetic "conversion" lifts her from an elemental, preverbal creature to a person who relates to the world through her body. As she grows she becomes open to touch, sight, and sound. An expansive, surging sense of life fills her. And while opening up, she continues to weave her own unique, enclosed self. With puberty she acquires language and asks questions in the process of a possible loss of innocence. The silence of the convent protects her like a womb. It bursts open with encroaching reality as the Germans approach. She discovers her Jewishness, and with it anti-Semitism and greed. Through it all she maintains her world as fantasy and epiphany. As the war draws to a close she is shot by the Germans.

The story of "Kitty" (as of "Bertha" and the later novel *Tzili*) is an intricate tale of girlhood and womanhood. Appelfeld is especially attuned to the fate of the young girls, whose stories carry autobiographical elements. Kitty's metamorphosis is from "cocoon" to "butterfly"; her new process of individuation involves the initiation of her own speech through a constant contact with the world that touches her: texture, touch, sound are all viable elements in her own initiation into personhood. She converses with whatever is present in her space and breathes life into inanimate objects. Here is the opening paragraph:

> She was expected to read slowly and to memorize the sentences. She felt how the words hit the stone and returned to her, chilled. They called her name, which rustled within her as in the starched linen dresses which made her shudder. The windows shimmered in the sharp yellowness, kindling the floor with little flames. Sometimes she felt the full impact of the air gripping the back of her neck, stifling the syllables in her mouth. But at other times the flow increased, the good words remained within her, like a warm secret which planted itself slowly, spreading its roots.[1]

In Kitty we encounter a solipsistic young woman whose trauma, undetailed in the story, causes a kind of "conversion disorder." Bertha symbolically and psychologically stunted her growth; Kitty's trauma returns her to a preverbal state of being and submits memory to the deepest and darkest recesses. Unlike Bertha, Kitty goes through a process of individuation connected with Christian symbolism. The Jewish girl feels that in her rebirth she is the daughter of God, whose tormented body on the cross she observes. Her encounter with the world around her shapes her new image. Like other of Appelfeld's characters, she senses a mysterious flow of movement which points to another reality embedded in the visual signs of the world. The protracted silence of the convent is her salvation. Penetrating noises unsettle her, creating deep anxiety. A forthcoming visit of the abbess and the sound of cleaning, scrubbing, and furniture moving unsettle Kitty, seeming to evoke unexpressed fears of the past and portending danger. The sound of the steps of the authoritative abbess evokes other sounds within her. But Kitty's suppressed past allows her to glow in the acquisition of a new self.

> Summer came, and with it the change. Suddenly, like the transition from budding to blossoming, speech burst forth. It surged in her, colorful and wild, crystallizing into French words which fluttered in her like caged birds trying to escape. They emerged only with the greatest effort, tittering syllables which took on a meaning only by virtue of the voice, the fluency, and the intonation. You couldn't call them words. They didn't seem to come from the speech center. It was her whole being which spoke. (Pp. 226, 228)

The nuns in the convent—except for Maria, her tutor—consider Kitty to be a handicapped child. Assigned to teach the girl, Maria understands her uniqueness. In comparison, Maria's own life seems unfulfilled. For Kitty the transition from innocence to experience comes with the posing of questions, with puberty and war, all portending penetration. The convent is surrounded by German soldiers, their half-naked bodies suggesting the sensuality and sexuality that have penetrated Kitty's existence.

The threat is coupled with the second visit of the abbess and the appearance of Peppi, the vulgar cleaning woman. Peppi is cunning, strong, and direct in manner; Kitty is attracted to her, knowing instinctively that many questions, unanswered by Maria, will be answered by the peasant woman. Peppi, with her loose tongue and down-to-earth manner, does not hide her sexual encounters with the Germans and thereby reveals a new world to Kitty. As the convent is besieged by Germans, Peppi suggests stealing the convent's gold candelabra. Kitty's refusal to go along with her scheme unleashes a barrage of anti-Semitic slurs. Peppi calls her "a dirty Jewess" and threatens to expose her.

Maria's departure and the revelation about her origin mark the beginning of Kitty's undoing. She is confined to the cellar. Yet in her descent is her ascent: through spiritual resignation and calm she weaves a new relationship with the things that surround her: jars of pickled vegetables in the process of fermentation. Two voices are at war within her. One, a sense of divine grace, leads her to think that she is one of God's chosen children and as such must suffer until his light shines upon her. The other voice repeats the question: "Am I a hairy Jewess?" Despite it all, in an act of spiritual resignation, she awaits her fate. As the war draws to an end, the convent is attacked and invaded.

> Kitty had grown taller in the cellar and when she was brought out into the light, dressed in her white nightgown, she looked even taller. The gown trailed behind her. She was led along narrow paths behind the fence. How marvelous it all seemed—like floating in space. Now all the people were gone. Angels embraced her arms and when the shot was heard, she stood for a moment, marveling at the miracle revealed. (P. 246)

The revelation of the wonder suggests the multilayered structure of the story: a spiritual, almost hagiographic element combined with a deep sense of the irreversible reality of the Holocaust.

Critics offer various readings of the story. One critic claims that it is Kitty's ignorance vis-à-vis Christianity that allows her to create an intimate relationship with Jesus and to conceive of herself as God's daughter. That allows her to experience her death not as a horrible murder but rather as a religious event.[2]

One theme that emerges in this story, as well as in "Bertha" and to a lesser extent *Tzili*, is the fear of growing up, of womanhood, of penetration. Kitty's emerging womanhood and the beginning of her menstruation are accompanied by both fear and guilt. The revelation of her Jewishness is juxtaposed with the forces that try to penetrate her and the convent. Only in a state of childhood, protected by a father figure or a convent, can the traumatized girl's wounded psyche find refuge. Guilt ties up the physical strata—changes brought about by puberty. If indeed she is a dirty Jewess, she is reponsible for the crucifixion. Sexuality—suppressed and expressed—is depicted by the women in the story—the nuns on one hand and Peppi on the other send differing messages to Kitty. Sexuality and self-awareness burst out simultaneously. Sublimation on one hand and repression on the other engulf the girl, who has to withdraw to her encased self and to the cellar, there to await her inevitable fate.[3]

Another story of the 1960s, "In Stone" (in the collection *Kefor Al Ha'aretz*), portrays a counterpart to Kitty, a boy of unknown origin who also lives in a convent. Various elements are reminiscent of the earlier story: the cellar, the character Maria, and the fact that the boy, like Kitty, has a speech defect and is considered mute. The boy, given permission to leave the convent, is assigned to work with a stonemason, and stone becomes his mode of expression. Silent entities prominent in "Kitty" appear in this story, too. War hovers, but the boy is in no danger. Enrico, in the story "Enrico's Journey," is, like Kitty, curious about his own origins. He is told that the neighboring village, where he was born, was set on fire and that he was brought to the convent as a baby. Revelations unite all these stories. The young boy of "In Stone" discovers the face of a young Jesus in the stone he carves, and a visiting bishop consecrates this image.

The Jew is almost always on the move in Appelfeld's work. Escape, flight, and pursuit unite his characters. At this early stage Appelfeld writes Jewish tales that combine Biblical, Hassidic and Kabbalistic motifs. That allows him to suspend any historical framework and to endow his stories with a mythic quality by depicting a repetitious pattern of the basic Jewish condition. The title of the story "In The Wilderness" brings to mind the desert wandering of the Children of Israel. Appelfeld introduces a religious authority into the stories in the character of a ritual slaughterer or a rabbi. In most cases, they have lost their power or their authority in a world gone awry. Time is not specified; neither is the place. We know that these parable stories take place in Europe. They seem to exist beyond an identifiable geographical terrain; war is in a distant background. Wandering is a major theme in this group of stories, where surrogate families are formed.

Appelfeld's early stories often present variations on the same motif, or a branching out from given basic units. The collective group is occasionally the protagonist, and the protagonist himself is a type rather than a clearly individuated character. In various stories we encounter the unit of three, most often composed of one adult and two young people. Appelfeld moves his characters from the center of historical events into peripheral locations. He strands them in forsaken places away from the eye of the storm. "The Hunt" opens with the tale of a nameless protagonist who was deserted by his nephews on the bank of a thawing lake. He joins a group of wandering gypsies, inhabitants of the nearby mountain, and becomes a storyteller and healer. He tells the children the stories of the Pentateuch, stories engraved in his memory. He wants to tell them about the last tragedy of the Jewish people, but they want to hear about the Biblical Joseph and his travails.

Their curse is their forgetfulness. Initially their wandering had a higher meaning, but they forgot it; their power to foretell the future is now their curse. As the wolves begin attacking their camp and snatching their children, the gypsies withdraw to the cave. They embrace death valiantly as free people. The story of the gypsies is mysterious; their enigmatic existence, with obvious comparisons to the Jewish plight, is an inverted mirror image: remembrance versus forgetting, past versus future, words versus deeds.

Until the 1990s Appelfeld's stories, characters, and plots are situated geographically away from the war and the concentration camps. We do not encounter a camp directly until his 1991 novel *The Railway*. Appelfeld's stories are fictional replicas of his personal autobiography. In this early phase of his writing, locations parallel those experienced by him after he was severed from his family as a child. The flight, the forests, the bunker, the monastery are stations in his own life, as are the shores of Italy. The stories against the background of Italy vary in mood, type, and tone. Some carry clearly autobiographical data, while others are highly fictional. Appelfeld succeeds in creating a similar but different world in the stories "By the Shore," "Cold Heights," and "The Isles of St. George." The terrain contributes to the atmosphere of the stories and is molded by them. The scorching sun, the Mediterranean Sea, and the sands are the background for the refugees of the DP camps. Some of the stories are character-oriented ("The Convoy"); in some a group of people serves as a protagonist. There are highly stylized tales as well as parables against the background of Italy. Small mountainous Italian villages, unaffected by time, are invaded by convoys of eternal nomads and refugees.

It is interesting and valuable to examine the relationship of an author to his characters, their actions and behavior. Appelfeld tries to adopt a nonjudgmental tone, but one nevertheless cannot avoid posing questions in regard to his feeling toward acts committed by his characters. From the early stories to the novels in the 1990s he attempts to maintain an aesthetic distance. That he chose to depict characters who commit immoral acts in the eyes of society but does not comment upon them creates an interesting dichotomy. We might claim that his traumatized characters move in a different world, one that does not abide by conventional morality. The question raised is in regard to whether this can serve as a complete and satisfying answer. Clearly he is not trying to teach a moral "lesson." The unparalleled circumstances of his characters shape his fiction. And yet the choice bespeaks an attitude—toward the self, toward Jews, and toward Europe.

The tone of the story "By the Shore" (also translated as "Near the Shore" or "Along the Shore") is established in the opening paragraph:

> Immediately after the war, a world of opportunities opened up, the trains rushed to the ports . . . a few succeeded in boarding ships, the rest remained here, on shore near the small huts left by the army . . . a bustle of activities ensued; there were even those who removed their clothes and offered them up for sale; the more enterprising set up stands.[4]

The theme of trade and peddlers appears in stories connected with the life prior to the war, taking place on the shores of Italy after the war, and later in Israel. A certain mixed tone is almost always attached to this form of life: mild criticism and understanding. Appelfeld personally joined a group of people who distanced themselves from the hustle and bustle and opted for meditation and silence. At the same

time he feels that those frantic activities should not be perceived su-
perficially—it was out of a deep need to taste change, life, and a way
of breaking away from suppressed horrors. The activities in this story
portray frenzy and madness. Most of the surface activities are somehow moored in self-deceit, in an externalization of inner turmoil. The
urge to move, to do, to act, answers deep-seated needs: "Memory was
still naked. There was a remarkable readiness to respond to every
rhythm, to every transaction, even to plundering of the army
camps . . . which had been deserted" (p. 140).

It seems as if only the tangible and the immediate bring any certainty. Ideas, words, mores—all have failed. Freedom means movement without hindrance. Reb Israel, the son of the Kumchul Rebbe,
calls for repentance and a return to a modicum of spirituality. When
he tries to approach the British authorities, people don't hesitate to
drug him with sleeping pills and put him on a freight train going
south. The attempt to break away from authority knows no bounds.
The deep sense was "how marvelous it was to be alive, to be in the
thick of the transactions." (p. 143). The burgeoning of petty commerce
consists of small stands under the scorching sun: dealing came first,
the search for relatives was left for later.

Excessive eating and general surfeit bring on an epidemic, in the
form of smallpox. The army's enforcement of quarantine has led some
to the idea of escape. Two cases of typhoid and the plan to fence the
area off have accentuated the desire to escape. Excessive sun and excessive food have taken their toll. The quickest have fled to the ancient
Italian village perched on the hill. At this juncture Appelfeld could
have opted for a story with a collective protagonist, but he brings forth
three characters and focuses on a major instance in their life. The
opening sentence is repeated as an introduction to the characters: "Up
there a world of great opportunities opened up." Berl and Fischl infil-
trate a slumbering village with their zeal and frenzy for business. The
village is awakened to cries of "nylons, nylons." Both have survived
and are set on having a "good time." Their attempt was to do, not to
think. There is a void between the hustle and bustle of the days's
empty activities and the equally vacuous sleep.

Another epidemic breaks out, forcing the two down from the mountains against their will. Everyone has returned, even Reb Israel, who
was in a state of Yerida, a state of "descent," which in the Hassidic
lore is a condition for Aliya, "ascent." Not uttering a word, he sits all

day long eating sardines. Quite late in the story the reader is introduced to Gitl. She was nine years old when Berl found her in the snow
and brought her into the bunker, and since then they have been together. Despite her attempts to please both men by serving them, Gitl
feels that she is a hindrance. So do the two men, who decide to leave
the girl behind. In the glorious search for new opportunities, there is
no room for a child. The decision is to leave Gitl in a convent: "There
she'll learn French."

The surrogate family and partnership bear a variety of forms in
Appelfeld's fiction. Usually the nonsexual tie, between a mature man
and a young girl, involves desertion as well. The desire for movement
and freedom is acute; it is the existential desire to be that goes beyond
emotional ties to the past. Saving Gitl's life was a noble human act;
committing her to the convent was a cruelly cynical one. Conversion
is a very sensitive issue in Jewish moral consciousness. Fischl, as Berl's
alter ego, brings the girl to the convent; his voice is muffled when the
"transaction" takes place. He signs the form the nuns present to him:
"With faith and complete awareness I have brought my daughter to be
brought up in holiness, all the days of her life, blessed be the worship-
ers of God" (pp. 168–169). Gitl is forced to believe that French is good
for her. As we see the last of the two they are heading south.

Another problem that emerges frequently in Appelfeld's fiction is
the suspension of the ethical: the character's actions here point to just
such a suspension. Presented with the actions depicted in this story
and others, we may ask whether the reader is called upon to resolve
the ethical dilemma. And what can the reader infer about the attitude
of the author? Despite Berl's hesitations, the deed is done. Self-denial
and self-deceit are a part of the mentality of the two. Their cultural
and moral opaqueness makes them light and mobile. Memories are
suppressed as a load that can have tied them down, and they are therefore discarded. It is interesting to note that the scene depicting the
betrayal and desertion of the girl is conveyed through dialogue. This
enhances the dramatic nature of the event and creates a distance between the author and the text. Toward the end of the story the dialogue between Berl and Fischl takes over: it is terse, repetitious; everything said is repeated and echoed, depicting hesitation and coercion.
One senses Berl's moral anguish, yet he is being led into self-deceit
willingly.

In the midst of "petty transactions and grander schemes," Mintz points out, "one realizes that opportunity is mobility."[5] Despite the nonemotive depiction of events, there is a surfeit of the grotesque and of parody. Awkwardness emerges from the lame energetic scenes depicted. Opening paragraphs are often independent units which can be attached to a variety of stories, facilitated by nonparticularized plot and character, with the reader acting as an organizer, creating the narrative continuity by combining independent, often disjointed units into a story.

In this regard, the story "Cold Heights" is different. From the beginning we are given time, place, even particularized descriptions. Despite ambiguities, the story begins affirmatively, with a detailed description:

> The tower of Larma, commanding the scene from stark heights, soaring like a statue which blends with the rocky landscape. The ocean lies in front, and from behind, jagged gorges surround it, a dank dwelling of eternal gloom. . . . Relics indicate that the place was originally used as a lookout post for one of the princes. Later, due to its unusual virtues, it became a fortress. . . . Eventually it became a retreat for monks.[6]

The inhabitants of the tower are convalescent war refugees. A contrast appears between their emaciated bodies, which "had nothing but a network of nerves to cover them . . . , their souls flickering within, and the open expanses of the sky." Under the seemingly quiet, hushed atmosphere, madness and violence are waiting to erupt. Outwardly the patients changed, their wounds were healed, their cheeks were flushed —all to the satisfaction of Dora, their nurse. In other characters the choice of inertia and a state of stagnation is typical. Voluntary change, as we have observed, is highly demanding, often a risky and even damaging process. Language and expression, too, endanger the status quo. Some of the patients are catatonic; some look like skeletons. The bursting spring outside bespeaks rebirth.

"Cold Heights" is one of the few stories by Appelfeld that feature a narrator as a presence. He observes the small movements of the convalescents and knows that neither generalizations nor details could capture their being. A smile, a single syllable, a stammering utterance are the paroles of these maimed people. These sparse signs are shrouded in secrecy and silence. How does one combine all these signs into a body language amounting to a comprehensible text? How can a writer, even one who is a witness or a survivor, penetrate the mystery of the other person? Two characters emerge and come to the center of the story. Despite similar motives and situations, each has a unique nature.

> There was one man by the name of Spillman. When chairs were brought outdoors he could be seen sitting beside a girl, who, to judge by her resemblance to him, must have been a niece. . . . Certain facts concerning their life were known and could even be pieced together. . . . They were among those who had fled. This incredible escape story is worth describing in greater detail, though I doubt whether I can do it justice. We must make the oversimplified distinction between those who faced the torture through to its end, exhausting it, as it were, and those who fled to the forest disguised as peasants or circus clowns. Carrying death within them they roamed about. They joined a troupe of clowns who did the rounds of villages, drawing crowds and entertaining them with acrobatics, pantomime and rowdy dances. (Pp. 94–95)

Appelfeld's fascination with the circus is also expressed in *Essays in First Person*. It is possible, however, to see another connection. Fascination with time and movement is expressed in Kafka's fiction, and one of its symbols is the trapeze artist, whose desire to avoid touching the ground—to exist freely, independent of outer factors—is echoed in the hungry artist's desire not to depend on food.

Tragically, many inhabitants of the tower in "Cold Heights" have become emaciated as a result of their torture at the camps. There is no particularly esoteric message to be attached to their bare bodies. Tightrope walking, performed by Spillman and the girl, can serve as a metaphor for any number of Appelfeld's characters. The two have a mystic aura around them—they sit in the sun like two majestic frozen figures, evangelists of a hidden meaning. There is an ambiguity in the way they are described: "they seemed to be clarifying their thoughts, contemplating the crucial words" (p. 95).

The connection between Spillman and the girl is unclear. Is she his daughter? His niece? His mistress? Did he save her? The presence of a narrator does not help in eliminating ambiguities. The story is, in a way, about the writer's limits on knowing and expressing. And thus the slow awakening in the cold height is marked with cryptic sentences that allude rather than state. Despite silence and sedation, questions seem to be suspended in midair: What for? Where to? We observed that some of the inhabitants are in a catatonic state; others have awakened to life and its possibilities. Again the themes of food and sickness are connected. Liuba, the girl, contracts measles, but she is not alone. The textile merchant, with his dreams of commercial trans-actions, is ill, and so are the two children in the tower.

The role of the narrator is at best ambiguous. At times he is one of the characters in the plot, at other times a director who steps in and out of the play-text; at still other times he is silent. The emerging question is: whose play is it anyway? His hesitations and doubts are expressed:

> What right had he to tell the tale of the group? If Liuba were to open her heart, the warm flow would purify them, give them the redeem-ing word, restore friendship, revive the days in camps and bunkers. Someone said that Liuba was sealed in silence and suffering, and hadn't said a word yet. (Pp. 108–109)

It seems as if the redeeming words are sought by the narrator who faces the mystery. Those words, the healing words, did not come, words that could recreate a bonding, a connection between the people. The feeling is that sometimes living in the twilight zone was safer; a dazed state of inaction was preferable to a state of change. The noncommittal self desired no change. And at times, silence was a cover to a seething rage. Spillman, in a moment of rage, madness, and pain, drags Liuba along the veranda and tries to hurl her over the cliff. The process of healing is connected to the emergence of memory. Liuba is the one to recover—the fate of Spillman is unclear. He claims that she, the girl he saved and carried on his shoulders, was defiled by the gentiles while in the circus. Between violence and silence the subterranean life of the inhabitants of the tower draws to an end. Liuba and Spillman are left behind, awaiting the decision of the health authorities.

The departure from the fortress has a comic-tragic bent. As they leave, the refugees are clad in colorful donated American clothes, painting a picture of a slow, uncertain, and grotesque exodus. "Cold Heights" consists of several tales. One is the story of twenty-four ref-ugees in the fortress, which serves as a rehabilitation camp in Italy, probably established by United States forces. The nurse Dora, who is probably a nun, takes care of her wards. She mediates between the patients and the outer world, while the narrator, the silent observer, relates his own story and theirs to the reader. In a manner suggesting Pirandello, there is a search for characters. The story of Liuba and Spillman is the story of the artists and the story of the surrogate family. It is Spillman who dreads separation and desertion. His acts of violence are desperate acts to maintain his hold on Liuba, who in her white dress evokes purity. In the midst of it all there is a game (as Spillman's name suggests), a serious deadly game of love and betrayal, of faith and doubt.

> Uncle and niece have become wasted in spirit and vitality, and the other survivors know that they must go about reconstructing their life with no expectation of solidarity. The consequences of remembering, it is implied, cannot be otherwise. To survive is to have done terrible things or at least to suspect others of having done them. When memory comes, it decimates, because, for the survivor the only contents of memory can be shame and accusation, real or imagined. Now, the return of memory is not inescapable. The way out is never to let it surface or to force it back underground by clinging tenaciously to a state of present-mindedness.[7]

At this stage the Appelfeldian characters oscillate between a desire to suppress memory by silence and the adopting of activities that seemingly proclaim freedom. Both action and inaction are modes of suppressing memories of the past.

The novella "The Isles of St. George" in the collection *Kefor Al Ha'aretz* (Frost on the earth, 1965) also belongs to the cycle that depicts the life of refugees in Italy. It is an outstanding study of a man who has reached a point of no return on a deserted island near the shores of Italy. This third-person narrative sums up various themes and places experienced by the Appelfeldian characters: home, the flight, the forest, Italy, Israel. The protagonist, a man sought by the police, is in a state of total fatigue, with his past memories encroaching upon him. During and after the war he was in a constant state of moving—he never stayed long in one place. In Israel, where his friends settled down, leaving behind them their shady dealings, he was still involved in black marketeering. The few moments of grace in Jerusalem have not changed him. The desolate Isles of St. George are his last resting place; the arid, desolate place is a last resort and a possible station in a hidden desire for purification and atonement. After being constantly on the run to avoid the authorities, he has been arrested by his own psyche, it seems.

The protagonist with multiple aliases, who bought the name Chohovsky, is being transferred to the islands by an old Italian fisherman. The motif is reminiscent of the crossing of the Styx in Greek mythology, when the souls of the doomed are transferred to the underworld. The protagonist has perfected the art of illegal dealing and the art of escape, thrilled by the danger and suspense. He despises his past partners in Israel who settled down to a life of middle-class acceptability and boredom. He thrives on danger, achievement, and freedom. The spirit of adventure was broken, however, and a yearning for his childhood besieges his dreams. He fears the encroachment of the past because he realizes that his strength lies in being on guard. The past is a disarming experience. The quest for the island is a turning point in his life.

The novella reveals various stages in the protagonist's life, and like many of Appelfeld's longer narratives, the opening establishes a framework for the unfolding story.

> During the course of his wandering Chohovsky arrived at the Isles of St. George. These little islands south of Italy were once inhabited, and the name they were given, although its origins have long been forgotten, bears witness to a certain sanctity which was attributed to them. The sparse vegetation lives its humble life under the sun. . . . Chohovsky was weary of his wandering: only long solitude would be able to absorb the poison of the years from his body. . . . He wanted to part from his fate and from his stupefying weariness.[8]

Once on the island Chohovsky senses that his life is going to be different. He, the man who had pursued sin and danger with elation, expects a certain expiation through seclusion. The story features two movements: one tells in a progressive manner about the protagonist's life on the island; the other reverts to his early childhood. The reader reconstructs Chohovsky's life and interprets the present in light of the past. Chohovsky, whose life resembles that of a trapeze artist, knows that the time for the dangling sensations has passed. His life of shady dealings and speculative ventures was a form of art. He always aspired to unattainable summits. He glowed in the life of walking on a tightrope but this came to an end; he senses that the rope has snapped—no longer can he enjoy an existence outside the law and restrictions. A feeling of resignation settles on him as he realizes that his long flight has come to an end. With trepidation he views the inevitable collapse. The island seems to be his solution.

The third-person narrator is a source of information and data. We learn the various stages in Chohovsky's adventures and their pattern: he has moved from place to place, from Vienna to Italy, to Israel and back to Italy, continuing his illegal transactions. When his speculative dealings "rose to dangerous heights," everything collapsed and he moved on to a new place. He did not desire the accumulation of capital, since this required deliberation and steadiness. What excited him was risk for the sake of risk. As noted earlier, in Appelfeld's stories memories are often suppressed because they constitute a heavy load. Time and again, characters adopt forgetfulness to facilitate movement or a state of no change. Chohovsky is different. He tries in a way to delve into his past through dreams and by so doing to unite the severed halves of his existence: blissful childhood and the life of an outlaw. As long as he was on the run, memories were suppressed; on the island, memories emerge. His hometown, Lischchik, is evoked in his conversation with a fisherman. Regardless of where a Jew finds himself, Chohovsky says, his home calls him back. The change for Chohovsky is not merely a change of place—he has a longing for home—he expects a miracle or a sign. Unprotected by either commercial transactions or constant movement, he is in a state of vulnerability. After twenty years of life on the run, he tries to shed the phony covers he adopted. He realizes, for instance, that his real name is Leibel Gutsman.

The exploration of the island parallels his exploration of his own psyche. Years earlier the island was chosen as an oil site, and the failure of prospectors in their endeavors left the unearthed rocks in a state of chaos. Chohovsky's Bukovina background emerges as he remembers traveling with his father in a convoy to the Sadigora Rebbe. They sang on their way as stones were hurled at them. This was a test, a trial, as was his whole existence. On the barren background of the island he is able to converse with his suppressed dreams and with the figure of his father. His existence gains a religious aura. His desire to kneel, to pray and confess, evokes a hidden sense of guilt. Chohovsky's prior life is reconstructed through dreams and visions. The dreams, reminiscent of Agnon's *Book of Deeds*, are always connected with childhood, with his father and with his name. Guilt in Appelfeld's fiction is connected with the act of betrayal and desertion. In one dream, characters from his childhood emerge; his borrowed name, Chohovsky, belonged to a man who was drowned in the Danube, and the dream takes place on the banks of the Prut, the river that runs through Bukovina. He feels a combination of deep guilt for his desertion and a desire to gain his old name/self.

The image of the father appears again and again—with his white beard and the flour the gentiles threw on his face. The father is shocked by the son's life; he considers it insubstantial, illusionary, witchcraft. The son tries to convince the father that business and speculation are God's gift to the people of Israel. The father's message is that a man must examine his own deeds and distinguish the real from the illusory.

Walking over the island, Chohovsky/Gutsman meets Vinter, a watchman guarding the deserted equipment and the drilling machinery of the oil prospectors. Vinter, a Jew, does not crave company, and he looks much like the petrified terrain he lives in. It seems that Chohovsky, too, will remain in this disemboweled land. Another discovery is the presence of smugglers who found refuge on the island. He befriends one of them, also a Jew, and they reminisce about their days in the forests and their adventures. Every meeting on the island points to a possible way of existence. His last encounter, the most meaningful one, occurs at the monastery of St. George.

> Many times he had sought refuge in monasteries. The monks rejected him. This time it seemed that he had not come to seek refuge, his legs had carried him there on their own accord. He remembered his speculations like a worn out adventurer with nothing left but his memories to delight him. How exhilarating his moments of happiness had been. (P. 67)

A month after his arrival on the island he reaches the monastery. The pleasant monk who greets Chohovsky/Gutsman resembles Vinter. At this stage of his life Chohovsky tells everyone he meets that he is running from the authorities, and he does not hide the truth from the monk, either. At the beginning the meeting is rather formal. Only when Chohovsky says that he was in Israel does the monk get excited. He has been assigned to go to Israel in six months. He asks Chohovsky to teach him Hebrew so that he can read the Bible in its original language. Chohovsky, who did not speak Hebrew in Israel, begins to teach the monk the portion of the week in its traditional Ashkenazi intonation which he remembers from the Heder of his childhood.

When the monk departs from the island, Chohovsky is left alone on its shores. But before he leaves, the monk tells Chohovsky that a man can begin again from the beginning. Chohovsky responds with questions.

> But where is that beginning? Perhaps it would be better to ask where is the end? and perhaps it would be better to forget. To sit and forget,

year after year, until forgetfulness eats you up from inside and then to rise again. A new man. A new Chohovsky. For that reason, and that reason only, I came here. Otherwise the cancer will find many places to take hold and grow, innumerable places. Teach me the art of forgetfulness so that I can begin again from the beginning. (Pp. 71–72)

The open-ended closure of the story indicates that the process of introspection and self-awareness has begun. Chohovsky's character will appear in a variant in the novel *The Immortal Bartfuss*.

5

FROST ON THE EARTH

Aᴘᴘᴇʟꜰᴇʟᴅ's ᴛʜɪʀᴅ collection of short stories, *Kefor Al Ha'aretz* (Frost on the earth, 1965) marks his choice to become a Jewish writer and not strictly a Holocaust writer. *In The Fertile Valley* may be seen as Appelfeld's attempt to wrestle with Jewish motifs. In the mid-1960s he tries to expand his historical and geographical territory, in an attempt to go beyond the experience of the survivors. Identifying himself as a modern Hebrew/Jewish writer, he expands his historical boundaries, like I. B. Singer and S. Y. Agnon. Appelfeld's new territory is the modern Jewish experience. He does not restrict himself to the experience of the survivors, yet he never abandons it. Some of the changes are detected in the novella "In the Isles of St. George," discussed in the preceding chapter. Self-awareness and self-questioning emerge as prominent aspects in the depiction of a character. The authorial distancing is relaxed; a more individuated narrator appears, sometimes a child.

Appelfeld now becomes fascinated with Jewish mysticism. His characters, like their author, often are "gatherers and collectors of visions." In a mythical depiction of timeless Jewish life, Appelfeld creates a synoptic view. By combining past events with visions of the future he breaks historical barriers and enhances the historical archetype, thus following the dictum that "there is neither early nor late in the Torah" (*Pesach Tractate* 6;b). Historical rules of perspective and irreversibility are abandoned. This artistic policy of the open border applies to time, place, and period, allowing for a great fluidity in Appelfeld's fiction: "This sameness of conditions is a way for Appelfeld to assert that the nature of existence is one, and that it matters little if one writes of survivors, who have gone through the event, or of their predecessors."[1]

Various narrative techniques continue to be applied. Realistic and surrealistic tales appear side by side. Appelfeld's claim that he is a Jewish writer, not exclusively a Holocaust writer, is substantiated by his stories. Stories of the 1960s can be seen as chapters in an extended saga of Jewish life. Wandering and movement are maintained as themes. The Jew continues to define himself and his movements conscious of the constant presence of the gentile. Throughout Appelfeld's fiction, the Jew is depicted as the "other." Basic symbols appear and reappear: winter, a state of siege, the Hassidic pilgrimage connected with the theme of quest. As observed, Appelfeld tends to imbue realistic depiction with metapersonal dimensions by introducing mysterious authorities. Their presence seems to introduce both an air of determinism and a tone of ambiguity.

Winter is a major factor, almost a connective tissue, in some of the stories. "Frost on the Earth" tells about a town besieged by snow. Only two wandering Jews challenge the elements: a traveling salesman and a matchmaker. One hotel in the town awaits the wanderer; the moment the nameless wanderer sets eyes on the two candlesticks he knows he is at home. This place is the last haven to homeless Jewish traveling salesmen. They routinely return out of despair and in hope of consolation. Like Mother Courage, they are constantly on the move. They return after their yearly rounds in the villages to hear a Jewish word, to eat Jewish food. They have forgotten their origins, and the hotel owner is the keeper of their memories; he knows one of them to be the son of Reb Pinchas. The son does not remember his father; his years on the road have erased his Jewish look and his Jewish language. The hotel owner is a gatherer of information and memories; he dedicates his existence to the maintenance of past existence. He awaits the return of the wayward sons to help awaken his own memory. They too, like other characters, cannot carry the load of responsibility and guilt. Mobility necessitates forgetfulness, and in turn, mobility enhances forgetfulness.

Hebrew literature written in Europe between the 1870s and the Second World War is replete with "exits" and "returns." Young people left the *shtetl* and moved to the big city, only to return home from time to time. They left home in quest of knowledge, education, and personal emancipation from the strictures of tradition. The reasons for Appelfeld's exits and returns are more obtuse. Many of his characters are taken up with the world of commerce and success, never to return. "Authority" still plays a central role in Appelfeld's stories of the mid-1960s. "The Station" is a first-person narrative about a man going to the provincial capital to plead with the local governor because his concession was revoked. These can be regarded as containing texts behind the text. The journey, the trial, the appeal—all are connected in a cycle of unspecified detaining/preventing agents that make all missions into failures. Even the success in gaining the license does not bring joy to the man. He returns from his journey fatigued and parched. Appelfeld succeeds as a chronicler of unexpressed moods and obtuse states of being, depicting anxieties of the one, the Jew, who is forever an outsider.

Flight from the naked self is a theme common to author and character. Appelfeld continues in his reluctance to reenact, to recreate, to restate his own life story at this stage. In the 1970s Appelfeld openly returns to childhood landscapes of Bukovina; at this stage he chooses to depict Jewish existence in Bukovina and in neighboring Galicia and Bessarabia. Hassidic lore and forced conscription into the army occasionally are combined with Kafkaesque elements in the same story.

Modern Hebrew literature is rife with Biblical motifs: the Akeda ("the binding of Isaac"), Exodus, the time in the wilderness, and others. Agnon makes frequent use of the topos of the Exodus, most noticeably in the novella "In the Heart of Seas," where he artfully combines folk motifs and saga with Kabbalistic and Hassidic mysticism. Despite thematic allusions to early literature, Appelfeld does not establish a clear connection to a specific canonic text. He does not search for a clear prooftext. His connection to earlier texts might be thematic, but very rarely does he create a network of linguistic allusions. In the story "Expulsion" his characters are the "mute Hassidim," a clear allusion to the disciples of Reb Nachman of Bratzlav. They are referred to as the "toite Hassidim," the "dead Hassidim." No dynasty followed the Rebbe's death, and they continue to worship with the dead Rebbe as their ultimate "authority." Reb Nachman, a descendant of the Baal Shem Tov, the founder of the Hassidic movement, left parables studied to this day by his disciples. The truth rests, his disciples believe, behind those simple parables or "tales" (maises). The Rebbe's tales are allegories, metaphors, and "Meshalim," examples and parables of mystical depth. In the introduction to his collection, the Hassid editor hastens to warn the reader that those are not simple tales ("proste maises"); inherent in them are the secrets of the Torah. Agnon was a master of composing "simple" tales with deep moral and mystical underpinning. Reb Nachman's writings are models of the art of the tale.

Appelfeld, with his deep interest in Kabbala and Hassidism, uses the theme of expulsion in conjunction with the theme of Exodus. Expulsion as a decree is interpreted as yet another opportunity for union, for liturgical chant (niggun), for stories about the miracles of the Rebbe. The mission of the convoy is to go to the provincial capital to get a decree rescinded. Yet the interest lies somewhere else: it is the hidden (nistar), embedded in the revealed (nigleh), that occupies the convoy. Only when Reb Hershl asks "Whither?" does the convoy slow down.

The journey containing the motifs of expulsion and exodus is an attempt to break away from the world of the gentiles and from the world of commerce and its transactions. Against the movement of Enlightenment (Haskala), with its dominant motif of Emancipation and the attraction of secular civilization, the Hassidim are armed with a story, its dedication, and the belief that the world is in a constant state of revelation and concealment. Appelfeld subtly introduces himself in the character of the orphan on the convoy, the one who absorbs the sights, the sounds, the melodies—but as yet does not have a language of his own. The potential storyteller is the child-witness who will mature and make stories of remnants of memories recalling and reconstructing. The last Shabat is inscribed in the orphan's memory. The fable makers say that this Shabat was like the original sabbath on the seventh day of Creation. With the Havdala service at its end, celebrating the departure of the holy day, secular reality sets in. Some Hassidim try to chant the niggun of "Thou didst reveal thyself" ("Ata nigleyta," part of the musaf service for Rosh Ha'Shana), connecting the text to the Exodus and to the Revelation on Mount Sinai.

The "mute Hassidim," on their way between home and the provincial capital, portray a reverse Exodus. Their silence and their attempt to unravel the decree will fail; this failure is seen as part of a mystical process whose hidden intentions are not revealed to man. Introducing the mystical Hassidic lexicon with its themes of "revelation" and "concealment," including the "chant" (niggun), "intention" (kavanah), "clinging" (dvekut)—all endow the story with meanings that transcend the mere anecdote. Mintz writes: "Expulsion is inscribed in the cosmos; as in Appelfeld generally, such a fate is a defining condition of existence rather than a product of history."[2]

For the child, the visions on the road are corroborated by verses from the Bible, especially from Pentateuch. The Jewish child in Eastern Europe who was brought up traditionally integrated the canonic texts into his vocabulary and everyday reality. In the last part of the nineteenth century and the beginning of the twentieth, stories by Mendele, Bialik Feierberg, and other writers of Hebrew and Yiddish fiction portray young impressionable children for whom the Carmel, the Golan, and the Bashan were actual pulsating realities. This synoptic view of Jewish existence through the eyes of the child is not reiterated in Appelfeld's later fiction. The child on the Hassidic convoy accumulates visions, sights, niggunim, stories as foundations for his mature life as a storyteller. As if fictionally, Appelfeld points to the process of storytelling that began for him early as a child.

A story that corresponds in theme and sentiment is "Gonev Ha'Mar'ot"—the title translates as "The thief who steals visions" or "mirrors" or "reflections." Implied meanings are reflected/deflected by this first-person narrative. The man, a lame, misshapen individual, is a messenger in the rabbinical court. He sleeps in the poorhouse attached to the synagogue. Not unlike other Appelfeldian characters, there is a journey in his past that went awry. Upon his return, he appointed himself to be the night chronicler of the community, an unofficial recorder who does his writing in secret. Despite his lack of knowledge, he loves the written word and would have liked to be the official scribe of the community, the one who writes its history. He is the collector of sights and sounds. Barred from the holy books, which are beyond his comprehension, he creates his own text. Appelfeld (like Agnon in his tales), uses the word *sofer* in a variety of meanings: author, religious scribe, one who counts (recounts).

Getzl, the protagonist, does not grow up. His deformed body is not affected by the years. His deformity is a refuge to him and a constant benign siege. He records all the doubts, the uncertainties (the official chronicler would record only certainties). Marginality and deformity, inadequacy and ignorance, all pertain to the role of the writer in a time of eclipse. Implied in the text is Appelfeld's own self-perception as a writer at that time. Hassidic tales tell of the miracles performed by the holy man (*zaddik*) detailing his powers to save and heal. Appelfeld portrays the twilight of Hassidic lore. His characters are descendants of great *zaddikim*, all in a state of fall or descent. He continues to focus on marginal characters, the handicapped child, the deformed, as observers of reality. Attracted to the mystical spirituality of Hassidism, Appelfeld portrays matter versus spiritual quest, the world of temptation versus the world of restraint. The urge to tell, in words or on a carved stone, is the province of the child, the outcast, depicting a world of unuttered truths.

The last stories in the collection *Frost on the Earth* are highly autobiographical. Appelfeld's commitment to the past, to Bukovina and

Czernowitz, has been constant through the years. He recreates shreds of memory and fashions it into a tale.

"A Meeting" opens with a simple statement: "I met a man a year ago." There was nothing distinguished about the man; he was from Lischchik, the narrator's hometown. The story takes place in Jerusalem. "I believed that Jerusalem was my city. I have been living in the city for many years, and I know every corner of it. Sometimes I imagined that I was born in Jerusalem and orphaned in Jerusalem."[3] The name of the hometown evokes the aroma of the spring he has carried with him since his childhood. The narrator confesses that he remembers only the forest; even the image of his parents has been blurred. The man, a merchant, probably a sometime smuggler, carries his demolished city within him. The narrator recalls:

> In my childhood we went to visit my grandmother, God bless her soul. Heavy snows delayed us in a Jewish inn. We were surrounded by snow. A child cannot remember what happened. . . . But I remember the wondering yearning we all experienced. . . . A bookcase full of hardcover books was there. (P. 126)

This is probably Appelfeld's own private recollection of his childhood. We know that his grandmother's place was the last connection with his family before his escape. This germinal scene, short and concise, appears in a variety of fictional guises in his short and long narratives. The autobiographical tone continues as the narrator muses:

> Eyes deceive you. A person thinks that he lives in Mediterranean climate, lives in the city of the Prophets, crosses streets named after Tanaites, Gaonites, and the revered poets of Spain. . . . But not for a moment does he forget that beyond many a river, there is one river, most probably the smallest among them, and its water continues to flow as of old, and a young boy stretches his hand, delighted at the sudden revelation." (P. 126)

This minor plotless story reveals two elements prominent in Appelfeld's fiction: the roles of memory and of childhood on the banks of the river Prut. His recollections are the bedrock for his fiction, its real/fictional scaffolding.

6

ON THE GROUND FLOOR

Appelfeld's fourth collection of short stories, *Bekomat Ha'karka* (On the ground floor, 1968), continues to portray the Jew surrounded by a Christian society. At the center is the Jew who typically has lost his/her Jewish self-image and immerses himself/herself in the life of the Ruthenian-Ukrainian village. The flight of the Jew into "gentileness" is a study in metamorphosis: distinguishing characteristics disappear; skin, muscles, and facial features seem to have changed. This is usually accompanied by the forgetting of Yiddish and the Jewish ways of life. For the Jew, adapting oneself completely to a non-Jewish environment often involves the demise of one's Jewish identity.

In the story "Escape" the change is described in organic terms: "His Jewishness lay at his feet like the fallen leaves of autumn. It shriveled within him and around him. The gnawing sadness was lost too."[1] The protagonist escaped the pogrom when the Yaroslav Riders demolished his town. He moves, talks, and crosses himself like a local peasant. Secretly he marvels at the change, and he enjoys it as he drinks and carouses with the gentile peasantry. Within a year his metamorphosis is complete. He is a peddler, going among the local peasants selling salt, kerosene, and vodka. Occasionally the metamorphosis is challenged; predictable and unpredictable factors do not allow for the finite change. Some Jews have survived the massacre by hiding in the tall grass, and they unsettle him. They have become subterranean creatures, overlooked in the rush. The protagonist is aware of their existence and is drawn to their voices and melodies. He listens to the voices of the children studying the Pentateuch in the traditional chant, in Hebrew and Yiddish.

The path of possible return to the fold is connected with the ancient language and the traditional chants; sounds and sights are often the main markers in Appelfeld's characters' attachment to childhood. At dawn the protagonist discovers three emaciated Jews, their black clothes hanging loosely on their thin bodies. They look like moles or giant beetles. The nameless protagonist is like the Biblical Joseph as he reveals his identity to his brothers. They in turn tell him their story: as the massacre broke out, the landlords closed their castles and the church demanded the Jews' conversion. During winter their feet froze and they assumed a subterranean existence. Their hope lies in the summer.

The encounter poses an enigma for the Jews and for the protagonist: how can one forget so much within a year, and how can one adopt the local mannerisms so completely? He talks in a mixture of Yiddish and the local dialect characteristic of gentiles who served in Jewish homes and knew Yiddish and the Jewish customs. He offers his horse, but the Jews are frightened by it. When, as creatures of the night, they disappear, he feels as if a bodily member has fallen off him. Despite his mobility he is bound. To his brethren he poses a challenge: they do not trust him; he is either feigning Jewishness or he is indeed a Jew. In either case he poses a danger.

If we expect a modern repetition of Joseph's story, that expectation does not materialize in "Escape." The revelation does not bring recognition. No miracles occur—the protagonist's metamorphosis is complete. The encounter with the traditional Jews proves to him that he is a Jew no longer. The change, an act of duress and survival, succeeded, but at the price of a loss of identity. The landscape of Bukovina continues to be the background for the stories, and so is the desire of various protagonists to shed their Jewish guise, the Jewish mentality and Jewish mannerisms.

"The Betrayal" uses the theme found in Appelfeld's early stories and his later novels. The theme has a variety of manifestations in his fiction and is often connected with a deep, unexpressed sense of guilt. The horse trader Berdinsky detests the religious Jews who come into the villages to trade. He had severed all connection with Judaism and Jews, yet he did not convert to Christianity. The sudden unexplained blossoming of his childless wife leads him to think that she is betraying him. In the past she expressed a wish to go down to the town, to visit the graves of her forefathers, and to be among Jews. Berdinsky always denied her wishes, and she continued to work in the yard like a peasant woman. The summer harvest has brought the inexplicable change within her. Her rejuvenation is astounding: she looks like a young peasant woman. Obsession and madness now control Berdinsky's life; his lame attempt to throw a rope around her neck fails: "She turned her head slowly as if it was not meant for her."

The story is bitterly ironic. His desire to break away from Judaism has materialized in the metamorphosis his wife is undergoing; she who wanted to return to her origins has been transformed and looks like a young woman; he who betrayed his creed does not realize that she is the embodiment of his betrayal. On the background of the bountiful summer the man's obsession is heightened. The women portrayed in this collection all depict unanswered, unrequited yearning. They are portrayed either as submissive or as unbridled creatures yearning for freedom. Most of them do not talk, seldom making their voices or their wishes heard.

Appelfeld's interest in the Jewish lore in Bukovina and the Carpathian Mountains continues throughout his work. Jewish farmers, dairymen, millers were part of the environment he briefly experienced as a child. The Jewish women of the Carpathian Mountains will appear as God-fearing Jewish women (as in the novel *The Healer*) and as simple, peasantlike women, as in the story "Infertility" in this collection. The month of Elul, the last month of the Hebrew calendar, is traditionally devoted to prayer, forgiveness, and repentence in preparation for the Days of Awe, the period between Rosh Ha'Shana and Yom Kippur. Infertile Jewish women from the mountains come to the house of the ritual judge (*Dayan*) for a month of supplication. They are tall, strong, and unused to soft words; the mountain air has hardened their features. The powerful women fill the air with their cries; their grief is of tremendous proportions. Despite their sensuality and power, their bodies are denied fertility. The Dayan's wife reads to the women and interprets the Scriptures. They in turn express their grief, singing gentile melodies mixed with Jewish sorrow. As the month of Elul draws to a close and with the Days of Awe approaching, the women go through a change. They have lost their peasant bearing. Their submission reaches its peak on the Day of Atonement. At the end of the day, after the concluding service of Yom Kippur, they leave for their homes only to return the next year.

The themes of change and submission are corresponding themes in the stories. "Together" is a story of a Jewish peddler and his growing daughter. His wife has died, and out of love for his daughter he has decided not to remarry. The girl is attracted to the young local men, and they in turn are attracted to her. When she comes home she brings with her the smell of dark places and bad language. The father's attempts to take her along with him on the road do not help. As a last resort he ties her to him with a chain. His total devotion to her grows and so does his pain. The girl has some inexplicable mysterious quality about her, and this quality is being repressed. Wrist to wrist they move. Her constant pleas to be released are not yielded to.

The father is looking for a healer. They travel toward the town of Radom in search of a cure. At a certain point in their wandering the father, no longer able to take responsibility, releases her, and here a reversal occurs: her spirit is broken and she asks the father to put a chain on her. They move on their way like two yoked animals. Reaching Radom they are barred from seeing the doctor, who attends only to rich people. The girl has changed—losing her youthfulness, she has gained weight and now looks like a full-grown woman. She scurries from place to place in search of food and firewood. She is no longer attractive to men.

> The painful awareness gnawed at him: only for his sake did she trudge along after him. It was this devotion of hers which distressed him most. "Let me alone." It was now he who wanted it. He slept. She could have walked away and left him. She stood close to him, as though his sleeping frightened her. After this they walked along as if at the beat of a hidden drum. The snow turned to ice. The close of winter bore on at a steady pace. It seemed that they would never separate, and the clink of the chain was like the chanting of a vow.[2]

This sensitive story can be interpreted on various levels. One cannot overlook the hidden sexual suggestiveness. The girl grows to look like her mother, and the father will keep her chaste forever. Earlier stories have revealed the desire of a young girl to refuse to grow up by avoiding sexuality. In this story it is the father who tries to keep his daughter a young girl, chained to him on an endless road of wandering.

The connection between submission and change gains an ironic twist bordering on the tragic. Her free spirit, her uniqueness as a young girl, is interpreted as an illness, as if a *dibbuk*, a demon spirit, had entered her. Another reading will reveal the attraction of the Christian world, with the church bells tolling in the background and with the young men and their explicit masculinity. After he has killed the free spirit of his daughter, he is eventually chained to an ungainly woman, a phantom of his wife's image. By now she will not release him; it is she who is the provider, he the dependent.

The transformation of a Jacob into an Esau—the Jew into a gentile—has a variety of manifestations in Appelfeld's narratives. In the story "Transformation" there is a suspension of time and place that is almost complete. As in the other stories, the seasons are activating

agents in the plot. For unspecified reasons, a couple has been persecuted by the villagers and is pushed to the marshes and the land of
the cattails. Through hidden mutuality, both partners change. New
skin has grown on his face, his hands have become hairy. By spring
they swim, climb trees, live among the animals, and greet the peasants
in the local dialect. They have accepted a new existence—he has made
himself a fur coat and she has braided a skirt. By now they have lost
the old language. Their ability to survive in nature has been perfected:
they dry fish, and they know how to decipher the movement of the
clouds. There occurs a certain reversal to a strange Eden. The woman
is willing to be absorbed by the life of the peasants; she attends church
and is attracted to the local peasantry.

This story is a reverse mirror image of "The Betrayal." It ends with
the woman deserting the husband, whose legs are frostbitten. In a last
glimmer of sanity he plans his eventual revenge and her eventual
death. When the spring comes, he hallucinates, he will bring her back
and bind her. Change and submission are also connected with the
change of seasons. Puberty, growing up, newfound femininity—all are
connected with the burst of spring or with the opulence of late summer. Winter points to stagnation, to a state of no change; with the
thawing of the snow, liberation comes. This applies as well to the
liberation after the end of the war and the woman's liberation to womanhood. Yet, sadly, women rarely escape the cycle of submission.

The story "Rushka" depicts another aspect of change, first introduced in "The Betrayal," where a husband suspects his faithful woman, whose blossoming is perceived as betrayal. Rushka yearns for
the male gentile world and becomes its victim. Most of the Jewish men
depicted, despite a seemingly successful process of transformation,
suffer a certain malaise. In most cases wives follow their husbands; at
times it is they who want to immerse themselves in the new existence.
In all cases the couple is childless; little is known about their previous
life, and they hardly converse. "Rushka" is a tragic story about a free-
spirited woman who cannot escape her fate because she is a woman.
Rushka loves to swim, to bask in the sun, to enjoy the admiration of
the villagers. Her husband, a fisherman, tries to coax her into returning to town to be with the Jewish community. His own wish to return
wanes with the years.

Rushka leaves her husband to live with Vasil, their gentile neighbor.
Vasil treats her cruelly. One day the husband discovers Rushka in the
grass. She looks like a plucked bird: thin, blue-skinned, with a pro-

truding nose. Her broken spirit bespeaks torment and misery. She cannot utter a word; she only gurgles, or chirps come out of her mouth. She is no longer the beautiful wildflower; she is transformed into an ugly bird. She cannot touch food. Only her eyes, or rather the light in her eyes, is reminiscent of her old self. The husband's dreams of returning to his hometown are blurred. He can hardly remember whether he or his parents left town. He remembers his forced conscription into the army. He looks like a gentile and behaves like one. With the onset of the cold season, the frozen river brings life to a halt. White ice encircles the fisherman.

> . . . the suddenly altered state of Appelfeld's characters probes a critical ambiguity about the nature of the link between before and after. Is the metamorphosis a fate visited by the decree of unspeakable events beyond their control? Or is it a chosen destiny, the certain consequences of willed evasion, or even the accelerated culmination of tendencies already latent?[3]

The theme of return is closely connected to that of transformation. This is part of Appelfeld's mythification of the Jew who was transformed into a gentile peasant. The assimilation into the host society is a basic concern in Appelfeld's fiction, together with the fundamental transformation of Jew into gentile. He raises the question: how can one become another? He tells stories of organic assimilation and of intellectual assimilation typical of the urban Jew. The capacity to grow another self on the old self later appears as the major theme in his novel *Ha'or Ve'hakutonet* (The skin and the gown, 1971).

The dictum "know thyself" is highly problematic in the modern parables of Kafka, Agnon, and in turn, Appelfeld. The stories do not provide motivation for the submission to change. There is a hidden challenge and pleasure in being another self; yet the loss of language and the suppression of memory fracture the psyche. The return home is a painful process connected with the loss of the old self and an attempt to regain it through physical return. In most stories the characters themselves are oblique and evasive and do not articulate their inner state of being. The overvoice of the narrator provides a framework for their movement. The characters, in constant movement, do not remember factual details, although sights are sources of familiarity. Sometimes the characters develop an almost animalistic sensitivity to a place, and recognition can occur through a sense of smell. Spatial presence rather than cumulative memories individuates characters.

"The Return" tells of a horse trader who arrives at his hometown after many years of wandering. He arrives without a horse, and the wanderlust dies within him. Like many of the characters, he is nameless. He knows that a man must return home. At the outskirts of town he drinks from a well. He has vague recollections of his grandfather, who used to bathe in the well's water when he returned from the fair, a custom of early Hassidim who aimed to "cleanse" themselves of worldly things. After thirty years away, he recollects the town's structure. A whiff of a smell coming his way creates recognition and familiarity. Appelfeld wisely does not move his protagonist from his position by the well—his memories move; he stays.

Appelfeld's characters continue to be marginal. There are those who have chosen to live on the periphery of Jewish society and those who were closer to the local rural scene. Return is often connected with purification. Washing his face, the protagonist of "The Return" remembers the Bratzlav Hassidim, who used to hide and meditate among the reeds. Sights and sounds evoke memory, and memory in turn brings forth a forgotten past. The protagonist remains by the well. He does not enter the town. An encounter with a stranger, an ex-military man, probably a Jew who was kidnaped to serve in the Tsarist army, reflects on the protagonist's own situation. The stranger always suffered because he was called a Jew. Now, when he wishes to be a Jew, he does not know how to be one. The question is not merely "Who is a Jew?" but rather "What is a Jew, and how is a Jew?" Both characters have altered through the years; they talk about Jews the way gentiles talk about Jews. The two spend the night talking. At dawn they ask a passing peasant about the name of the town. He tells them that this is not a town, but just a military barracks. They go in circles, never to arrive.

The state of neglect and the demise of spirituality in the Jewish community are symbolized through the decline and disarray in the Hassidic community. Baffling were the actions of Reb Nachman of Bratzlav, who left his town to go to Uman, where he stayed in the house of a wealthy Maskil, to the horror and disbelief of his followers. A rabbi's lost authority is depicted frequently in Appelfeld's fiction, as in prewar and postwar existence. The spiritual malaise is intimated by the growing power of the merchants, aggressive men who defy the rabbi.

Appelfeld returns again and again to the theme of spiritual malaise that afflicts the Jewish community, both at its center and its periphery. The last story in the collection combines themes and motifs that were present throughout: the transformation or the loss of Jewish identity, the failed return home, the state of perplexity that afflicts individual and community. The story "The Pilgrimage to Kassansk,"[4] portrays (again) a man returning home after having served in the army for over twenty years, having been forcibly conscripted. In Appelfeld's fiction the prodigal son is often not recognized and not embraced by the community. The returnees from the army had to face a ritual court, and the judges decided their fate with regard to their rejection by the community or their acceptance. In this story, the judges do not acknowledge the Jewish identity of the man. Despite his official discharge, his certificate, and two medals, he is rejected. Like other characters he remembers—but the details escape him. Remembrance is recognition through spatial familiarity, not through articulated factual details.

His frozen memory prevents his acceptance as a returning son. At the communal poorhouse, he is advised to go on a pilgrimage to Kassansk; there he will find repair to his soul. Given some provisions for the road (prayer book, phylacteries), he sets out on a new voyage, perhaps a new pilgrimage. The road will offer its temptations. Most of the characters he meets on the road reflect his own situation. They have been captivated by the past. They are bound to the past, unable to extricate themselves from it. Kassansk is in a total state of neglect and decline. The Hassidic courtyard was broken into by the merchants and is in ruins. A state of siege prevails: the old Rebbe who could work miracles is dead, and the court has turned into a marketplace. Everyone is in a state of captivity—those who remember the old Rebbe are captivated by their memories. The community was taken over by the merchants, the speculators, and the pilgrims who joined them. The Rebbe's oldest son is forced underground, where he teaches and studies.

The narrator tells the Rebbe who he is and where he comes from. The Rebbe cups his ear and his eyes shine, but he cannot speak because of the commotion. Malaise afflicts all. The spiritual world suffers decline and divine eclipse.

7

THE FOUNDATIONS OF THE RIVER

The talmud speaks of Adnei Hasadeh ("Foundations of the Field"), mythical creatures in human form who are umbilically connected to the center of the earth, from which they derive their sustenance. Appelfeld's fifth collection of short stories is entitled *Adnei Ha'nahar* (1971). The noun *eden* (pl. *adanim*) has multiple meanings: foundation, base, pedestal. The English translation of the title, *The Foundations of the River*, suggests a purposely ambiguous sense of both fluidity and substance.

Characters in Appelfeld's world are often rootless, faceless people who inhabit fragmented stories with tangential plots. Many relate to life in a most distracted and fatigued fashion. Many are devoid of an expressed will. As marked people, some have lost all desire. The relation between man and woman is a joyless thing for them. The woman is often the provider of basic necessities; at times she can even evoke hopes for a new start, but the shadows of the past are relentless furies that never let go.

Blindness is a major theme in this collection; it is the most prominent expression of total solipsism and inwardness. Facing the new demanding reality in Israel, blindness, both physical and emotional, allows for a detached existence.

"Bronda," the first story in the collection, opens with the celebration of Israel's Independence Day. Against the background of public jubilation, the humiliated existence of the characters gains an added dimension. They do not take part in the celebration. Against the distant sounds of the military parade, the shattered existence of Kendell, the moneylender, strikes a grotesque note. He lives like a mole, buried, leaving his lair only at night. This nocturnal existence is a continuation of the previous life in the shadow of fear; the nights are too loud and too lit for him. Kendell is a pariah, even among the other moneylenders and black marketeers in Jerusalem. He finds shelter in the cellar inhabited by the blind Bronda, her narrow room which is "lit by a thin darkness." Bronda is a recluse who rarely leaves her place.

There are strange alliances in Appelfeld's fiction, deep and binding and wrought by dependency and a desire for freedom. Kendell promised to buy Bronda a home, knowing full well that the merchants who owe him money will never pay him back. A deterministic element suffocates the characters—a deep chasm exists between their words, their reality, and their aspirations. Their dreams are small and simple, but they will never materialize. Even a change for the better carries its inherent dangers. Bronda is Kendell's moral rod. She knows his shiftiness and believes that he is devoid of godliness—the god within him is dead. What defines him to her is his mode of life, not necessarily his actions.

Unlike other alliances between man and woman, this one has a clearly sexual connection. A grotesque scene, bordering on the tragicomic, ensues at night when the two are in bed. Bronda tries to unravel Kendell's sleeve to get the money sewn in the seam; the struggle sometimes lasts the whole night until she manages to have her way. Kendell's trouble is not specified—whether moral or psychological. Bronda tries to reconstruct his life, "to repair his soul," but the details he provides her about his past are sketchy. He was born in Lodz; during the war he found refuge in the home of a gentile woman; and after the war he moved to Germany where he began his business.

Kendell is in a slow process of disintegration, both financially and mentally. Not unlike Kafka's characters, Appelfeld's shrink in size, fortune, or perception. After the parade, in the deserted streets of Jerusalem, Kendell meets his archrival, Deemer, and the other people who impoverished him. Kendell's diminished fortune is hidden in his shoes, and he is heavy of movement. A confrontation occurs in the post office square, but nothing happens. When all is said and done, Kendell is closer to those who robbed him of his money than to the Israelis.

Bronda's death on that day marks Kendell's total demise. He enters the open door of the cellar and creeps into her empty bed, shoes on, wrapped in the torn blanket and trying to embrace forgetfulness. In a way, Kendell is the "man from underground." Unlike Dostoevsky's character, however, he is presented as devoid of clear awareness, consciousness, and judgment. Like other Appelfeldian characters, he is almost birdlike in his capacity to move lightly from place to place, yet his heavy feet pull him downward. Self-sufficiency is the key to existence in his unexpressed perception: his occupation is based on absence of trust. Nevertheless, the strange union between Kendell and the blind woman is convincing. Kendell clings to Bronda because she challenges his opaqueness; his implicit need to be challenged is answered by her domineering manner. Their relationship is almost a master-slave relationship in the Hegelian sense: Kendell needs Bronda for defining himself to himself. This violent symbiosis answers terrible needs not verbally articulated. Kendell looks for dark places—the cellar and the body of the blind woman who can see him only in his voice. His opaqueness is reflected in her blindness.

No desire to acculturate is expressed in this story. The Israeli scene is meaningless to the characters—they don't even relate to it. They have created their extraterritorial territory, which subsists on its own accord. Bronda and Kendell represent aspects of blindness. Bronda, like other women in Appelfeld's world, presents a verbal aspect somehow connected with an ethical quest. Kendell embraces an existence of lingering vacuity. Whereas Bronda evokes the past, Kendell tries to avoid memory. Paradoxically, he needs her laceration, her clinging, her moralizing, and her fight over his diminished fortune. Both are earthbound; their feet are heavy. Toward the end of her life, Bronda walks barefooted with margarine smeared on her feet to alleviate pain—a poignant image for the end of a journey. Like the mythical creatures connected to the center of the earth, they cannot take flight or change.

Water is a central element in *The Foundations of the River*; it evokes the animalistic world analogous to the Jungian perception of the psyche. In the story "The Hunt" the protagonist is on a barge heading toward an unnamed destination. The absence of identifying time or place enhances the mythical atmosphere of the tale. There is a sense of ritual embedded in the story, based on the primordial picture of the hunt. The aim of Janeck, the protagonist who is being ferried on the barge by an old fisherman, is to reach the lakes. The movement of the barge as it enters the narrow straits is paralleled by the movement on the shore. At this turning point there are dark people who seem to have descended from the trees. The people, Jews, emit a certain transparent quality despite their darkness. It seems as if they have gone through a change, a physical change—their bodies look heavy and short. The fisherman tells Janeck that as a young man he trained himself to hunt Jews, for which he got respectable sums of money. Janeck shudders at the thought that "their blood runs in my veins," and as the barge enters shallow water the confrontation is almost inevitable.

The black Jews give Janeck insights into his own fate: he realizes his father's denial and his own attempts to erase his Jewish identity. Janeck feels deeply that he, like the Jews he observes, is doomed to death. Janeck, who passes for a gentile, asks the fisherman whether the Jews cannot change. The fisherman does not answer; he is certain of one thing: they cannot hide. Janeck's ultimate fear is that the same metamorphosis awaits him. To the fisherman, the Jews are animals and as such should be hunted.

The tale has elements of the fantastic. The reader is struck by a sense of hesitation—the Jews seem to be human and at the same time, in an ambiguous way, they have developed qualities of animals and birds. Appelfeld does not distinguish between the literal and the metaphoric levels, and thus an embedded ambiguity emerges. This, coupled with the absence of a clear point of view, adds to the uncertainty experienced by the reader. The Jews can neither hide nor take flight. The slow pace of the story, along with the slow movement of the barge, lulls the reader while creating an ironic rift between the horror and the acceptance of it.

At twilight Janeck senses the fatigue and sadness of the dark Jews. He reflects upon his own fate and wonders when he will go through a change, when his clothes will darken and his face lose its tan; then he too will become a wanderer and a hunted man. The desire to hide, to camouflage oneself, is frequent in Appelfeld's fiction. Was Janeck successful in deceiving the fisherman who was an old hand at the game of hunting? When he checks Janeck's hands he notices that they are not the hands of a fisherman—"you are not one of us." As night falls the image of the Jews changes; now they are compared to birds perched on trees. Sometimes they are compared to beetles trying to shed off their carapace unsuccessfully. It seems as if they are losing their sight.

The story can be perceived as an allegorical tale about the state and position of the Jew in Europe. The continuation of the story bears out this image. The old fisherman, out of sheer boredom, has decided to hunt the Jews. He lures them by expressing a wish to buy salt. As one of the men leaves the pack, having been cajoled into drawing nearer, the fisherman hurls a knife at him and does not miss. The Jews withdraw, carrying their injured with them.

A smell of fresh blood mixed with plucked feathers filled the air. The finite silence absorbed the wail of the wounded man. The silence was disturbed by the cry of the predatory night birds. As if they were awakened from their sleep and descended like after a murder to be witness and partners . . . "[1]

Janeck knows that he is caught in the net. The Jews have left their gaze with Janeck, as if their total substance has been reduced to this glowering stare.

"The Birds" is yet another rendition of the mythical man-bird motif. The tale can be perceived as a midrash, an interpretation of a certain reality through a narrative alluding to an earlier text or prooftext. Simultaneously, the impossible becoming fictionally possible gives the stories their poignancy. "The Birds" is a story of a group of wandering Jews, followed constantly by a group of birds. The birds form a wing of sheet metal that darkens the sky. They hover and dive, as though suggesting that the group of people is their prey, and at times they walk alongside the group. The barren, mountainous domain is a foreign place for the birds, an element that underscores the allegorical, fantastic nature of the story. Attempts to ward off the birds are few and futile. In this no-man's land, Jewish fragility and vulnerability are emphasized. Zender, the ex-peddler, tries to find a solution. He had always dealt with the gentiles and could bribe them with gold coins. He applies the same tactic: bribe the birds with dead carcasses. The ironic-sarcastic tone, not found in "The Hunt," is present in this story. Nachtigal ("nightingale"), a nonpragmatic man, presents an anxious argument: if they continue to serve the birds with carcasses, the birds will never leave them alone; can this commitment continue forever? As long as the Jews are alive they carry the symbol of death upon them. This is the secret of the hunt and the chase.

Three movements are operating here: those of a small group of Jews, a group of birds, and the hunters who follow the birds that follow the Jews. The patient birds walk alongside the Jews, then fly above them. The Jews bring water to the birds, since the terrain is so rough and rugged. The old ailing ritual judge is carried on a stretcher. The people cling to the stretcher, hoping for a word. The familiarity between the Jews and the birds is broken when the impending death of the old judge becomes a certainty.

No resolution is given in either "The Hunt" or "The Birds." Both seem like chapters in a continuing saga. A resolution of a story emphasizes the fictionality of the tale: when a story ends with a resolution the reader closes the book with a sense of completion. Matters have been put to rest. Open-ended stories linger with the reader, who is often asked to provide his/her own resolution or solution, and thus the fictionality of the tale is challenged. Both tales seem to follow the strange movements of a dance macabre, combined with a bitter sense of wry irony. The impending death of the silent judge and sage points to a spiritual demise. He begs to be left behind, but the group refuses. The prophetic birds anticipate his death. In the past he used to admonish the members of the group for immoral behavior, especially the women. When the white-bearded man realizes the finality of the situation, he adopts silence. Despite realistic elements in "The Birds"— names of people, personal history—the story has a certain ritualistic quality. The birds are reflectors, mirror images of death. The Jews are being identified by external omnipotent powers represented by the birds. On another level the Jews gain the quality of moving like birds though incapable of taking flight—in an existential state of no exit.

The story "The Last Revelation" presents Janeck, the protagonist of "The Hunt", in another phase of his mobile existence. (Appelfeld uses the same names in a number of stories; occasionally the characters are the same. In the short stories, the characters are not clearly defined; thus the similarity of names can be accidental and nonintentional.) This story is structured around an encounter of two men in what seems to be the last leg of their journey. Janeck knows that he would not escape his undefined fate, since his pursuers are on his heels. Walking in the rainy open plains, a stranger joins him. The stranger could be an accidental wanderer or the one who is destined to inflict the last blow. The theme of disguised identity is another frequent element in Appelfeld's fiction. The dialogue between the two men is terse, laconic; the veracity of their speech is uncertain. Janeck's body is on the verge of disintegration. He recalls the time when a flock of birds hovered over him, recognizing that he was a marked man. The stranger is clad in peasant's clothes. In a recognition scene, the two confess to their Jewishness. Zatka, the stranger, cannot fathom the reason for the constant persecution of Jews. His only explanation (one of the traditionally anti-Semitic ones) is that Jews are detected by an odor uniquely theirs. Jews are born with this odor and will die with it. This carries the mythic component one step further. Anti-Semitism is neither logical nor historical, but is embedded in the way the Jew is perceived. In the same way that the two men's getting together is unexplained, so is their parting. As in other stories, the unresolved ending emphasizes a timeless quality and points to an inevitable death.

Instead of posing philosophical questions, Appelfeld creates situations, often highly improbable, in an attempt to cover the gamut of the Jewish-gentile relationship in the twentieth century. He stretches the narrative over an extended line, always curious to know when the Jew stops being a Jew, when he becomes an "other." Kafka took the idea of metamorphosis to its limits by entering a different biological order. Appelfeld's characters, not infrequently, find themselves in the midst of an irreversible process that "befell" them. There is a psychological subtext to this phenomenon. But the tight mode of narrative and the opaque, two-dimensional characters do not allow for a psychological reading, unless one accepts a process of self-denial and self-hate as a subtext. The reader can opt for a story with no implied allusions, for an allegorical reading, or for accepting the story as a metaphor or an open-ended parable that can be interpreted in more than one way.

Imperceptible changes take place in the lives of these characters. Appelfeld takes conventional images from his own inventory and combines them anew. Stories combine elements of Hassidic mysticism and modernistic parable. There is no clearly causal connection in the various units that comprise a tale. Characters grow more opaque and further apart as a story unfolds, until the fantastic enters in the form of an intimated final metamorphosis.

Appelfeld combines the realistic and the metarealistic, the fantastic and the impressionistic. He moves in an unpredictable rhythm from one pole to the other, often infusing very realistic stories with highly improbable elements. At this stage of Appelfeld's writing, as we have seen, the stunted emotional life of his characters does not allow for a connection to the past.

Appelfeld often creates an almost pointillistic picture from mundane recognizable reality. He chooses a particular place, such as a central location in Jerusalem. He places one observing character in its midst. Familiar characters enter the observer's field of vision as a voice retells their lives in a detached, uninvolved manner. There is no story qua story; nothing happens except for the promenade of characters. The underlying message is the loneliness of the observer. Despite quiet familiarity, there is a sense of displacement. The aimlessness of the promenade, the slow motion, the sustained movement emit a sense of loneliness. Even when the characters are in the heart of the city, they create their own domain inhabited by people who came from "there."

Appelfeld's survivors in Israel are city dwellers. They live in urban centers: Jerusalem, Tel Aviv, Jaffa, Netanya. Their occupations, their socializing, and their general frame of reference are their own. Appelfeld adds a surrealistic dimension by introducing a certain airiness to the city through its changing light. The characters seem to move in a sphere they have created, rather than entering a given space. Their own space is limited, but it suffices. And if they do fall in love, as in the stories "After the Wedding" and "The Robbery," the results are disastrous. People carry with them slender slices of life that cannot be diffused or enter into contact with other realities. Existence on the verge of the precipice adds a bizarre quality to these stories unfolding against the background of Jerusalem. The bold juxtaposition of the familiar, the opaque, and inexplicable adds to the strange atmosphere.

The vitality of the woman and the impotence of the man seem to run as an underlying theme in this collection, underscoring the universal nature of the Appelfeldian character. Occasionally, memory is the only viable thing left. In "After the Wedding" one of the characters says: "We are simple people, we have lost our faith but we can't make the cursed memory subside. And even though few are the memories we are left with, we can't exist without them."

Appelfeld's collections of short stories are not arranged chronologically or thematically; even stylistic differences are not a major point of departure. Thus many of his stories are stylistically independent units. A harsh, terse style in one story may be followed by a story involving surrealistic, atmospheric, impressionistic diction. As stated earlier, like other writers of Hebrew fiction, Appelfeld attempts to break away from the literariness of the Hebrew language and its rich allusions. In this collection, Appelfeld's language is often plastic, and descriptions are occasionally direct. Yet it is hard to indicate a clear turning point in his language usage. These stories do not lead to a climactic point. We often meet the characters in the penultimate station of their life. Occasionally a false sense of a new beginning might enter their existence, to be shattered later on. Resorting to his own reservoir of stories, Appelfeld reworks them into new texts, thereby creating an interdependency, betweeen continuity and change.

Appelfeld published his five collections of short stories between 1962 and 1971. The central elements are the survivor's experience and Jewish existence as an unfolding myth on the verge of extinction. Yet he refrains from touching directly upon the Holocaust, preferring to emphasize the marginality of characters and the marginality of events.

The spawning ground for Appelfeld's stories is Bukovina, both as background and as foreground. In the first decade of his writing, the locale is the typical Ruthenian-Ukrainian village. From the 1970s on he will depict the urban assimilated Jew of Czernowitz and Vienna.

Dan Miron correctly observed in 1979 that Appelfeld's early stories were mature, controlled; his narrative technique managed to bring forward, in a delicate and restrained tone, the psychological and moral impact of the Holocaust. Refraining from pathos, Appelfeld clings to characters in the margin of the historical whirlpool. Nevertheless, they display the existential problematics of Jewish life as prefigured in the shadow of the Holocaust. Miron points to another issue, discussed earlier: the reader's expectation of what is commonly referred to as the "Holocaust writer." He observes that in Israel, where the audience has been accustomed to literature that maximized the horrific experience, Appelfeld's fiction was conceived to be static, since it continued to cling to basic formal and thematic subjects.[2] In turn, this observation can be applied to his fiction before the 1990s—namely, a subtle reworking of similar motifs while expanding the experiential and psychological map of characters and their movements.

III.

NOVELS: THE ISRAELI EXPERIENCE

8

TZILI: THE STORY OF A LIFE

THE MOVEMENT from the short story to the novel marks Appelfeld's transition into a more psychological study of character and an attempt at his own historicization of Jewish existence in the modern era. Complexity of character, the emergence of a clear protagonist, and a wider gallery of personae allow a deepening and broadening of narrative scope.

Tzili: The Story of a Life (1983) centers on the survival of the marginal, where marginality turns out to be power. It is a survival built upon an escape to nature and adaptability to nature. The marginality of Appelfeld's characters is one of their main attributes. His characters are shaped by events that befall them, by circumstances beyond their control. They prevail in their simple guarded existence in the midst of, or on the periphery of, cataclysmic events. Emotionally scarred, deprived, and forever changed, they nevertheless continue to move. Their traumatic projection into the unknown erases all traces of familiar terrain; in turn they create new thin familiarities despite the changing of time and place. They are either confined to one place or are forever on the move. Dominated by fear, silent, and in constant danger, single characters (children and adults alike) survive in the narrow path of an aftergrowth. Their seeming adaptability is misleading; it is a part of a survival mentality that continues to be with them years after the initial catastrophe.

The Jew, as the alien and the "other," is given a strong depiction in Appelfeld's writing. A sentence that appears repeatedly in his fiction is "A person is not a vermin." It is uttered by various characters in a variety of tones, and it stands for the ultimate in human dignity and morality versus the greatest indignity ever inflicted on human beings. The Nazis could exterminate Jews with great ease because when they looked at them they saw vermin; extermination is justifiable in excising an infestation. Appelfeld frequently places the utterance in the mouth of his characters when they are at the lowest point of their existence; they utter it as a credo, to say that dignity, morality, and self-worth are still valid human aims despite the utmost in degradation ever suffered by human beings. The answer to total humiliation is a strengthened sense of the self, even if it is unarticulated and unexamined.

Tzili, a young girl who survives the Holocaust, is a person of limited knowledge and expression. Her psychological makeup is simple, uncomplicated, basic. She is able to survive and become a strong person on her own. Appelfeld does not endow her with thoughts or ideas beyond her basic circumscribed domain. He is attuned to her unique being, which is at the same time far from unique. Being close to nature, she has the power of change, along with the power of adaptability to the periphery of peasant society. Her even temper, her placidity, her lack of drive allow for the change to take place. Once her family has fled the oncoming war, she finds herself alone. Her atypicality saves her. Even in school, before 1941, the gentile children would mock her as "a Jewish girl without any brain!" Despite countless hours of study, she either forgets what she has studied or gets it all mixed up. The highly charged, hysterical household, the terminally sick father, her sisters and brothers preparing themselves for the state entrance examination are in sharp contrast to Tzili's opaque equilibrium. Despite humiliation, ridicule, and scorn, Tzili Kraus continues to attend classes in the local school, and she perseveres.

An old Jewish tutor is assigned by her parents to teach her the prayers and basic precepts of Judaism. Judaism was not held in high esteem in the family, harried in its attempt to become a part of the host society. The old tutor and the small lackluster girl create a strange union. She recites "Hear, O Israel," and the serenity that accompanies his visits has lingered with her. She has also learned "to take up as little space as possible." One night Tzili is left alone to take care of the house. That night soldiers enter the town and destroy it. Tzili survives by hiding in the yards among sackcloths.

Pitted against the forced learning of the family and its emphasis on acquisition of knowledge, Tzili's body is her guide and compass. Despite haunting dreams, she does not have identifiable Jewish traits. Tzili becomes a native girl in speech and manner. She identifies herself as a daughter of Maria, a beautiful prostitute, who has had numerous daughters born out of wedlock. By so doing Tzili places herself on the margin of the peasant society, and that allows her a temporary refuge as well as mobility.

In Appelfeld's fiction the young child is often given the role of witness as well as that of protagonist acquiring experience in a world of uncertainty. Typically these children are opaque, silent, and highly cautious. Tzili begins her resignation and self-acceptance before the war. Like Kitty (see chap. 4), Tzili faces her puberty alone; unlike Kitty, however, Tzili leads an existence devoid of guilt or fantasy. The sight of blood makes her think she is going to die. The outbreak of war and the outbreak of the hidden secret of womanhood occur almost simultaneously in Tzili's life. In her first encounter with a local blind man, she faces rape but escapes. Tzili's strength is in her opaqueness, her succinct perception of things, and her self-possession. This innate sense of the self will allow her to become a completely mature person. In the first stages of her aloneness she knows that her family has gone, and "a kind of hollowness, without even the shadow of a thought, plunged her into deep sleep."[1]

Tzili travels light. She is not undone by memories, guilt, or speculation. Her nature has prepared her to merge, to append herself to her surroundings, and to continue to move. She fears her body and the changes it has gone through, "as if something alien had taken possession of it." Once she survives the test of unexplained menstruation, she walks on, washes herself in a stream, and overcomes her fears. This is an initiation into both womanhood and personhood. As parts of a rite of initiation, blood and water conclude one phase of her life. Her bodily physical strength and her noncontemplative nature save her from herself. "Day by day her body was detaching itself from home" (p. 26). Like an elemental creature she begins her life anew, as a wild thing living off the fruit of the field. Her birth, her ugliness, her reputation as a daughter of Maria all make her a nonentity and lend her a potential sexual allure in the eyes of the local peasants.

> She roamed the outskirts of the forest and the peasants who crossed her path averted their eyes.... Her ugly existence became a byword and a cautionary tale in the mouths of the local peasants, but the passing days were kind to her, molding her in secret, at first deadening and then quickening her new life. The sick blood poured out of her. She learned to walk barefoot, to bathe in the icy water, to tell the edible berries from the poisonous ones, to climb the trees.... She saw only what was in front of her eyes, a tree, a puddle, the autumn leaves changing color.... Her life seemed to fall away from her, she coiled in on herself like a cocoon. And at night she fell unconscious onto the straw. (Pp. 29–30)

Tzili chances upon the hut of Katerina, a prostitute, who adopts her because she takes her to be Maria's daughter. Tzili observes, in Katerina, an aging woman afflicted by illness, drinking, and unpredictable moods. Katerina dwells at the edge of the forest in a dilapidated house. The houses around, outside the village, serve as refuge to lepers and lunatics, horse thieves and prostitutes. Tzili, self-sufficient and instinctively wise, becomes Katerina's maid. Katerina tries to convince her to become a prostitute and flings a knife at Tzili—who realizes that the time has come for her to leave. Autumn finds her working for an old couple in a remote hut. The woman treats her like an animal; she beats Tzili mercilessly and indiscriminately, seemingly to exorcise the evil connected with her birth.

Tzili succinctly presents many themes, motifs, and characteristics that appear throughout Appelfeld's fiction. The acculturated/assimilated family, life in the provinces, the Ruthenian village, life in the forests and bunkers, the life of the survivors after liberation—all are present and are interwoven here. Appelfeld ventures to make a marginal character the centerpiece of a novel; the slow girl becomes a protagonist. Rejected, the "other" even in her own home and at school, this slow learner will become a full woman once she encounters a man named Mark. Mark brings old and familiar, now-forgotten words from home. Tzili was never endowed with words, and her stay with the local peasants has severed the roots of words for her.

Mark has escaped a concentration camp and left a wife and two children behind. Not unlike the characters in "Three" (see chap. 3), he is awash in guilt and doomed to disappear. His restlessness, his nervousness, his remorse move Tzili. Settled in with Mark, she manages to exchange his used clothes for food, drink, and cigarettes. Mark marvels at Tzili's metamorphosis, adding that

> "everything about me gives me away—my appearance, from top to toe, my nose, my accent, the way I eat, sit, sleep, everything. Even though I've never had anything to do with what's called Jewish tradition. My late father used to call himself a free man . . . but here in this place I've discovered, looking at the peasants ploughing in the valley, their serenity, that I myself—I won't be able to change anymore." (Pp. 76–77)

Mark senses deeply that he is doomed, that there is no way out. Tzili does not understand this sense of the temporality and facticity of his existence; she continues silently to be compliant on one hand and free on the other. She descends the hill into the valley to fetch food. She comes to a river and wades across it, bathed in light; she feels strong and fearless. Despite the absence of a physical description by the author, we infer that Tzili becomes beautiful and clean as she bathes in the cold river. Water, a continual motif, cleanses Tzili and engenders an unspoken femininity. Mark brings forth the image of the assimilated Jew as well as the built-in frustrations embedded in the process of acculturation and assimilation. Acquisition of the German language as a badge of honor for the assimilated Jew appears in another variation in Mark's words:

> "My late father's love for the German language knew no bounds. He had a special fondness for irregular verbs. He knew them all. And with me he was very strict about the correct pronunciation. The German lessons with my father were like a nightmare. I always got mixed up and in his fanaticism he never overlooked my mistakes. . . . In the provinces people are more fanatical about the German language than in the city." (Pp. 87–88)

Mark paints a caricature of the culture-hungry Jew with his absolute and tragic cry for acceptance. He creates a bunker for the two and tells Tzili about his childhood and his adult life. His family mirrors Tzili's family in many respects, although Tzili was never spoken to. Her femininity "blossomed within her, blind and sweet," her limbs rounded and she gained strength. Her blossoming both baffles and attracts Mark, and the two become lovers. But Mark cannot exorcise the ghost that has haunted him. He feels he must conquer his fear, a fear that has tormented him all his life. Feeling like a free man, he decides to go down to the valley, to challenge himself. Tzili was the provider up to this point—now he wants to test his new self. Tzili's pleadings are to no avail. He goes down, never to be seen again. In an indirect yet precise way, Tzili's fortitude, her lack of fear, and her direct, unconvoluted experience are a model for Mark. He loves the girl who is unencumbered by fear or by familial-societal expectations. She tries to remember his dictum: a person is not a vermin. Tragically, Mark was not prepared for his new psychological freedom—he is marked by his past and by his present anxieties.

Alone, carrying the heavy sack that belongs to Mark, and carrying his child, Tzili begins her long trudging walk. At fifteen she looks like a young Mother Courage. She is not on the run; she could have joined the peasant subsociety quite easily, but her unarticulated integrity moves her along in search for Mark. As the war draws to an end, Tzili joins a convoy of refugees. In a strange, roundabout way the young pregnant girl rejoins her people. Despite her love for the mountains and the brooks, she enters a new form of existence.

The world of refugees is a microcosm of Appelfeld's characters in various stages of their existence; we have encountered them along the shores of Italy. In the midst of the march southward Tzili realizes that the world she knew no longer exists. She realizes that her losses have rendered her alone—that she will never rejoin her loved ones. In the midst of refugees who wrestle with everyday existence and with ethical problems, the heavy and strong young girl walks along. The growing life within her gives her strength and inner happiness. She misses Mark. As she walks, she instinctively knows she leaves her past behind her, as well as her dead loved one. On the stages of her walk with the refugees, she has been adopted by various people who create a stretcher to carry her, and cling to her. Tzili loses her child. In order for her to enter the new reality she has to lose everything she owned—and loved. She finds herself, on a boat going to Palestine.

Tzili's four years in the forests, the marshes, and the bunker are depicted by the changing seasons, connected to the passage of time. Within this span of time Tzili creates herself in her own image. Lacking charm, limited as she is, though not half-witted or feebleminded, the young pregnant woman of fifteen speaks in actions, not in words.[2] The obsessive anxiety she experienced at home (depicted by Mark's instability) does not affect her. Her strength, strangely enough, is indirectly drawn from the old Jewish tutor who taught her her prayers. Unlike Helga in *The Healer*, Tzili knows the secret of the holy words. She is her own healer and, for a short while, she heals Mark. There is something almost deliberate about her focused self. She bears humiliation and physical torture by the peasants who brutalize her, but she does not lose her dignity. The brutalities inflicted upon her create and mold her strength. The austere character is depicted in an austere manner, moving against the background of open sky, forests, rivers. Tzili purifies herself as she goes along. Water and blood initiated her solipsistic existence, the loss of her ill-fated baby leaves scars, but somehow the image of the sea, as a huge body of water, gives her yet another chance for a new start.

Tzili is a totally independent person. She draws her strength from herself alone. Bertha was symbiotically connected to Max; Tzili is not a parasite. In contrast to the totally dependent young woman, Appelfeld posits Tzili as an emblem of independence. Tzili points to a way out of her predicament, and this self-engendered advantage saves her.

The opening paragraph of the novel alludes to its covert truth: "Perhaps it would be better to leave the story of Tzili Kraus's life untold. Her fate was a cruel and inglorious one, and but for the fact that it actually happened we would never have been able to tell her story" (p. 1). Beyond being a rhetorical device, the opening sentences tell the story of Appelfeld the child. Asked in an interview if transposing himself into the body of a girl was a deliberate distancing, Appelfeld answered that

> from a technical point it's very difficult to write. I wanted to write about my life in the forest, with the peasants. I wanted to chronicle what happened to me. But a writer cannot write chronicles, because the moment you write a chronicle you are no longer a creative person. You are linked and bound to memory, and memory is only one of the elements of the creative force. So I tried several times to write my story . . . and I could not write it. Then, suddenly, through a girl, not a boy, a bit older than I was, I found a new perspective. Because you cannot write about a girl as a memory, you have to create atmosphere, the objects, the environment. *Tzili* is really my story, my inner story, not a chronicle.[3]

9

THE SKIN AND THE GOWN

Tʜᴇ ɴᴏᴠᴇʟ *Ha'or Ve'hakutonet* (The skin and the gown, 1971) marks the end of a period in the fiction of Appelfeld.[1] Thematically it ties in with the short stories and thus serves as an appropriate close in the analysis of his early works. The novel's opening chapter employs a visual technique reminiscent of French Impressionist painting. The picture is composed of areas of light and shadow, depicting an evening in Jerusalem where things happen in space yet no clear action can be detected.

The slow movement of many of Appelfeld's opening passages creates a sense of pantomime or dance of marionettes. Often there is twilight. Objects in and of themselves devoid of interest enter the domain of a two-dimensional composition, somewhat like a still-life painting. Appelfeld is careful to establish the right mood, atmosphere, and space for his characters to move in. Often he does not rush into specificity of character or action. The three characters screened in the opening scene are Gruzman, the protagonist; a woman in a doorway; and a man with an umbrella. All seem to be frozen in space. As Gruzman utters "Evening" the scene comes to life; there is the sound of church bells, and characters become distinct, as though moving from darkened background to foreground.

Gruzman, protagonist of Appelfeld's first published novel after two decades of short stories, resembles characters from Appelfeld's earlier narratives. The reader is presented with two voices. First is the objective "overvoice" that sets the tone for the opening scene, an unidentified voice describing spaces which are in the protagonist's field of vision and beyond. The second voice focuses on Gruzman and the characters around him. Appelfeld uses two lenses to depict scenes in many of his narratives: the broad wide-angle lens and the more direct telephoto lens, which centers on the characters. The opening chapter serves as an introduction to the novel, yet it exists as an independent unit redolent of atmosphere and the terse dialogue of earlier stories.

The novel will dwell on characters and depict them in a detailed "realistic" fashion. The reader is again introduced to survivors in Israel.

Into Gruzman's life of quiet desperation enters Betty, his wife. Her appearance after twenty-five years of separation betokens an unwelcome change. Gruzman's solitude is broken; the sleep he engulfed himself in for years is disturbed. Betty spent the war years in Siberia. She has gained weight and size, and she now looks like a young peasant woman. Had she returned tormented, emaciated, broken, things might have been different between them. Her belated blossoming, however, portrays her as a foreign power that had infiltrated his life. His blissful life of neglect, untouched for years, is now under attack. Betty begins to work like a maid around the house—without complaint or demand for reward. Monosyllabic in her answers, she knows that speech has carried with it some unwelcome consequences. Years in Siberia taught her that the present must be disconnected from the past.

Gruzman works in a warehouse with three other men. They constitute a family forged in Holocaust Europe; they continue their opaque existence in Jerusalem. Gruzman, Ortze, Pitjak, and Blutter are bonded by unarticulated ties. As spring comes, buried memories are evoked. The four feel that they are strangers in the hot climate. Like migrating birds whose course was shifted by a wind, their necks are strangely twisted, as if in constant flight. The four came from different places in the Jewish "Pale of Settlement" in Eastern and Central Europe, and yet each has his characteristic litany—a chant which pierces his shattered life. The chant is connected with childhood in Europe. Despite the strong bond between them, they do not ask questions of each other. Only after many years of togetherness does Blutter, the youngest, dare to ask Gruzman for the name of his hometown. For generations in Eastern Europe it was a ritualistic question between any two Jews who met, to inquire where the other came from. Following the traditional greeting of "Peace unto you" ("Sholem Aleichem") came this question, which created the verbal Jewish geographical network. Blutter was saved by the others as a child and grew up among them and the trucks in the warehouse in Jerusalem. Despite his young age they decided to raise him and not place him in an institution.

Betty's past is visited upon her in Jerusalem, too. Friends from Siberia who settled in Beer-Sheva come to visit her in Jerusalem. Gruzman observes their vodka drinking, their speech—a mixture of Siberian, Russian and Yiddish words. The Siberian bond is different from the bond between Gruzman and his friends. Evenings in the Siberian *cantine* were spent singing, playing the balalaika, and drinking. Betty's friends behaved like Siberian peasants: they came with their suitcases and sat on the floor. Betty and her partner were one step from becoming certified entertainers in the Soviet Union. Their sudden liberation shattered their lives.

Betty continues her past existence in Gruzman's home. She weaves, fills the house with textures and smells reminiscent of Russian villages and churches. As she tries to weave her life in silence and obedience, Gruzman's life is challenged. Gruzman's Jewishness is pitted against Betty's peasant looks. As his strength dwindles, hers mounts.

Jerusalem evokes past memories within Gruzman. A shabby celebration of the First of May in Jerusalem reminds him of the young socialists in his hometown. A walk to Mea Shearim, the ultra-Orthodox section of Jerusalem, gives him a sense that the people were cutouts of his dreams. Appelfeld's characters try to remake Jerusalem in their own image—a city whose meaning is gained by evoking memories of their own past. Jerusalem qua Jerusalem is a nonentity to his characters—they would like to fashion it in the image of their hometowns in Europe. Even the churchbells, so prominent in his earlier stories, evoke nothing more than past memories in Jerusalem. For centuries Jerusalem had attracted bizzare people of all faiths, people with messianic dreams and visions who now abound in concrete and literary Jerusalem. Appelfeld's Jerusalemite visionaries are connected with Europe and the past.

In Jerusalem Gruzman meets Spiegelmeister, one of the leaders of the Bund (the Jewish Socialist party created in 1897 in Lithuania, Poland, and Russia; the name is an abbreviation of General Jewish Workers' Union). An old mad ideologue, Spiegelmeister adheres to a conspiracy theory: the European proletariat was not vanquished; it is hiding underground awaiting the day when all workers unite. Polish Jewry too is awaiting the winter, the clarity of Israel's heat consumes them—with winter and snow the power of Polish Jewry will rise. The traitors are the ones who claim that Jews are a pragmatic nation; yet the Jewish nation is a poetic nation. Spiegelmeister's fervor is undiminished: he sends letters all over the globe and fights those who dissent. At the center of his Jewish Empire lies Warsaw—and he believes that after a period of purification the faithful will win.

Gruzman and Betty continue their life. He can never sleep; she wraps her life around her like a blanket and sleeps deeply. However, it is Betty who undergoes a major change. As long as she was sheltered by her Siberian cover, the memories of the past could not penetrate the skin and self she acquired in Siberia. Coming to Israel and to Gruzman marks the beginning of her end. The shell she had put on in Siberia is slowly breaking, giving way to memories. The Siberian self celebrated the body and its resilience; in Jerusalem she begins to lose weight, thoughts torment her and bring pallor to her face. Her Siberian skin begins to peel, and sickness takes over. Memory is an enemy of the new self. Only with a total suppression of the past is a new individuation possible. On arrival in Jerusalem, Betty's looks bespoke the resilience of her physicality. Her health and appearance denoted sexuality, vitality, and power, all underscoring Gruzman's impotence. Something almost pagan surrounded her labor, her weaving, her nonverbal acceptance of things. Gruzman, on the other hand, was vanquished by the tragic demise of European Jewry.

Now, within a year of her arrival in Jerusalem, Betty's face begins to resemble her mother's. Betty's sickness is her barrenness. Her emerging memories bring forth the image of the barren women who used to come to her parents' home in the Carpathian Mountains, seeking healing from her father, a religious judge. (Appelfeld reworks themes of his short stories into the novel.) In Jerusalem, Betty is in a parallel position to that of the Jewish peasant women. The coarse, tormented women have entered her being. She is afraid of thinking. It used to be said in Siberia that when a person thinks excessively, it is a sign that he or she will shortly die. She joins a group of women in search of healing in the holy places in Jerusalem. Adopted by two blind and barren Ladino-speaking women, she makes the rounds from the physician to the holy places; they serve as her guide. The healer in Jerusalem is a physician, who is supposed to be a miracle worker. But he does not bring a cure to Betty. Her barrenness reflects the infertility of a helpless man; Gruzman has infected Betty with his impotence.

Gruzman attempts to continue his life of numbness. After years of being "vomited" from one climate to another, one language to another, one land to another, he is by now his own creation. His faith is but a fading ember. No longer is he the extension of his parents; his life symbolizes a desire for forgetfulness. Severed from his roots, they strangely continue to blossom on the banks of the river Prut. The pain of the severed roots can be dulled, but the wound will never heal. Gruzman believes that those who survived are dried-up seeds; no healthy continuity will spring out of them. Dead fathers feature in the life of Gruzman and his friends—and in turn in the life of Betty. Characters are doomed by their silence and their speech, by their forgetfulness and their remembrance. They continue to be dislocated individuals with shattered psyches.

A change of roles occurs in the life of the couple. Gruzman, who was curious about Betty's life when she first appeared, now adopts silence. Betty, who was silent on arrival, remembers her childhood in full detail and wants to relate it. Betty begins to read her life like a book, and after a year of incomprehensible existence things begin to fall into a meaningful pattern. Gruzman tries to escape Betty's memories and her voice; he wishes to divorce her. Betty, by now totally resigned, looking like her Jewish foremothers, accepts her fate. The rabbinic court is inhabited only by people from "there." No mention is made of any other Jewish communities in Jerusalem. The place looks like a meeting place of people from the same town—a "Landsmanschaft." People have been waiting for years for their divorce decree, and the couples look content; no rancor is expressed; the rabbinic court resembles a social gathering.

Betty becomes a healer. She works in a clinic for chronically ill women. Mornings she cleans, and in the afternoon she sits with the sick women and teaches them singing and embroidery. Tragically she transmits what she excels in to dying women. But Betty's personal fate is sealed. She goes through her last metamorphosis. She becomes critically ill, and as her illness progresses, her body shrinks, not unlike Bertha's. She becomes another being. Was Gruzman her killer? Was his inability to allow her into his life the beginning of her demise? Is she the true metaphor of the man as the living dead who continues to walk the earth? In Appelfeld's score these are implied probabilities. And yet the power of the woman to change and heal, and the impotence of the man, continue to serve as prevailing themes.

The body continues to be a reflector of change in the Appelfeldian character. External change serves as a metaphor for an unexpressed inner change. In a paradoxical way, the characters in their own domain exercise a unique freedom. The dead present makes for a direct bond with the past, so that we become the past. Toward the end of the novel Gruzman resembles his father and Betty resembles her mother; in the Jerusalem of the 1960s both experience the live presence of the dead parents. They leap over years of pain and suffering and rebond with childhood landscapes and dead people. Thus they become Jewish archetypes of a seemingly timeless quality.

The Skin and the Gown

Appelfeld departs here from an early technique of his linear stories. The novel's story is enriched by digressions, bringing past information to the present unfolding story. Kierkegaard's dictum that "life is lived forward and understood backward is reversed in this novel: life is lived backward but no understanding can be found to serve the future.

10

THE SEARING LIGHT

The highly autobiographical novel *Michavat Ha'or* (The searing light, 1980) tells the story of a group of young people in Israel. Using a first-person narrator, the son of a Jewish-Austrian writer, it is a collective *Bildungsroman*—a group's coming of age through puberty and trial. The group finds itself on an educational farm not dissimilar to the one Appelfeld himself was sent to. The regime of the place is not to the liking of the young men, who experienced their first taste of freedom from authority and taboos on the shores of Italy. The Spartan spirit of the educational personnel and their Zionist zeal are foreign to the boys. As with other Appelfeldian protagonists, they go through a process of putting on new skin, and the process is painful. They have brought with them their anxieties, their cunning, their sarcasm, and a total lack of faith. These war-smart survivors are at odds with the newly burgeoning society with its highly ideological bent. The host society, in which many individuals have lost loved ones in the Holocaust, expected the young people to replace its losses, its family members who perished. This expectation is unmet; the boys are uncooperative and unyielding to rules.

The "reality" created by the young boys is shocking: a boy temporarily becomes a pimp; several boys rape one of the girls. There is considerable cruelty within the group; a brutal beating is designed to teach someone a lesson, and when he persists in his ways he is beaten senseless. There is suicide and association with smugglers, black marketeers, loose women. All this shocks the high-minded personnel at the farmstead. The boys are not replacements for lost ones; they are strangers without a language of their own, seeming to lack all memory of their own past. The suicide by drowning of one of the boys raises the question of where he came from. When his roommate is asked, he says they never discussed it. Despite the group spirit, the individuals are entirely enclosed within themselves.

The boys differ in their reactions to the new reality but are united in their rejection of it and its rules. Their sexual awakening is at odds with the harsh reactions of the educational personnel. The immoral behavior of these young men is a form of freedom, and they resent the moralistic ethos imposed upon them. The enclosed place and the guards (who serve in a defense capacity on the eve of the 1948 war) inevitably bring to mind the dire past. At the end of the novel the boys are, to their delight, conscripted into the army. Despite their glee on leaving the farmstead, they realize that the army will again mean camps and regulations.

The title of the novel, *Michvat Ha'or*, alludes to leprosy as referred to in Leviticus: "when the flesh hath in the skin thereof a burning by fire . . . " (13:24). The word *or*, in different spellings, means both "skin" and "light," and Appelfeld plays with this homonym. "Searing light" thus refers to the leprous condition as well as to the harsh light of the new land. As we have seen, physical impairment is a frequent part of Appelfeld's imagery. Two of the boys suffer from skin afflictions. The "searing light" has both a therapeutic and a scorching effect.

The novel clearly has autobiographical elements, elements that correspond in time and experience to Appelfeld's own. He emigrated to Palestine in 1946 with Youth Aliya, an organization that took care of orphaned children and youth. Appelfeld indicates the depth of the trauma experienced by the young people. He adds that many years passed before he realized the intensity of the darkness within himself. The trauma is absorbed in one's cells and later manifests itself in gestures and body language. Like himself, the young boys did not experience free choice in their youth: theirs was a childhood of external decree ruled by the instinct for survival. Yet despite the sense of being on the periphery of Israeli society and a sense of inferiority vis-à-vis native Israelis, there was a felt sense of superiority. Those who came from "there" were richer in experience, having been where others had not. At the same time, the newcomers wanted to prove themselves, and absorption into Israel was a stimulating factor in their existence, a challenge. Some tried hard to become Israelis in manner and speech; others aimed at irrelevent development, such as bodybuilding.[1]

In the beginning of *The Searing Light* the young boy encounters his father's former archenemy, a journalist named Sturm. The boy is reminded of his literary home. By now his German is faulty and he speaks Yiddish, mixing dialects and accents, reflecting a loss of linguistic identity. The loss of language is typical in the life of the young survivor. Further, the encounter with the Hebrew language is difficult for him: "We spoke very little, as if we were born without words; the few warm words we brought from home were extinguished. The foreign Hebrew words irritated the senses like salt."[2]

If the fictionalized "Appelfeld story" were told in proper sequential order, it would comprise these parts: (a) the experience of the twelve-year-old narrator prior to the war; (b) the boy's experience in the concentration camp, his escape and life in the forest; (c) the boy's postwar experience as part of the group that emigrated to Palestine; (d) the boy's return, as an adult, to his native town. Parts (a) and (d) form the two halves of *Tor Ha'pelaot* (The age of wonders; see chap. 14). Part (c) is incorporated as a distinct narrative in *The Searing Light*. What is deliberately omitted by Appelfeld is the putative part (b), describing in explicit detail his experience in the concentration camp. In his novel *Mesilat Barzel* (The railway; see chap. 21) this phase is alluded to, but that novel was not written until 1991. In the 1970s Appelfeld had his own reasons for not employing this part of his life as literary material. Instead he chose to amplify the pre- and postwar phases.

II

THE IMMORTAL BARTFUSS

For most of Appelfeld's afflicted characters, as observed earlier, Israel brings no change into their lives. The expectations of the host society were high. The ingathering of the exiles was one of the main tenets of Zionist ideology, especially when directed at Jews who suffered so inhumanly during the Holocaust. The survivors who came to Israel were the "surviving remnant" of European Jewry. For the Israelis who had come from Europe in earlier waves of immigration and whose former communities had now been destroyed, expectations were immense.

Israeli literature is rife with stories of newcomers to the land of Israel, from the close of the nineteenth century to the present day. Most of the novels, novellas, and short stories form a literary subgenre by now. The narratives tell of the problems of absorption as well as acculturation to what seemed to the newcomers a homogeneous Israeli society. The novels belong to types of *Bildungsroman* depicting a process of individuation which often included a change of name, accent, and mode of behavior. Appelfeld's characters, young people and adults, are at odds with Israeli society. As we saw in *The Searing Light*, the young boys resist the Israeli ethos with its highly moralistic demands. Older newcomers hardly touch Israeli society. They move in their own circles, carving out an existence that will brook no interference, especially by the authorities, and will allow them to continue doing what they did after liberation from the camps. Surrogate families, created in the bunkers, the forests, and the DP camps, often were maintained once the people reached Israel. This unarticulated mutual reliance was rooted in a deep sense of mistrust of the outer world and based on a desire not to venture into the "new." Many of Appelfeld's characters continue to wear the same clothes they wore in Europe, to speak the same language they spoke there, and to deal in the familiar. Some seem to embrace their self-imposed alienation and to continue the initial post-Holocaust sense of freedom they experienced on the shores of Italy.

Appelfeld himself did not embrace the burgeoning Israeli reality as a subject for his fiction. From the early stages of his writing he was committed to depicting those who, like him, had been in Europe and had experienced the Holocaust. His characters in Israel often adopt a hermetic stance as their way of coping with the piercing sun and the hectic activities of Israeli life. In a tragically grotesque way, many of his characters cling to illegal or shady deals that could secure future mobility if catastrophe threatened to reappear.

Bartfuss, the protagonist of *The Immortal Bartfuss*,[1] guards against sentimentality and emotional reactions. Living in the port city of Jaffa, he is estranged from his Balzacian, money-hungry family, which consists of a wife and two grown daughters. His bare room reflects his barren existence, his self-reliance, austerity, frugality, and stark financial and emotional independence. His cruelty toward his family manifests itself in his silence. His contempt is pure, hard-edged, unyielding. He despises their materialism, their self-satisfaction, their cunning, their garish tastes. His independent existence is that of a man for whom existential facticity is an everyday reality. His solipsism and solitude are not as yet decidedly "modern"; still, in an uncanny way he resembles characters in Beckett plays. His activities do not differ from day to day. This repetitive pattern gives his actions a ritualistic quality.

Pitted against Bartfuss's leanness is Rosa his wife, with her kitchy taste and crudeness. Bright dresses and cheap eau-de-cologne occupy her thoughts and those of her daughters, according to Bartfuss. He especially detests his wife and his married elder daughter, Paula, whose wedding he did not attend. Their pragmatic, calculating nature repels him. He feels an affinity to the young, slightly backward Bridget. The European gentility and petit-bourgeois mannerisms of Rosa, his wife, sicken him. He hates them all for his own incapacity to break away from them. They are his jailers, and in a way his hatred is self-hate, the hatred of one who needs his jailer.

An air of conspiracy and suspicion engulfs the home. Mutual distrust and repulsion have turned it into a tense, unyielding battleground of arrested speech and silences. Most of Appelfeld's male characters feel a great affinity with their life in the forests of Europe or on the shores of Italy. There, in the morally and socially vacuous no-man's land, survivors could tell themselves they were in a transitional state.

Sexual freedom and minor commercial opportunities gave the characters an additional sense of freedom rarely experienced elsewhere. In Israel, Bartfuss continues his shady illegal financial dealings, but he limits the time devoted to business to fifteen minutes a day and the rest of the time he is free. In Jaffa, on the Mediterranean, the coffee shops he frequents are also frequented by other dealers with a similar background; all are survivors. Yet he despises them and does not join them. On the other hand, they admire him—for them he is a legendary figure. He is known for his heroism and for having survived fifty bullets. Some people wish just to touch him.

Bartfuss leaves home in the mornings and returns there at night to sleep. His treasures, including pictures of his family who perished, are buried in the cellar, away from the searching eyes of his wife, daughter, and son-in-law. We perceive the Bartfuss family from his point of view. Consumed by the suspicion that all the members of his family have but one goal in mind—to get hold of his hidden money—he believes his wife has turned their daughters against him. The question is: how reliable is this notion? One cannot tell if Rosa is motivated by greed, cunning, or perhaps even love. Of the two characters, which is distorted? Does Rosa represent normality and adjustment, while Bartfuss is still enslaved to his past?

Bartfuss's sense of dignity does not leave him. During the war, Rosa found refuge with a peasant family; she slept with the old man and his sons. For Bartfuss, it was a shameful act he can neither forget nor forgive. Twenty years of marriage are marked by Bartfuss's attraction and repulsion of Rosa. *The Immortal Bartfuss* is a study of a man who, in the words of Appelfeld, swallowed the Holocaust whole. In a minimalist sense, Bartfuss is an epic hero whose movement asserts his existence: "The movement intoxicates him" (p. 8). In a strange way, it is a novel about a quest for spirituality. Bartfuss lives his life in one fashion while hungering for a different reality. In his unique way, however, Bartfuss is moralistic. He does not view mere survival as an ultimate value. In his past he constantly endangered his life in order to save the lives of others; this was for him the natural and right thing to do. He is bothered by shame, degradation, calumny. He tells Rosa: "Life is valuable, but there's a limit to disgrace" (p. 21). Before coming to Israel, he tried to leave her, but she managed to find him. Deprivation of emotion is a two-edged sword for him. He is deprived of familial love and care while he deprives his family of his emotions.

With middle age, his solitude and independence begin to erode his fortitude. He is gnawed at by his growing loneliness and by the ascetic way of life he has imposed upon himself. "He had invested a lot of energy into blocking up the opening through which thoughts could push out. In recent years he had managed to seal them off almost completely" (p. 36). His is an alienated and humiliating existence, and he knows it. Bartfuss is forever vigilant—he never indulges in deep sleep, forever expecting the unexpected. Closely connected with his instinct for survival is an element of denial. His distancing himself from others turns eventually to distancing himself from his own self —losing touch with his emotional-psychological self. Bartfuss found his true expression during and immediately after the war. In essence he is a trapeze artist for whom existence on the edge of danger gave him a true sense of freedom. In Israel he becomes a creature of habit, and he despises himself for it.

Bartfuss's past is at odds with his present existence in Israel. He survived one of the most notorious camps in Europe, and he now lives a reduced existence in his new homeland, where a certain stagnation has taken over his life. He does not divorce Rosa; he takes financial responsibility for her and their daughters. Occasionally he has a short sexual encounter with another woman. His basic needs are coffee, cigarettes, sex, the sea, and noninvolvement. His shady business dealings are reminiscent of the daring days when he was smuggling illegal goods and illegal immigrants into Palestine.

Bartfuss is a three-dimensional character, self-aware and introspective. His hospitalization and a series of encounters create a possibility for change. He tries to meet and create a connection with people from the past. Dorf's history is similar to that of Bartfuss: he too was interned in a camp; he too was shot at many times and was left for dead. They first met in the forests, where they spent several months in a foxhole. Dorf is one of the few characters who regards his immigration to Israel as a spiritual ascent. He works in the port. When he realizes the source of Bartfuss's income, he questions: "Why pollute this place?" (p. 40). Bartfuss resents Dorf's attitude; as far as he is concerned, his friend died in the forests and his evil spirit wanders around in the guise of Dorf. Dorf's sincerity, the fact that he does not use worn-out clichés, pains Bartfuss. Dorf is in a way Bartfuss's alter ego, and Bartfuss's resentment lies in the fact that another option was offered him which he did not take. Since the reader gets Bartfuss's point of view, and since all the other characters are perceived from this point of view, there is a certain indeterminacy: was Dorf a victim of new slogans and propaganda, or was he indeed an authentic man who chose to be a laborer rather than a black-market dealer?

An encounter with another friend from the past presents a further possibility. Scher, a handsome, daring young man, a swimmer and climber, was famous on the shores of Italy. In Israel he has become the owner of a housewares store in the center of town. Prosperous, religiously observant, a pillar of the community, Scher has lost his former luster. Like his forbears, he has become a cautious merchant. This option is repugnant to Bartfuss, and the loss of the friendship of Scher as well as of Dorf leaves him bereft.

Encounters with women are stages in Bartfuss's spiritual odyssey. His first encounter with Theresa in Europe is recorded:

> On a long trip, which had taken nearly a year, to that little camp known for its horrors . . . in one of those hidden warehouses on the long road, he met her. He was in his twenties, with no father or mother, already thin and longing for death. When everything was locked and dark, Theresa's face had broken through. There were many faces there, thin and tortured, but a clean light, tinged with deep blue, covered Theresa's. All that night they spoke about *The Brothers Karamazov*. In her high school, in the literature club . . . they had discussed *The Brothers Karamazov* that year. . . . Even afterward, when they had already been expelled from school, in the ghetto, they kept meeting in a cellar to read and discuss. One evening, upon returning home from the discussion group, she hadn't found her parents. (Pp. 48–49)

Bartfuss cherishes the memory of this encounter when he was mesmerized by the inner voice of the soft-spoken young woman. In Jaffa Theresa has become an unfeeling and domineering woman, drained of any vestige of spirituality. This fat woman with an excessive appetite is rude to Bartfuss, who desires to remind her of their first encounter; she is uninterested. Theresa's unyielding rudeness to one and all is not dissimilar to that of Bartfuss, who rejects those who evoke his glorious past. Bartfuss's fascination with Theresa continues—she unlocks within him a dark buried memory. The encounter allows him to relive the horrible journey and to come closer to the self he denied. Bewitched by her, Bartfuss stalks the cafe where he first saw her. Through this illusive woman who resents memories, he tries to break away from an existence of passivity and mental depravation, believing that she holds the key to his lost spirituality. He approaches her when she reappears in the cafe, again expressing a desire to exchange memories. She snubs him with laconic answers. In Bartfuss's last encounter with Theresa and her obstinate lover, she refuses to go to Café Budapest because she hates the false, genteel, "European" atmosphere it aspires to. She prefers the coffeehouses along the shore, those frequented (according to her lover) by "Jewish trash." She proclaims: "I love them, and I won't exchange them for any imitation. Even the word 'Budapest' disgusts me" (p. 67). Bartfuss, not unlike Theresa, resents the people from "there" who have a "mask of staleness imprinted on their faces."

Bartfuss is put to a test by an old man who asks him for money. Bartfuss hesitates; and once the money is handed over, the old dealer returns it. The old man had gone through the war with him, and when he tried to make Bartfuss come out of his shell, Bartfuss acted like an untrusting moneylender, no longer as part of the family forged in Europe. The old man poses a question Bartfuss does not answer: "Did the war make us any better people?" and continues, "Don't you agree that man is an insect?" (p. 64). Bartfuss, the trapeze artist, failed when asked to act immediately and without calculation. His various encounters are reflections of his real or potential modes of existence. A major reason for his silence is his hatred for hackneyed words. He continues to question the lessons of the Holocaust. He believes that people who went through the Holocaust should be more generous, knowing full well that he himself has failed the test of generosity.

Can Bartfuss, who once was a sensitive young man longing for death, a hero and a daredevil moved by Dostoevsky, change after years of humiliating existence? Can his inactive, self-imposed solitude change? Bartfuss tries to break away from his own cell by self-awareness and by beginning to act for the benefit and welfare of others. He visits the office of the Holocaust museum and entertains ideas of donating his buried treasure to the organization. The offices eventually close down, and the group breaks up. Like a modern quest-hero, he has to gather experiences in order to be saved. Bartfuss begins to open up in his search for friendship and camaraderie. In his encounter with his friend Schmugler, it is Bartfuss who opens up, speaks, shares feeling; his friend is silent. Bartfuss brings up stories told by Schmugler in Italy about his sister, a pianist. Schmugler, who represents an earlier Bartfuss, denies remembering. He remains taciturn and refuses to join in an attempt at reweaving a lost existence. The ascetic Schmugler was weary of words such as "mercy" and "generosity." His adherence to the purity of words has impoverished him, but his integrity could not be compromised with words bearing lofty meanings. He preferred to become a night watchman rather than accept money from his brother abroad, who added the phrase "God willing" to his letter. Bartfuss observes elements of arrogance and contempt on Schmugler's face; he hits him again and again. Psychologically, he continues to exist in a hall of mirrors.

Bartfuss's territory spans the Mediterranean shore. Years ago on a visit to Netanya, a coastal resort town, he met a woman with whom he spent a night. In years gone by, in cafés, people would tell about their past. In his present visit he encounters bitter people. The woman reappears and manages through threats to get money out of him. He knows that he is being blackmailed, but he yields and pays. Jaffa is the citadel of Bartfuss's territory; Netanya, but a short trip away, points to the outer provinces of his spatial domain.

As we have seen, seasons are markers in the lives of Appelfeld's characters and Bartfuss is part of this scheme. He becomes ill in the spring. His failed attempt to reconnect with his friends occurs in the summer. With the coming of fall the seashore is deserted and the cafés are his refuge. There he meets Sylvia. Like Theresa, she represents and reflects his quest for spirituality. Sylvia is a thin, outspoken woman. Intelligent, knowledgeable, a graduate of a Hebrew high school in Europe, she still maintains her intellectual world view. Melancholy and pain exude from this chain-smoking woman. She has strong ties to her home: she loves the memory of her dead parents and at the same time knows that she has been cursed. She is a demanding lover, and Bartfuss's generosity is limited. She craves a coffee service, but he does not grant her wish. Sylvia and Bartfuss ask questions, both personal and philosophical. Sick and on the verge of death, Sylvia connects with her dead parents. Her love for her parents and her love for literature never diminish, for her love transcends the boundaries of life and death; it vanquishes death. The young Theresa and the dying Sylvia are guides in Bartfuss's voyage into himself. Now he can relate to his parents and sister, whose photos are part of the buried treasure in the cellar. Despite Sylvia's harsh, demanding manner, Bartfuss is attracted to her. Both know that their only humanity is in their solitude.

Barred from the seashore, his home and his past, Bartfuss clings to Sylvia. With the worsening of her illness, she is moved to a hospital, where Bartfuss encounters her good-hearted first husband. The two survivors engage in conversation. Bartfuss poses questions: "What have we Holocaust survivors done? Has our great experience changed us at all?" (p. 107). Bartfuss says that he expects greatness of soul from those people who survived. The man does not know what Bartfuss is talking about. Do these utterances reflect Bartfuss's genuine thoughts, or are they merely wishful thinking?

The death of Sylvia throws Bartfuss back to his usual existence. Financially he is more generous toward Rosa and answers her demands for money for Bridget. Clara, who works in a café, is another assertive woman who knows herself. She too has strong ties to her past. She speaks with her dead parents daily, and they are for her a living presence. For their sake she is even capable of praying. She derives her strength from the deep feeling that someone in the world to come loves her and awaits her. With the help of a measured amount of cognac, she manages to ward off fear. Like Sylvia, she believes that death and fear can be overcome through pure love.

Women in this novel fall into two categories: the fat, pragmatic woman, occasionally dumb and uncouth, and the sensitive, articulate woman with a tragic aura. Bartfuss is sexually attracted to the earthy one, yet seeks the spiritual one. His attraction to the heavyset woman is embodied in his relation with Rosa. The women reflect his divided self. One night, overcome by sexual desire, he stalks the deserted streets of Jaffa. He knows that there he is bound to meet a woman he can drag to one of the darkened entrances of the abandoned buildings. He expects to meet a bosomy, comfortable woman, but the woman he meets is his younger daughter, Bridget. She too is restless, wandering, looking for a mute encounter. "She followed him the way a woman follows a man who has motioned to her to come with him" (pp. 117–118). Bridget represents the woman he is attracted to, and her utter resemblance to her mother endorses it. In Italy, Bartfuss encountered females like her: girls with no will of their own, yielding women of a tacit and passive nature. Bartfuss knows that he can do whatever he wants with her. Walking together along the deserted beach of Jaffa, they look like a couple. Though nothing happens between the two, the encounter is suffused with intense but suppressed sexuality. Bridget eventually twists her ankle and they return home together, to the horror of Rosa, who devoted her life to making her daughters her devoted allies.

Later, Bartfuss encounters Marian. He remembers her from the shores of Italy as a thin and pretty young woman, dumb and innocent, who was seduced by men for a promise of candy. Her stupidity and innocence made her a prey even to adolescents, old men, and idiots. At present Marian is a short fat woman who lives in a deserted house.

She does not remember Bartfuss, even though he was the only one who actually gave her chocolate and did not exploit her. "But it was very important to Bartfuss that this miserable, stupid woman remember him and thank him for what she had received from his hands, for nothing in return, the candy" (p. 134). He is now stunned by her poverty, and realizes that she subsists on apples given to her by a grocer. He tries to give her a large amount of money, pleading with her to buy food and not to take it as a gift from men. Marian has lost her sexual allure, and obviously it is charity on the part of the grocer and not sexual favors that provide her food. Bartfuss most probably sees in Marian a projection of Bridget's future. Bridget too could be lured with promises of gifts by men like himself. Bartfuss manages to frighten Marian. He stuffs her pockets with money, which she probably will lose or have stolen. Her stupidity enrages him, and he slaps her face. Nonetheless, all experience fills him with satisfaction. Is this the generosity he was referring to?

Appelfeld's characters can be compared, as stated, to archaeological sites. Earlier characters often consist of a single layer almost suspended in midair. The reader meets them at a certain juncture of their life and does not know a thing about their past or their next station. Those characters are devoid of an acknowledged past or memory. As consciousness and awareness enter the lives of his later characters, an attempt is made to connect with the pre-Holocaust experience—with home.

Bartfuss does not choose the options offered by either Dorf or Schmugler. The novel ends with this paragraph:

> on his way to the apartment, he felt no revulsion or pain. His limbs were warmed up properly. When he entered the house Rosa and Bridget were already sunk in sleep. In his room there was no sign of a strange hand. Only when he drew near the bed did he feel that mighty sleep, that full sleep, which he had been struggling against for years, had gathered strength and now it was about to spread its iron web over him. He managed to take off his shoes and socks, to put his shirt on the chair, to look about the naked room, and to say a sentence to himself that he had heard by chance: "From now on I shall remove all worry from my heart and sleep." (P. 137)

Can the end of the novel be perceived as pointing to a new beginning or a change? Can it be understood as a resolution, an indication that Bartfuss indeed is beginning his recovery? Or is it just another chapter in a life of denial? Can a man so thoroughly changed by the

Holocaust go through yet another change? Throughout the novel there exists a gap between his actions and his verbal declarations. Posing questions about the moral message of the Holocaust is a tremendous step forward in the painful process of coming to terms with oneself. From the unuttered depths of desperation, alienation, and mental dislocation, words are found. The sense of vacuity coexists with a dim notion that life has a value: "Man is not an insect." Even in the depth of despair and solitude, Bartfuss does not denigrate life. He must unlock the memories buried within himself and literally in the cellar.

Bartfuss is a modern epic protagonist in quest of spirituality. His own inner space must be explored. He must begin to trust words and verbal expressions as signs of his healing. Even in borrowed, worn-out words, there is a chance for salvation. Change can be achieved by two simultaneous actions: breaking his self-imposed isolation and beginning to introduce his youth into his present. That does not mean entering Israeli society. It implies creating a bond with the people with whom he shares memories; accepting his family, which represents one aspect of his own personality; and acting in a generous manner.

Bartfuss must look for the missing layers in his persona in order to become a more complete person. He is a modern post-Holocaust man from underground who exists in his psychological lair. His existential malaise seems to portray a no-exit situation. And yet, unlike elemental characters in earlier Appelfeld texts who opt to live while exercising only a part of their being and leaving other parts untouched, Bartfuss attempts to break out of his cell. At the beginning of the novel he appears as a member of the living dead, a brooding, intractable shadow with only basic needs. The emerging Bartfuss has to find the power of language and the line of memory that can save the soul of the immortal Bartfuss.

IV.

NOVELS: DEPORTATION
AND BEYOND

12

THE PUPIL OF THE EYE

Appelfeld's three major novels of the 1970s—*Ke'Ishon Ha'ayin*, (The pupil of the eye), *Badenheim 1939*, and *Tor Ha'pelaot* (The age of wonders)—mark a change in his narrative technique. These highly stylized narratives do not attempt to delineate Jewish life in its totality; rather, they focus intently on the penultimate stage in the life of the Jewish intelligentsia and they center on the totality of change.

Appelfeld's short stories often serve as blueprints for extended narratives that employ a theme, story, or motif that appeared in the earlier writings. *The Pupil of the Eye* (though it has not been published in English, I will use the English title)[1] has a precursor in an atypical Appelfeld story, "At the Height of Autumn," in the collection *Frost on the Earth*. The time is the later years of the Hapsburg regime. The protagonist, Mr. Rapoport, is a wealthy Jewish landowner who espouses the values of the Hebrew Enlightenment. He owns an estate in the region of Bukovina. The twilight atmosphere is reminiscent of Russian writers such as Chekhov and Turgenev and Hebrew writers such as Uri Nissan Gnessin and David Vogel.

Rapoport, unlike many other Appelfeld characters, is a mature observer. He observes his own life and the life of his grown children, and he realizes that despite his wealth and success, his life is on the brink of dissolution. The abundance of the fall is staggering; the early harvest is plentiful. Yet it portends a violent and unnatural growth, challenging the cycle of nature. A message is hidden in this abnormal phenomenon, and Rapoport tries to decipher it. Observing his beloved daughter, Gusta, walking the estate grounds with her Polish tutor, he knows she will marry a gentile. His son, a gymnasium student on vacation from school in Vienna, looks like a stranger against the background of the estate. The son resembles neither his enlightened father nor his grandfather, a Sadigora Hassid. A question emerges: who is a stranger to the time and place—father or son? It is probable that Rapoport himself, the master of the estate, is the stranger.

Occasionally Rapoport is attracted to Vienna despite his contempt for Jewish lawyers, whom he terms "the new Jews." His son most probably will settle down in Vienna and join their ranks: the Jews who fill the cafés, who work in the stock market and light industry. Rapoport can imagine his son going on summer vacations to fashionable resort towns. For him the new Jew is inauthentic. As a well-versed intellectual, Rapoport reads the latest Hebrew periodicals from all over the world, and realizes that he is in the midst of a transition he cannot articulate. As a Jew his central position in the community reflects his own marginality.

His uprootedness is typical of the uprootedness of the Jewish intellectual in Hebrew literature in the late nineteenth and early twentieth centuries, the difference being that the place of the self-lacerating, poor, idealistic young writer is taken by a wealthy, middle-aged estate owner. In his own way, Rapoport represents an extinct Jewish archetype, an ideal that represents the combination of erudition, Hebrew roots, Jewish consciousness, and European culture. Not assimilated, he is proud of his heritage. Emancipation and enlightenment coexist in this benevolent character. And despite it all, he senses that the foundations beneath his feet are shaky.

Aberration penetrates the seemingly tranquil state. The implied question, unstated and unanswered, is what lies behind the excess. Clearly, a sickness afflicts Rapoport's world; he knows that his existence will have no continuity. The question repeated in the subtext concerns the source of the sickness, the eroding powers that afflict the Jewish spirit. Rapoport is horrified by the idea of "crossbreeding," a strange combination of things that do not belong together or coalesce. This idea unites the various parts of the story. The abnormally excessive harvest on one hand and the emergence of the new Jew on the other are connected and reflect one another. The new Jew is the fruit of a strange combination of a particular encounter between the Jew and Western civilization. Rapoport, the intellectual freethinker, and his religiously observant wife gave birth to children who do not reflect them. They probably will be neither intellectuals nor observant Jews. Rapoport is not unaware of anti-Semitic sentiments toward him on his own estate. He is nauseated by the idea of excess. The idea of accumulation, be it money, property, or anything else, sickens him. One of his acquaintances, a stock broker in Czernowitz, tells him: "Franz Joseph will drown us all in sweet cream."

Struck by a fatalistic stance, Rapoport knows that the change is inevitable and preordained. He merely wonders why the process of liquidation takes so much time. He is surrounded by the mystery of change, as comprising both noncontinuity and aberration. As an estate owner he himself is involved in experimentation and crossbreeding of fruit trees. He manages to reduce the size of the trees and to get an exponentially higher yield. Who is the creator of aberrations? How far does he predict? It is difficult for Rapoport, who tends to see his personal fate in the prism of history, to articulate the change he senses. The metaphor/parable of the forthcoming change is embedded in the huge misshapen apples. Rapoport does not find answers in his library (periodicals from East and West do not carry encouraging news). He goes down to the cellar, where he looks at his preserves: beets, apples, cherry cordial going through a process of fermentation; they change their shape, their color, and some become intoxicants. Another metaphor is added to the text.

"At the Height of Autumn" foreshadows not only *The Pupil of the Eye* but also Appelfeld's other novels of the 1970s and 1980s. The sense of foreboding is portrayed in organic terms. A process of growth has been afflicted by a devastating sickness. In this short story Appelfeld poses questions about the very nature of Jewish life. Written in the 1960s, it questions the process of enlightenment and emancipation of European Jewry. The three novels of the 1970s, depicting the penultimate stage prior to the Holocaust, all end in deportation and doom.

The death of the narrator's maternal grandmother opens *The Pupil of the Eye* (1973). The Hebrew words of the prayer for the dead (Kaddish) reverberate in the country estate that belongs to the narrator's father. Two of the three major novels of the 1970s employ a first-person narrator in an active role of observer, witness, and recorder of events. In both *The Pupil of the Eye* and part I of *The Age of Wonders*, a young person or a child stands at the threshold of unfathomable changes. The last year is depicted in three stages: the total decline of the estate, exile from the estate, and the deportation station. The structure of the novel is of interest. Appelfeld could have opened the novel when the family was rounded up by the Gestapo and then regressed to preceding events. He chose instead to depict the decline of family and estate in a slow Chekhovian pace, depicting each step of the rich and tragic life as an irreversible process.

The implied question posed earlier continues to haunt this novel:

what was the source of the breach in the Jewish psyche in the first half of the twentieth century? What was the source of this tragic excess? Was it hubris? Not knowing the right measure of things? Uprootedness? Was it the attempt to erase stereotypical Jewish traits? A quest for the unattainable? A deep guilt feeling for leaving the fold? Was it self-hate and self-denial? Appelfeld may be posing questions to the last one hundred years of modern Jewish history in Europe. The penultimate year in the life of the characters is depicted in almost an iconic manner to parallel the penultimate stage in the life of Jews in Europe in the 1930s.

The family replaces the individual protagonist in Appelfeld's longer narratives. And to a certain extent, this is a *Bildungsroman*, a novel about a young man growing up. The narrator's father, the owner of the estate, appears, wearing riding boots and carrying a revolver. These virile symbols are but a cover, however. He represents the impotency of the Jew. He cannot prevent the estate from being taken over by peasants, gypsies, and others. He is helpless, a broken man being driven from his own property. The city, Vienna or Czernowitz, and the estate create an interesting axis. The Jew who became a rural landowner is nevertheless attracted to the big city. The "new Jew," the assimilated city Jew, continues to appear in Appelfeld's fiction. He talked about that in an interview with Clive Sinclair.

> *Appelfeld*: You see I'm a great admirer of the assimilated Jews. It's not only that I was born as an assimilated Jew. But, first of all, that these are people, uprooted people, culturally uprooted people, they became, . . . the most sensitive people. In modern literature there are three figures; Kafka was Jewish, Proust was Jewish, and even Joyce wanted to give us an example of a kind of modern sensitivity. He chose Bloom, an assimilated Jew, who lives in Dublin. So, the assimilated Jew represents the best of Europe. Of course it has a price, sometimes a very high price, denying yourself. But they are the real Europeans.
>
> *Sinclair*: What your novels make clear are this desire for assimilation, and as you say to assimilate means to want to be something other then you yourself. Although you've made them vulnerable, blind to what's going on around them, and although you said that sometimes a Jew was the best European, there must have been some kind of flaw there (a) that made them want to change; (b) which made them blind. What do you think that flaw was?
>
> *Appelfeld*: . . . blind, because they believed, believe up till today that they are some sort of universal people, that they belong to the

universe and not some type of nation. This was of course a very naive
concept, and we are seeing it during the Holocaust. . . . So that the
tragedy that we saw during the Holocaust is that you cannot escape
yourselves. You cannot run away from yourself, the blood in your
body condemns you.

Sinclair: But your books imply that there is something inherently
wrong with this, because you now say that "the blood in your body
condemns you" but you're also implying that there's something in-
trinsically wrong with assimilation. Not only because of the punishment that is meted out upon you by your enemy, but also because of
this self-negation. I'm trying to get at what this self is that is being
negated.

Appelfeld: . . . the assimilated Jew had a feeling that he should deny
his being, his culture, his heritage, his being a Jew. This was a part of
it. To become a universalist you should deny yourself. This is of
course a tragedy, you can't deny yourself. The moment that you deny
yourself, you are punishing yourself. Another danger is that you become a superficial person, because you are an uprooted person without a past. This is a kind of ambiguity, a kind of richness and sensitivity from one side, and poor from the other side. Being a part of the
great world on one side and then you are punished by the world. They
do not accept you. They accept you as Jewish—this is a tension that
we feel, up to our day: between that deep desire to leave our old
heritage, but from the other side you cannot escape it. . . . The Germans, the Austrians have seen [the Jews as] an alien element, demons
from another world, that have penetrated into their culture. And this
they could not accept. They tried to expel them, because the first war
against the Jews, in Germany, in Austria, was against their culture.
Against the role they played in German and Austrian literature. Then
they burned their books in the streets. Because the books were the
symbol of a spirit. These weren't Jewish books, these books were
written by people that wanted to become Austrian that wanted to be
European. This is the tragedy. But they were accepted by the Austrians not as universalists but as Jews.[2]

Appelfeld does not try to come to terms openly with the causes of
the assimilation. Through careful signs and symbols he depicts the
detrimental effects of the assimilation and the psychological dislocation it has produced in his characters. He moves characters from one
extreme to another: Paul, the narrator's uncle, tries to escape his intellectualism by marrying a peasant woman who degrades and hu-
miliates him, then disappears; Paulina, his cousin, a gifted cellist, is
haunted by the demanding impresario Rosenwasser. She leaves Vienna,
returns to the estate, becomes the abused mistress of the estate agent

Krill, and goes mad. Breaking away from intellect and talent does not bring solace to the afflicted spirit.

A most disturbing portrait is presented in the image of Tropich. His small, Jewish-looking head is mounted on a huge peasant body. His father was a Jew, his mother a local peasant. The peasant women and his Jewish relatives ignore him. A half-wit, Tropich eventually takes his mad revenge—he kills and is killed. Depicted in a grotesque yet visibly palpable manner, Tropich is one expression of an afflicted abnormality.

Diametrically opposed to Vienna, the site of culture, is the Ruthenian village. Both extremes are foci of attraction for the assimilated Jew, and both prove tragic. The intellectual-creative attempt to reach perfection through music must fail, as does the flight to the seemingly "simple," "wholesome" village.

And the estate is in ruin and disintegration. Through the broken windows, wild growths break in. There is nothing more to steal, yet the gypsies continue their pillage. The maid Fissula parades in the mother's clothes after she has ransacked all the closets. Religious Jewish relatives gather around. Only Carola, the old servant, remains faithful. After the death of the grandmother she is the one who reminds the family about their duty as Jews. She is the only one who knows Jewish customs and the Jewish calendar. The kind physician and friend of the family, Dr. Munther, is killed by Tropich, who sees him as responsible for his misfortune. The father, while attempting to intervene between the two, hits Tropich's head. Tropich dies, and his tiny head is slung over his huge shoulders like a broken tendril.

That is the turning point in the family saga. The father harnesses the two white horses and puts the two dead bodies in the carriage. Books are packed. Paulina, who is in a state of catatonic slumber, is placed between pillows. The family reaches Vienna at early dawn and the father heads directly toward the Jewish cemetery. The old grandfather says Kaddish over the two who did not live as Jews but died as Jews. The family finds refuge in a deserted cellar. Paulina is put in a community hospice for the poor; the father carries wood for a living, and the mother works in a lace-curtain factory. Silence settles on the family in the bare cellar. They eat their potatoes silently, sitting on the floor. The two famished white horses, a pale reminder of past glory, are eventually killed by the father. Rumors about expulsion, deportation, and persecution are brought by the grandfather, who has settled in the Galician synagogue. Bands of hoodlums stake out the streets, and a sense of danger looms. In total silence, the family continues to act as if it exists on borrowed time. When the order of deportation arrives, the family reports at the time and place decreed.

The Pupil of the Eye is a carefully structured novel. Characters complement and contrast with one another. Devoid of a psychological dimension, their state of being is depicted by metaphor, image, metonym. It is a novel about resignation, about acceptance devoid of rebellion, self-laceration, or self-questioning. The family is beyond redemption—it cannot be revived in either the big city or the village, and consequently it wishes its own death. The violent peasant world heals itself and rejuvenates with time. The returning gentile soldiers beat their unfaithful women to death; this is accepted as an old and unchallenged ritual, and life will go on. In its final year, the Jewish family seems to exist outside time and outside a predictable and repetitious pattern. And pitted against the peasants' virility is Jewish impotence.

Appelfeld is preoccupied with the fictionalization of an incomplete memory and the filling in of autobiographical and fictional gaps. His first-person narrative is a reconstructive literary device, partially answering a need to restructure an unlived past. A deep sense of no exit afflicts the characters in the last year of their lives. There *is* a way out, however, and it is madness, a form of self-negation and self-hate. This is a story about centrality and marginality, as many of Appelfeld's narratives are. Ironically, what seems is not what is. Seemingly the family is rich, cultured, well off, and established. Its reality, however, is its rootlessness and lack of purpose. Despite the nonpolemic nature of Appelfeld's fiction, one cannot avoid grappling with the questions the characters do not pose for themselves. The failure of Jewish landed gentry goes beyond the boundaries of the estate. The estate realistically and symbolically "exiles" its Jews.

The modes of transmission of a text also carry a message. The first-person narrator, at this stage in Appelfeld's work, does not orchestrate the text. The omnipresent voice of an all-knowing narrator organizes the material by creating a map of contraries, contradictions, similarities. Appelfeld's treatment of his subject matter points to novelty and experimentation. He subverts the reader's expectations and sentiments. The reader's built-in, prestructured reactions are challenged. Appelfeld does not choose an avant-garde mantle; nor does he lament a world devoid of meaning. His fiction is not overtly nihilistic. But one should not be lulled by the elegant sentences and the flowing rhythm. All over this elegaic text there is an arrested scream. A deep sense of alienation has been established here, and it will continue to appear in all of Appelfeld's novels and novellas that deal with the prewar era.

13

BADENHEIM 1939

Tʜᴇ ᴏᴘᴇɴɪɴɢ paragraph of "Badenheim, Ir Nofesh" (1975; English version entitled *Badenheim 1939*) introduces in germinal form the powers that will shape the fate of Badenheim and its inhabitants.

> Spring returned to Badenheim. In the country church next to the town the bells rang. The shadows of the forest retreated to the trees. The sun scattered the remnants of the darkness and its light filled the main street from square to square. It was a moment of transition. The town was about to be invaded by the vacationers. Two inspectors passed through an alley, examining the flow of the sewage in the pipes. The town, which had changed its inhabitants many times in the course of the years, had kept its modest beauty.[1]

The two powers are intimated in the romantic and tranquil depiction of nature and the presence of the Sanitation Department inspectors. The town, it is implied, faces an invasion, a state of siege.

What gives the small town its uniqueness, its attraction, is the annual spring festival, an event that brings musicians, actors, and singers to Badenheim. The festival, like mythical spring rites, revives the visitors, whose need for the yearly pilgrimage to Badenheim is vital. This reality is a wishful phenomenon on the surface of events. The subsurface reality is that madness and sickness have beset the city and its inhabitants.

As in previous and future narratives, Appelfeld gives us the penultimate phase in the lives of his characters in a tale where the beginning portends the end. We are first introduced to Trude, the pharmacist's wife. Like the mythical Cassandra, in her seeming sickness or madness she prophesies the future of Badenheim and its people. To Trude, "everything looked transparent and diseased" (p. 10). Then Dr. Pappenheim, the impresario of the cultural festival, emerges like a Hassidic miracle worker from the forest to preside over the festivities on main street. His annual task is to bring to town the best talent in the performing arts. Like Sisyphus, he never achieves his goal; he comes closest in his preparations for the very last festival in Badenheim.

Who are the visitors and vacationers? They are Jews and converted

Jews. Jews who married gentiles, Jews who married into the aristocracy and nobility of Europe, Jewish intellectuals. The town had grown used to them, those "foreigners who had insinuated themselves like diseased roots" (p. 4). When they begin to arrive, Trude observes their excessive pallor, though Martin, her husband, is unaware of it. Eventually Trude's prediction of doom will be validated—Martin will become sick and Trude will gain control of herself and the situation. As in many of Appelfeld's narratives, the ironic turn of events points to an ominous future, a bitter, tragic outcome. To Trude the transparent world looks poisonous. Her function, despite her marginal role in the novel, is to forecast the inevitable end of the Jews in Badenheim and, in a wider scope, to point to the fate of European Jewry as a whole.

Added to the themes of transparency and sickness is that of intoxication. This theme has multiple meanings in the novel. In the beginning we hear about a "secret intoxication in the air"—as Badenheim has been a source of intoxication for its vacationers. They are drunk with their desire for culture. Toward the end the pharmacy is looted by the vacationers to get drugs. Intoxication is also tied to the slow demise of Badenheim as a town.

The novel has no central protagonist with the possible exception of Dr. Pappenheim, who is more of a connecting tissue. A variety of characters are introduced, all well drawn. Each character and each utterance contributes to the novel's architecture. Seemingly innocent sentences carry a dark prophecy. At the beginning of the novel, for example, an unnamed woman is amazed that no letters are sent from Badenheim; she thought the place was completely isolated.

Bitter irony pervades the novel, bordering occasionally on the grotesque and tragic. There are two movements afoot, the preparations for the festival and the slow turning of the town into a concentration camp, and Appelfeld deftly orchestrates them:

> The inspectors of the sanitation department were now spread all over town. They took measurements, put up fences, and planted flags. Porters unloaded rolls of barbed wire, cement pillars, and all kinds of appliances suggestive of preparations for a public celebration. (P. 15)

In a highly stylized manner, the novel presents Badenheim as a microcosm of the assimilated existence of central European Jews on the eve of the Second World War. Concentric circles are hinted at: Badenheim is in Austria, the festival is in Badenheim, the artists and the vacationers are the Jewish inhabitants of Badenheim on the eve of the *Anschluss*. Under the guise of good manners and civility, a sense of doom besets all the characters.

As the novel unfolds, the sense of no exit becomes more and more apparent. The artists who appear in Badenheim reflect in their art and personalities the plight of the time. The twin poetry readers are one of the major attractions of the place. Dr. Pappenheim discovered the two in Vienna and "immediately sensed the morbid melody throbbing in their voice" (p. 17). His fascination with the two, whose passion is Rilke, is shared by the vacationers, and now Pappenheim cannot do without them. At the beginning the public's response was not enthusiastic, but with time people discovered the hidden melody in their voices and became intoxicated with it. The twins represent the motif of the double (the *Doppelgänger*), depicting the total immersion of the one in the other—a probable metaphor as well for the yearning of the assimilated Jew for absorption into European culture. In addition, there is a sickness in their voices that fascinates their listeners. Frau Zauberblit feels that life without them is pointless. Semitsky claims that their voice touched "his infected cells."

It was Rilke whose poetic attempt to reach "the thingness (*Dinglichkeit*) of things" bordered on depersonalization. The twins depict this quality of the selfless self and are eternally practicing in order to perfect their art. Their ascetic existence and their attempt to touch the very thingness of things continues as Badenheim's state of siege and confinement ensues. Their unceasing attempt to reach the "innerworld-space" (*Innerweltraum*) depicts simultaneously a blindness and an awareness, the essence of being rather than everyday reality. Paradoxically they are blind to the encroaching reality outside.

The preparations for the festival correspond to the preparations for the deportation. The posters of the sanitation department are chilling.

The Sanitation Department now resembled a travel agency festooned with posters: LABOR IS OUR LIFE . . . THE AIR IN POLAND IS FRESHER . . . SAIL ON THE VISTULA . . . THE DEVELOPMENT AREAS NEED YOU . . . GET TO KNOW THE SLAVIC CULTURE . . . " (Pp. 29–30)

The remote, alien Poland begins to seem an idyllic and pastoral place to many of the assimilated and acculturated vacationers. A return to one's roots is entertained, while the twins continue to intoxicate the vacationers with the poems of death.

For two hours they sat and spoke of death. Their voices were dispassionate. They were like people who had visited hell and were no longer afraid of it. When the reading was over they stood up. The people sat with downcast eyes. There was no applause. Pappenheim approached from the doorway and took off his hat. He looked as if he were about to kneel. (P. 35)

The vacationers at Badenheim seem captivated by powers beyond their control. Like marionettes they go through motions, featuring in a most civilized manner the stylized horror story of the twentieth century. The reading by the twins is a reflection of the true situation. They too, in their way, prophesy the future, and the listeners know that in a mysterious way the things said refer to them. As Ruth R. Wisse writes,

> The Badenheimers . . . have reached such a remote stage of acculturation that some of them have never even been recognized as Jews; the drama of their progressive unmasking is like the prolonged climax of a successful masquerade. Throughout the summer, as the town adjusts to every new discriminatory measure, the Jews, one by one, reluctantly or persuaded by an inner logic, accept the condition that has been forced upon them, and which culminates in their "return to Poland."[2]

Writing with a variety of agendas, commentators such as Marsha Rozenblit have tried to define the critical terms *acculturation* and *assimilation*. The term *assimilation* is especially problematic, as she correctly claims. For a Zionist, assimilation has always been a derogatory term implying subservient and cowardly behavior before gentile culture. Rozenblit takes the term to be of neutral value. Following Milton Gordon's definiton in *Assimilation in American Life*, she conceives it to denote "continuum." The first step in the process of acculturation is a cultural assimilatiom. Thus acculturation is not necessarily a step toward assimilation. In one view, total assimilation occurs when a minority group fuses with the majority. It is interesting to note Rozenblit's own observations of the Jews of Vienna between 1867 and 1914:

> Jewish assimilation in late nineteenth-century Vienna—and presumably in other European cities as well—was a group phenomenon. Jews acculturated into the larger culture and society adopted the cultural tastes and styles of Austro-German society, but did so in the company of other Jews. . . . As a result instead of merging into the larger society, Jews developed new social patterns and new modes of behav-

ior which continue to mark them as Jews to themselves and to the outside world . . . "[3]

Superimposing a transparency of common sense and causality on the Appelfeldian universe does not enlighten the reader. In a parallel to the world of Kafka, Appelfeld's fiction, in many cases, creates an enclosed verbal universe that answers only to its own inner laws. The message of doom is transmitted through the actions of the Sanitation Department and through Rilke's *Sonnets to Orpheus*, in which life and death reign, and the *Duino Elegies*, in which the threatening reality cannot be veiled. Rilke, the wandering poet, entered the psyche of the assimilated Jew whose hunger for culture is never sated. Thus, according to the common portrait, the Jew is portrayed as restless, anxious, intellectual. And yet the idea of a return to Poland, the original homeland of the Ashkenazi Jew in modern Europe, appeals to the vacationers. It seems as if the shards of collective tribal memory of the old country can bring respite to the ever-moving drive.

Instead of creating one complex protagonist here, Appelfeld gives us a rich gallery of characters, and each one adds to the collective persona of the assimilated Jew. Situations are constructed by a process of adding new characters to the novel. Whereas the Twins represent one aspect of the Jewish psyche, the Yanuka represents the other. The Yanuka is a child prodigy who sings Yiddish folk songs in Yiddish, his only language. He is loved, pampered, and adopted by all the vacationers. The Yanuka represents the Jewish character of Badenheim, the resort town. The expanding actions of the Sanitation Department are paralleled by the returning Jews. A barrier is placed at the entrance to the town and the movement of the vacationers is limited. They are forbidden to have picnics out of town. Only the hotel, the swimming pool, and the pastry shop are open to them. The Yanuka, like Trude and the Twins, is but another reflection of the impending catastrophe. His songs about the forests where the wolves dwell echo Trude's vision of the town being besieged by wild animals. The situation in Badenheim is a strange mixture of intoxication and hope. The idea of a return to Poland takes hold of many of the vacationers, and even Dr. Pappenheim becomes one of its proponents. Simultaneously, the closing of the swimming pool is yet another sign of the increasing confinement. Yet the idea of the imminent return to Poland serves as a temporary placebo. Dr. Pappenheim envisages a "New Jewish Order," a term that carries a tragic irony within it.

Appelfeld does not expose us to the inner thoughts and feelings of the characters. We observe their movements and their conversations. Outer agents represent the mood: the anaerobic atmosphere is depicted through locutions such as "cold light," "leaden sun," "cold horizons" —all are indexes of the abnormality of the situation. Another symbol of the approaching end is the parable of the aquarium. The head waiter tells Karl, one of the vacationers, of the catastrophe that befell the illuminated aquarium in the hotel lobby. Blue Cambia fish brought by a nature lover in the previous year massacred all the other fish. From that moment on, Karl becomes fascinated with the aquarium. On deportation day, he places two fish in a bottle, taking them along to Poland. The death of the fish occurs at the moment of deportation. Karl's sensitive son is sent to a German military academy by his army general grandfather. The demise of the prettiest green fish is Karl's own personal demise, the demise of Badenheim, and the demise of culture. The aquarium is a riddle whose answer is embedded in the riddle itself. Karl shares with Trude the "secret" of transparency and clairvoyance.

Trude is enlivened by the idea of the return to Poland; she knows that her beloved daughter Helena, married to a gentile who abuses her, will return home. But even open-eyed characters such as Trude have only a limited vision of the future. Some vacationers totally ignore all signs and try to complete their work. One of the representative Jewish intellectuals is Professor Fussholdt, who throughout his stay in Badenheim has buried himself in his room to proofread the last draft of his book on satire, leaving his young wife Mitzi to her coquettish affairs.

> Professor Fussholdt read the proofs of his book. At one time his lectures had given rise to quite a controversy in academic circles. It was he who had called Theodore Herzl "a hack writer with messianic pretensions" and his associates "petty functionaries who jumped on the golden band-wagon." Martin Buber too did not escape his barbs. It was Fussholdt who had said that Buber couldn't make up his mind if he was a prophet or a professor. If anyone deserved the title of a great Jew, according to Fussholdt, it was Karl Kraus: he had revived satire. And now the professor was sitting and proofreading his latest book. Whom was he attacking now? The journalists, the hacks, so-called "Jewish art"? Perhaps his book was about Hans Herzl, Theodore's son who had converted to Christianity. Or perhaps it was a book about satire, the only art form appropriate to our lives. (P. 62)

The assembly of all past residents of Badenheim and those connected with the place brings back to town the famous Mandelbaum

and his equally famous trio. Mandelbaum tells of the Jews of Reizen-
bach who were put into quarantine—while he managed to escape with
the help of a junior officer. Mandelbaum, president of the music academy
in Vienna, is incensed. The academy does not answer his letters and
ignores him, the founder of the academy. Dr. Pappenheim is elated. For
years he had been trying to bring Mandelbaum to the festival, with
no success. He tells the artist that if he agrees to appear to the intimate
crowd left in the hotel it will be a most memorable experience, to
which Mandelbaum answers:

> "Me? I'm just a Jew, a number, a file. If not for the junior officer I
> would still be rotting in Reizenbach. What do you need me for? Am I
> a rabbi, a cantor?" (P. 67)

To Dr. Pappenheim, Mandelbaum is "our maestro," the only one
they want. But Mandelbaum, like professor Fussholdt, buries himself
in his room, tormenting his musicians in a quest for utmost perfection. Restriction and confinement continue. Telephone services are
terminated, and the town is totally separated from the outer world. It
begins to live "a life inside itself " (p. 70).

Music is portrayed by Appelfeld as a possessive force that overpow-
ers the artist. Paulina, the young cellist in *The Pupil of the Eye*, runs
from the tyranny of the impresario Rosenwasser into the arms of the
virile, abusive Krill. In *Badenheim 1939* the broken spirit and the impotency of the Jewish intellectual are replaced by denial or by a re-
newed quest for roots, for an undisguised Jewish existence. Aberrant
nature, unnatural growth, is one of Appelfeld's markers for a cata-
strophic end. The creepers, the fish, and the flora grow in an abnormal
way, infringing on expected boundaries.

Since no supplies or goods are allowed into town, the hotel owner
opens his stocks. Delicacies saved for better days are given to the re-
luctant vacationers, who suffer from loss of appetite. As quiet desperation settles in, the Twins begin to mingle with the guests and Yanuka
is pampered by the aging demimonde. An atmosphere of mellowness
and forgiveness prevails. The quiet conversion to Jewish consciousness
is enhanced with the return of Badenheim's past rabbi. Dr. Pappenheim and the rabbi become the leaders of the community. The rabbi,
who has suffered a stroke, is led in in a wheelchair. When asked how
the transfer to Poland will take place, Dr. Pappenheim answers: "By
train. Train journeys are nice, aren't they?" (p. 74).

The omnipresent voice that opens most of the chapters sets the tone by depicting atmosphere and mood through changing lights and colors. The telling voice guides the reader by drawing the wider parameters of Badenheim. The characters fill in the gaps through their modes of movement and speech. The crowd is varied and colorful, and despite differences they all draw together for the coming end. The constant addition of new characters to the existing map expands the fabric of the novel and underlines the gathering of the Jews for their last station.

The cold horror of the story lies in its slow pace and the quiet process of telling the tale. The strength of *Badenheim 1939* lies in its power to portray the macabre, though not through garish colors and harsh sounds. Muffled utterances, everyday small talk, and bizarre behavior seemingly within the boundaries of order paint the picture. And yet the novel challenges the claims of order, culture, and civilization. Appelfeld shuns the melodramatic, the pathetic tone. He remains a student of such Central European Jewish writers as Wassermann, Schnitzler, and Kafka, and Mann's *Magic Mountain* clearly influenced this novel. The tone of the narrative is stoic despite the madness in man and nature. Tragically, the inhabitants of Badenheim are not the "desert generation" on their way to the Promised Land.

The infrastructure of the novel feeds on irony: the tension between seeming and being. The characters remain in the domain of seeming, whereas the reader combines the two realities, knowing full well that the train carries the vacationers to their doom. Here is the novel's final paragraph:

> An engine, an engine coupled to four filthy freight cars, emerged from the hills and stopped at the station. Its appearance was as sudden as if it had risen from a pit in the ground. "Get in!" yelled invisible voices, and the people were sucked in. Even those who were standing with a bottle of lemonade in their hands, a bar of chocolate, the head waiter with his dog—they were all sucked in as easily as grains of wheat poured into a funnel. Nevertheless Dr. Pappenheim found time to make the following remark: "If the coaches are so dirty it must mean that we have not far to go." (Pp. 147–148)

14

THE AGE OF WONDERS

A SENSE OF exile from the familiar and the known is the central theme of Appelfeld's *Tor Ha'pelaot* (The age of wonders, 1978). In this highly sensitive first-person narrative, the young storyteller (age twelve) observes a new reality steadily encroaching upon his family. A mixture of sadness and doom engulfs the boy as he watches the coming apart of his parents' marriage, reflecting the disintegration of his extended family and the eventual demise of his community in the small provincial town of Bukovina. This attitude of wary observation is by no means unique to him. Indeed, one might say it is typical of the Jew in general, and it is matched by a corresponding sense of being observed. That is, the Jew leads his life with a constant awareness of the observing eye of the outer world and tries to interpret the intention of the gentile framework within which he lives.

That applies especially to the newly assimilated Jew, for whom Judaism no longer plays a major role. In *The Age of Wonders* (the English version appeared in 1981), the constant awareness of the "other"— watching and assessing—is especially heightened in the opening scene on the train. The laughing Jewish woman in her vulgar behavior embarrasses the "civilized," good-mannered Jews, who do not identify themselves as Jews. Nonetheless they are on guard whenever a Jew makes a public nuisance of himself or herself. This is the same attitude of being ill at ease which secular assimilated Austrian Jews felt vis-à-vis Hassidic Jews. On a larger scale it reflects a tribal uneasiness (appearing in many of Appelfeld's works) along with an excessive sensitivity to possible criticism coming from the gentile world. It underscores the very sense the assimilated Jew does not want to acknowledge—that he is after all an alien, a stranger.

The Age of Wonders begins with a variation on the setting of a Jewish resort town. At the end, we leave the vacationers and residents of Badenheim on their way to a death camp. This novel (like *Badenheim 1939* and *The Pupil of the Eye*) ends with deportation. In addition

The Age of Wonders has an opposite movement: it opens with mother and son returning from a retreat in a desolate place that portends in its decline some of the forthcoming events. Of the three novels, *The Age of Wonders* is the most realistic and psychologically the richest. It is the story of an assimilated Jewish family told from the point of view of the twelve-year-old who, as noted, observes the world crumble around him. The opening sentence establishes the personal tone, the centrality of the narrator, and the moment of narration: "Many years ago Mother and I took the night train from the quiet little-known retreat where we had spent the summer."[1]

At the center of events is the atmosphere of prewar Europe, foreshadowing the fate of this Jewish family. We are also exposed to the inner life of the narrator, to his aforementioned sense of sadness and doom, along with the sense of void that permeates his being. The mother does not choose to go to a grand hotel or to Baden Baden; neither the "cure" nor the mineral water attracts her. Similarly, she chooses not to go to a "cultural" resort. Her choice of retreat reflects her arrested spirituality and the sense of doom in regard to her personal life and the world around her. The summer's demise is made obvious to the observant child in his mother's uncontrolled weeping upon leaving the retreat.

An obsessive theme running through the novel is reflected in the sense that life is beyond one's control. The theme of movement also reenters the Appelfeldian narrative. In *Badenheim 1939* the movement comes from the circumference of the town, slowly creeping toward the center, the hotel. The process of confinement has made movement impossible until the moment of deportation, when the vacationers are led to their train. *The Age of Wonders* consists of constant movement, by train and by foot. This movement is part of the undoing of the family and its last attempt at self-denial. The character of the father is burdened with self-deceit, reflected in his refusal to accept the new encroaching reality. The mother (like Trude in *Badenheim 1939*) is the prophetess of doom. Unlike Trude, however, she does not speak; she senses, and expresses herself in action. While she retreats to a forsaken log cabin, the father, a successful novelist, shuttles back and forth between Prague and Vienna. His volatile exhibitionist nature is pitted against the mother's solipsistic stance and her silence. Her sense of uncertainty and the uncertain course of events in general give the novel a sense of indeterminacy, both in theme and in language. Appelfeld's highly metaphoric language succeeds in portraying the sense of the ominous which is embedded in the everyday.

The train is a central element in this novel, as in other Appelfeld narratives. It is the ultimate multisign or multisymbol for both the pre-Holocaust and the Holocaust experience: a train ride opens and closes the novel; a luxurious train at the beginning is transformed into a cattle car at the end. In the opening scene the self-certainty of the upper-middle-class Jews in the first-class car is abruptly shaken. The express train stops at a deserted sawmill. Security forces order all Austrian passengers who are not of Christian birth and all foreigners to register in the office. The elegant woman whose voice is heard in the beginning of the novel becomes a woman thrown into the Temple where all Jews are rounded up. Her desire "not to be lumped together" with the coarse, loud Jews is not fulfilled. In Appelfeld's own conception (as expressed in interviews) the train station is strongly connected with Jewish fate. The small train stations entailed great and positive hopes for the Jews who left Europe before the Holocaust on their way to Palestine, the United States, and other destinations. It is at the same time a symbol of the worst. Thus the railway station in its very ambiguity is an important part of Jewish history.

That touches upon yet another aspect of the novel: the self-criticism of the Jew that verges on self-hatred. From both the economic and (more noticeably) the social point of view, the traditional East European *Ostjuden* are a source of embarrassment to the assimilated Jew. Unlike the affected residents and vacationers in *Badenheim 1939*, who shared a romantic yearning for roots and origins, the characters in *The Age of Wonders* differ in their personal quests. Appelfeld also gives much attention to a further ambiguity. He frequently suspends day-to-day time while emphasizing the unceasing movement of his characters. Using the motif of the Wandering Jew, Appelfeld grafts another layer onto the stories, touching on the period that precedes the Holocaust.

In *The Age of Wonders* the movement of the characters is constant, poised against the uncertainty they feel and the certain doom we know awaits them. In the first half of the novel the roads lead eventually to deportation. A reverse movement appears in the second half of the novel, which takes place years later: the protagonist, a child in the first half of the novel, now emerges as an adult returning home to his birthplace. The experience of the Holocaust itself is not depicted; it is simply alluded to through the basic image of movement in the first part of the novel. Thus its footsteps pervade the early part of the book, which may be read forward and understood backward. The Kafkaesque nature of the opening scenes, in which the mother and son face the authorities, echoes *The Trial*, in which Joseph K. is arraigned but not arrested. The family in *The Age of Wonders* is marked for doom from the outset of the novel.

The family members—father, mother, and son—are constantly on the move. From the first-class compartment they are relegated to freight cars and slow milk trains. Accompanying the various travels and travails of the family in the first part of the novel are two colorful suitcases. The incongruity between the mental and physical anguish of the family and the resortbound suitcases casts an ironic light on the state of affairs. Clearly the last train, unmentioned in the first half of the novel, will lead the family to its deportation and eventual fate.

The impending Holocaust is already apparent in the seemingly unimportant elements introduced: the registration, the trains, the movement. At this point the movement goes beyond the merely geographical, functioning also as a cathartic element in spirituality—from home to the Catholic convent, from home to the country, from home to the Jewish old-age home. The map of these movements underlines the inner map of the Jewish psyche. The most striking movements are those of conversion/inversion. Theresa, the narrator's spiritual, graceful aunt, converts to Christianity in her quest for solace, silence, and escape. The half-Jewish sculptor Stark embraces Judaism despite his gentile appearance and bearing.

Thus Appelfeld, in his novels of the 1970s, introduces various aspects of Jewish existence in prewar Europe; the Hassidic Jews are constantly in the background. Their behavior is a source of chagrin to the father, who abhors their exaggerated manners and movements. At the end of the first part of the novel, all Jews face the same fate. They are finally brought to a common point, a leveling, those who denied their Judaism and those who affirmed it. The "Jewish Order" is cynically referred to by assimilated men and women, both in *Badenheim 1939* and *The Age of Wonders*. The disillusioned assimilated Jew is awakened by circumstances that cannot be controlled. The attempts at self-negation are expressed by the father, who blames the *Ostjuden* for all the troubles that are visited upon the enlightened Jews. His fiction is praised for bringing new beauty to Austrian literature, a beauty tainted

by malaise. Yet his attempts to enter and imitate his intellectual society fail as his fiction is attacked. George Steiner writes of Simone
Weil's fascination with Christianity:

> Weil's is not an isolated case. Other Jewish contemporaries of an up-
> rooted and questing nature felt tempted by the aesthetic solemnity of
> Catholic worship and by the sheer eloquence of the Catholic message
> within European art and civilization. . . . As devastation neared, much
> in the psyche and the sensibility of the European Jewish elite seemed
> to cast about for refuge.[2]

In *The Age of Wonders* the broken spirit of Jewish intellectualism
expresses once again the sense of the looming catastrophe. Intellectual
Jews were outsiders even in the "good" days; they knew it, yet refused
to accept it. In the father's attempt to defend his work (a "defense"
reminiscent, as noted, of Kafka's *Trial*) it becomes clear that his re-
puted motherland is not his motherland. Nor did it relate to him as an
adopted son. Clearly, then, the sense of security the Jew felt in Central
Europe was a false one. The multiethnic nature of the Hapsburg monarchy allowed many diverse nationalities to come under its flag. This
gave a sense of security to those who could congregate under the benevolent reign of Kaiser Franz Joseph. But with the dissolution of this
ancien régime in 1918, and with the emergence of nationalistic feelings among the various nationalities, the old submerged resentment
against the Jews reemerged. And yet the father did not embrace traditional Judaism but attacked traditional Jews: "Father cursed the little
Jews who could think of nothing but money and who stirred up strife
wherever they went. Their dark avarice drove them crazy" (p. 54).

Vulnerability is especially characteristic of Appelfeld's female protagonists, and we cannot overlook the assumption that the Jew's sensitivity and vulnerability are identified with that of the woman; osten-
sibly the Jew was perceived as the "other." One can surmise that hate
for the *Ostjuden* was part of a certain element of patricide. The old
father, in the image of the Jew in his traditional garb, made such Jews
fossils in the eyes of Appelfeld's protagonist, who represents the assimilated enlightened Jew—as if centuries of history refused to be
erased from the face of the earth. M. A. Meyer has suggested that "the
history of the German Jews is popularly perceived as an object in the
perils of naivete and assimilation." Meyer's further observations can
be applied to the German-speaking assimilated Jews beyond the
boundaries of German Jews:

Irony heaped upon irony: the German Jews sought to escape animosity through assimilation, but the assimilation only brought increased
animosity, and that animosity in turn—where it did not induce escape through conversion—led to increased awareness of themselves
as Jews. . . . Marked as Jews from the outside, some of the most assimilated were forced to confront their Jewishness. They came to realize
that they were regarded as Jews in spite of themselves. If so, they
concluded, they would be Jews—out of spite. The talented Viennese
novelist Jakob Wassermann may serve as an example of these trends
in a single life. His Jewishness was the product of rejection by non-
Jews; he noted its lack of positive content. Wassermann was neither
religiously nor nationally Jewish. Yet his greatest admirers were his
fellow Jews. . . . Much as he tried to write as a German for Germans,
Wassermann came to realize he would always be regarded as a Jewish
writer. He once noted down what he regarded as typically Jewish
faults that shamed and disgusted him, as well as virtues that he found
worthy of praise. But in the last analysis Jewishness . . . was a fate he
could not overcome. There was no choice but to accept the reality of
antisemitism.[3]

Constant presences in Appelfeld's fiction, from its beginning, are
the convent and Christianity. In *The Age of Wonders* the convent is
central. Theresa, the narrator's aunt, who suffers from depression, is
sent to St. Peter's sanatorium for healing. There she embraces Christianity. In her dubious mental state and in her failed attempt to excel,
Theresa joins earlier characters in Appelfeld's fiction such as Paulina
in *The Pupil of the Eye*. The young gifted woman attends the university, breaks down, and embraces her depression. Like every other character, she is a symbol and a sign of the general state of malaise, uncertainty, and insecurity.

As noted earlier, the second part of the *The Age of Wonders* is in
the tradition of the belated return home. Details that were unknown
to the reader in the first part of the novel are explicitly stated here—as,
for example, the name of the protagonist: Bruno (who comes from
Jerusalem to revisit his hometown). The relationship between the parents is here shown to be strained and difficult.

The technique of the third-person narrator as applied in the novel's
latter half creates a certain distance between the reader and the protagonist. To the reader he is now a different persona, with memories.
Yet the belated return to the same place, with different people, is an
exercise in vacuity; the protagonist is trying to reassess his strained
relationship with his father. The excuse for the trip, the revived interest in the writings of the father, hide an attempt to come to terms

with the most influential figure in his life. In the first part, the child observes the decline and debasement of the father, who did not change to the very last moment. The element of disgrace accompanies the son's image of the father from the outset: his love affairs, one even carried on at home, his attempt to find favor in the eyes of his early admirers, and so on. The fate of the father is unclear.

> They said he had died half-mad in Theresienstadt, and that before he died he had tried to convert to Christianity. Another rumor said that he had not been sent to Theresienstadt but to somewhere near Minsk, where he had been seen a number of times in the slaughterhouse. And that was not the end of the rumors. (P. 209)

The town, though it has not changed its physical character, is depicted as a place gone awry. Instead of a seemingly respectable provincial town where culture reigns, it looks like a place afflicted by aberration. Instead of the gifted Jews who were craving culture, instead of the dedicated artists who drove themselves out of their minds in their attempts to reach perfection, the city is now being fascinated by Oriental midgets who perform in the bar, by a loose singer who drives men mad, and by a bunch of young people of mixed origin, Jewish and Christian, who live on the borders of middle-class morality. The stay of the returned son is both unclear and unwelcome. Those who know him await his departure, and those he meets are unaffected by him.

Before the end, the priest, Mauber, feels that the Jews should leave quickly for Palestine. The father, who was never enthusiastic about Zionist ideology, dismisses the proposal: "I, for one, will not emigrate. I would rather be persecuted and disgraced than emigrate. I've done nothing wrong. I am an Austrian writer. No one will deny me this title" (p. 257). A sense of incompleteness accompanies the protagonist and the reader. The belated return is almost always doomed. Here parallels exist between father and son. The son faces marital difficulties just as the father had; the son has reached the age of the father and yet somehow still feels like a son. The latest miscarriage of his wife, a daughter of Auschwitz survivors, points to afflicted blood that cannot bring forth continuity. In many of Appelfeld's narratives the men are impotent, having been emasculated by their concept of gentile society and by their own inability to cease being the "other." Bruno finds a cousin, the illegitimate daughter of his womanizing uncle Salo, who was too drunk and too frightened to go to the final deportation place. She is engaged in a lesbian affair with another girl, who is of mixed origin. In a manner suggestive of the fiction of Heinrich Böll, and Günter Grass, the fiction of post-Holocaust experience depicts behavior shunned by accepted Judeo-Christian morality.

In an interview with Clive Sinclair, Appelfeld was asked about the transition from the first-person narrative in the earlier part of the novel to the third-person account in the latter part. Appelfeld remarks that when he is writing in the first person he is "looking" at his past despite the distance in time and place.

> I used the first person for Bruno, because when I began to write the book I felt a deep darkness. Some memories . . . just pieces is what I had. . . . It was very difficult to reconstruct from the small pieces. . . . The second part [is] the known part. I cannot return to Czernowitz, though I have returned to Europe. My returning to Europe was a kind of homecoming, it was known to me. Then I decided to write it in the third person, to give it a more objective view.[4]

Appelfeld's unpublished play "Locked In" is an elaboration on and extension of the last scene in the first part of *The Age of Wonders*. The play takes place in the sanctuary of a synagogue in a small Austrian town in 1939. The play hovers thematically between Kafka's "Before the Law" and Sartre's *No Exit*. A year after the *Anschluss*, some of the characters still deny the signs of the impending disaster. Thrown or forced into a situation about which they have no prior knowledge, they expose their truths and lies through the new conditions imposed upon them. The challenging presence of the others reveals, in some cases, the depth of self-deceit. The reader or viewer provides the historical framework for the characters' fate. Against this background, everything uttered in the play gains a tragic dimension, accentuating human frailty.

15

THE HEALER

THE SUBJECT of *Be'et Uve'ona Aḥat* (1985; English title *The Healer*, 1990) is many-faceted: unfulfilled hopes, the return to one's roots, the attempt to find meaning in life, and the loss of direction. What motivates the four members of a family to leave Vienna and travel to the Carpathian Mountains is the desire to seek a cure for the ailing daughter, Helga. They seek the help of a zaddik, a Jewish Hassidic holy man. The undefined disease is portrayed at the beginning of the novel as an incurable mental illness. Illness and malaise also seem to infect the other members of the family: the father, Felix; the son, Karl; even the mother, Henrietta. Felix, who lacks faith, regards the trip as pointless and sees the village healer as a charlatan, a cheat, a witch doctor.

The trip seems to be a withdrawal from Vienna, from the cultured world of theaters and cafés, to boorish country life. The experience in the country serves as a turning point in the life of Felix; he becomes willing to delve into his past. After his father's death, his mother, the only Jew left in the provincial town, took her own life. Helga, the talented daughter, has inherited Felix's susceptibility to illness. She is also expected to fulfill his hopes. Her talents have destined her to be a concert pianist. Helga's illness reveals to Felix his own true situation. He himself is at a crossroads. He has no connection with traditional Jews; he is not, however, willing to convert to Christianity.

After staying for six months in the Carpathians, locked in and besieged by the winter snow, he leaves his wife and daughter in the mountains and returns to Vienna with Karl. On the train he meets a Jewish woman physician who has converted to Catholicism, and he is shaken by that discovery. Faith led the woman to take the step. When Felix tells her that his wife has returned to faith in the power of Judaism, she is deeply affected. She believes that without faith and a deep sense of spirituality a doctor is but a sorcerer. All the negative traits which Felix attributed to the healer are forgiven him: life without faith is self-delusion, which inevitably culminates in emptiness.

The sojourn in the mountains has shown Felix that life has reached its end. It will merely continue in its unchanging routine while the danger to his existence increases.

At the first station on the trip to Vienna, two Jews, dealers in old clothes, are robbed, and no one comes to their assistance. The train is halted for an exceptional inspection, and when the policemen discover that Felix's last name is Katz, they insult him for being Jewish. When he arrives during the night at his house in Vienna, his Christian house-keeper refuses to unlock the door for him. When he persists in his knocking, she shouts, "There are no Jews here." Apparently strangers knock on the door every night. Once inside the house, Felix finds that pictures of Jesus and John the Baptist have been hung on the walls.

Karl, Felix's son, has been forced to drop out of school, preferring sports, coarse food, and women. The stay in the Carpathian Mountains brought out his coarseness. He befriended peasants and servant women, and came to resemble them. He represents a new generation for whom Judaism is neither a problem nor something to be desired. The appetite for knowledge and studies is far removed from him. Felix had dreamed of becoming a physician but could not because of his family's poverty, but Karl (for whom that goal would be possible) does not share the dream.

Despite their simplicity, the pious, faithful Jews of the Carpathian Mountains seem to have roots and to live in fullness and harmony with the nature around them. *The Healer* touches on the tragedy of the middle-class Jew who lacks an intellectual foundation. The intellectual Jew and the middle-class businessman, however, share a sense of uprootedness on the eve of the war.

Henrietta's response to Helga's illness is a return to her sources. Her own mother had come from the Carpathian Mountains and wanted to return but had not managed to do so; Henrietta's return is a completion of her mother's wish. Illness in this novel is connected with the loss of words. The discovery of the right words is a key to the discovery of the self. The loss of words signifies illness and lack of continuity.

The Holy Man suggests drawing close to the holy letters and contemplating them as the road to redemption—an old Kabbalistic faith in the magic power of letters. He instructs Henrietta to teach Helga the Hebrew characters, telling her that reading the prayerbook will be the beginning of her cure. Helga seeks a voice; playing the piano symbolizes the attempt to find a voice in European culture. But other voices burst from her lips; strange sounds are strangled in her throat. Those wild sounds seek a tongue. Helga tries to free herself from her demons by burying herself in the snow. There is a desire in her for peace, calm, sleep, and death. In a similar manner, Felix tries to find repose in the deep snow; like Helga, he is saved by the local people.

Helga finds aesthetic value in the letters. She tells the Holy Man that they are beautiful. His response:

> "The holy letters bring us closer to our home—like a person returning to his home village after years. The smell of the trees and the grass drives foreign parts away from him. We have a great many foreign parts within us, do we not? But we, thank God, have a home. We can return home. . . . Foreign parts are large, broad, assailing us with sadness. The holy letters are our home. When darkness falls, we simply enter our home. Our home is warm and light, and it has all manner of good things."[1]

Language itself is a central protagonist in this novel. The disintegration of the family is expressed in external words; the members address each other with words which do not touch. The thinning out of their conversation, of words, illustrates the gaps which are exposed. The simple peasant who takes Felix and his son to the train does not understand why city Jews do not speak Yiddish. When Felix argues that German is a more elevated language, the peasant answers, "German is the German's language isn't it?" Against the background of the Holocaust, with all its horrors, a painful question is asked regarding the curative power of words.

As we have seen on a number of occasions, the theme of return is a basic motif in the fiction of Appelfeld. It gains depth and dimension in his fiction after the 1970s. The return is often an intermediate stage in the character's existence. In pre-Holocaust narratives, the last station is deportation and death. In narratives depicting the survivors, the return can have a variety of destinations: Israel, home, or, mostly, nowhere—what can be termed "sites of forgetfulness." The Holocaust and beyond had proven to many that a Jew does not have a home in Europe. This sentiment was expressed in Appelfeld's early stories. Even in the early neo-Hassidic tales, the return home was always problematic. Thus the motif of return has more than one meaning in the fiction of Appelfeld.

Healing is another motif that continued to appear in Appelfeld's fiction. Many of his characters are left without solace. But despite their state of desperation, some aspire to a cure for their malaise. Combined with the motifs of return and healing is the constant motif of movement that informs most of Appelfeld's work. *The Healer* combines the three motifs and evokes earlier stories in which mystical Kabbalistic themes were prominent. The illness of Helga reflects the sickness of her father and grandmother. All suffer from the malaise of being severed from their roots. By the same token that her mother returns home, Helga returns to her sick roots. Helga alludes to another facet in the assimilated psyche. Despite appearances, her condition indicates that something was implicitly wrong in the process of acculturation and assimilation. One of the conditions that marks Helga's behavior is her dark elegy and her withdrawal into herself.

The Healer, however, takes a different route: the attempt is to find *tikkun* (repair) and healing from within. The family's pilgrimage is in the tradition of the Hassidic custom to seek the help of a rebbe or a zaddik. Young women such as Tzili, Kitty, and Helga represent the inner crisis of identity of the Jew disconnected from roots or home. A gallery of characters from all walks of life, from the Hassidic to the converted, inhabits the novel.

16

THE RETREAT

A~PPELFELD'S UNFLAGGING~ fascination with the prewar years is clear
in *The Retreat*, a 1982 novella.[1] Here he is trying to capture the mood
of the Jewish intellectual in that crucial time. It is the same fascination with the life of the Jewish intellectual that is reflected in *The Age
of Wonders* and *Badenheim 1939*, where the craving for culture is obsessive. It is the supposed remedy for Jewish angst, a putative cure
through Europeanization. Thus *Badenheim 1939* offers the most intense expression of the Jewish yearning to become fully European, but
at the same time it displays the painful awakening of the need for
Jewish sources, home, and authenticity.

The Retreat introduces a further theme, one almost diametrically
opposed to that of *Badenheim 1939*. The characters in *The Retreat* are
assimilated Jews of Austrian nationality; they are either intellectuals
or merchants, and they have married gentiles. But in contrast to the
craving expressed in *Badenheim* for the pleasures of food and culture,
the austere mountain locale in *The Retreat* points to attempts to shed
Jewish traits and to gain what is perceived as the "naturalness" of
gentile values. The Jew is perceived as "twisted," "unnatural." One
proposed remedy held that the Jew could achieve "normality" by avoiding the world of the here and now and trying to perfect one's body and
soul. Yet the question has been asked: can the Jew go through a metamorphosis and at the same time be true to his original self? Will conversion genuinely change the Jew? Will the return to the soil, to physical labor, make the crooked straight?

The chief protagonist in *The Retreat* is Lotte Schloss, one of a gallery of characters assembled on the mountaintop in the desire for
change. Lotte is an actress who was fired from the provincial theater
for being Jewish and now finds this place her last resort. The year is
1937. Her daughter, married to an Austrian estate owner, is a dull,
unimaginative woman who, without self-searching, has gone through
a metamorphosis: she looks and acts like a hard-working gentile. Her

husband beats her, and her three sons are beer-swilling hunting men and boors. Lotte and her husband, an assimilated Jewish musician who has found his way back to the traditional culture of the Jewish hamlet, have left no mark on Julia, their daughter. In her stoic acceptance of her lot, she does not resemble her parents.

Lotte's spoken German is perfect, and she is often not taken for a Jewess. She realizes that despite all her efforts and influence, she cannot reverse the decree that led to her firing. Her son-in-law clearly despises his actress mother-in-law, and she is utterly estranged from her grandsons. She therefore decides to go up to the retreat. She tells her daughter: "And now I'm going to the Jews. You know yourself how unwillingly. But one thing I have to admit, they have more generosity." At one time, in her daughter's home, she realized that her grandchildren would grow up to be common, ordinary Austrians. Her most penetrating realization was that she herself was utterly different from the accepted norm.

As a further contrast, the daughter's frugality is pitted against the mother's extravagant manner. But now, a woman in her middle years, she is without income, savings, or pension. It is the generosity of strangers that she relies on for her stay in the retreat. She is welcomed by one Herbert Zunz, a journalist who, like Lotte, was fired from his position for being Jewish. In her attempt to come to terms with who and what she is, she takes hikes around the peak; at the same time she tries to order her life by dwelling on memories of her childhood. The summit retreat, with its ascetic ways, is the last resort of the guests, who have severed all connection with the world down below. There are no letters or visitors. It is a self-imposed isolation, and at the same time it is a colony of those who have been rejected by family and society.

One of Lotte's first encounters there is with the theme of suicide. There is one character, Isadora Rotenberg, whose blinding self-hatred is stunning. She speaks of Jews as thinking only of money. She cannot abide them, yet still finds herself in their midst in a last attempt to purify them of their "Jewish traits." Lotte, by contrast, turns toward Jews when she realizes that her thirty years in the theater have amounted to little. Suicide had entered Lotte's consciousness before Isadora's suicide. While walking down the hill, Lotte stops to lean on a tree and discovers a sign noting the suicide of Sophia Traube in June 1937. The disturbed spirit of Sophia and her writing will be a source of strength to the people in the retreat.

The owner of the retreat is one Balaban, a Jew who has found, through nature, a way to a different type of existence. His first intention was to teach Jews the lessons of nature, the virtues of the horse, the benefits of a correct diet, and the true pleasures of sport. His wish was to alleviate the pain and suffering of his race. Balaban's plan had been to build a sanatorium, and what was originally planned as a business venture turned into a labor of love. "Balaban promised that within a short space of time he would painlessly eradicate embarrassing Jewish gestures and ugly accents. No one would have to be ashamed any more" (p. 62). Born in a small village in Poland, Balaban seems to have been successful in his own transition. In his high-minded idealism, he neglects his other affairs and dedicates himself to his new creed and vocation, to turn "the sickly members of his race into a healthy breed" (p. 63).

The experiment proved very successful in the first year, when it emphasized running, horseback riding, tennis, and healthy food. But because of various miscalculations and misunderstandings, things went awry. Balaban himself has grown flabby, has begun to smoke, to play cards, and some of his old gestures have reemerged. Balaban's experiment is an attempt to impose nineteenth-century romantic aspirations on his twentieth-century compatriots. Many of the residents of the retreat are romantic souls, forced by political and personal changes to "find themselves." Lotte too is afflicted with the romantic spirit. She believes that her tired body might find calm and refuge by the side of a simple man in a remote cottage. From her youth, influenced by romantic literature, she has dreamed of such encounters. She has now found that simple men are not simple. Like Balaban, she too, in her past, felt the need to erase the "Jewish" qualities, in her case by turning into a gentile.

A point that emerges again and again in Appelfeld's fiction is that in some cases the gentile may find in the Jew certain positive characteristics such as generosity but will still dislike him; and in other cases, the Jewish influence has detrimental effects on the Christian. The present mentor of the retreat, the one who maintains its equilibrium, is the journalist Herbert Zunz. Like many another of Appelfeld's characters in similar situations, Lotte finds that all attempts to secure help from erstwhile friends and connections end in nothing. Zunz had had an illustrious name in Austrian journalism; he was a pupil and disciple of the famous Karl Krauss and fought the evils of the period, as well as the corruption of language and morals. Ironically, it is this linguistic and moral corruption the Jews are blamed for. Yet Zunz, a man of gentle strength, does not relate to the past. He subtly fills the gap left by Balaban's deterioration.

One evening, in the hall, some of the residents are playing poker. In earlier years poker was forbidden, since Balaban viewed it as "a Jewish disease" and vowed to root it out. Yet the game has taken over, and Balaban himself watches it with fascination. In Appelfeld's works, fascination and intoxication are early signs of spiritual disease: abnormal growth and intoxication are always connected with a decline, a demise, an ominous end. In the retreat, the situation has been deteriorating. Though winter has come, no heat has been provided. Incessant rain has added to the gloomy atmosphere, and Balaban reiterates his old complaint: "The Jews could not be changed." The reason given is their weakness. "The weak are always devoured in the end. That is the lesson of the countryside" (p. 74). In principle, Balaban believes that the Jews could be changed, but because they are slow, sensitive, argumentative, and pampered, true change cannot occur.

Isadora's suicide is one sign of the no-exit situation in which the inhabitants find themselves. Elegant and witty, Isadora was mocked by her daughters, who felt she was "a Jewish mother." Her last requests are that she be buried without Jewish rites, that her daughters not be notified, and that there be no eulogies at her graveside. Lotte reads some poetry by Rilke at the funeral. Rilke was Isadora's beloved poet, and his literary presence in *Badenheim* and *The Retreat* is significant. One poem that might have been read is his "Herbsttag" (Autumn day), which suggests the absence of a permanent "place" or domicile in all the manifold senses of the term.

> Wer jetzt kein Haus hat, baut sich keines mehr.
> Wer jetzt allein ist, wird es lange bleiben,
> Wird wachen, lesen, lange Briefe schreiben
> Und wird in den Alleen hin und her
> Unruhig wandern, wenn die Blaetter treiben.

> He who has no house by now will never build one.
> He who is alone now will stay that way for long,
> will wake up, read, write long letters
> and will wander restlessly to and fro
> along the avenues, driven by the leaves. (Trans. by Leo Rauch)

Lang (literally, "long") is a short man who is one of Balaban's successes. Born in Galicia, Lang is trying to improve himself, to heal his "corrupt" inheritance and mend his heavy accent. He runs downhill, goes in for sports, eats peasant food, and builds his muscles. He liked Isadora despite her clear disdain for him. She calls him Kurz (Shorty), and sees in him the epitome of the incorrigible Jew. But even Balaban confesses that he has never managed to forget the dirty little town of his birth, that as long as it was lodged within him, no improvement could take place. Total separation from one's past is a condition for change. Mixed marriage is closely connected to the problem of identity. Most of the characters in *The Retreat* are faced with this problem. Like Lotte, many come to terms with the marriage of a daughter to a gentile. Further, the act of conversion is not viewed as cowardly; rather, it is often viewed as the right thing to do, for a variety of reasons.

At the base of all of Appelfeld's characters there are nagging memories. Sometimes they are muffled or unexpressed, yet despite their buried presence they shape the lives of the characters. Bruno Rauch, one of the long-time residents, tells Lotte of the earlier days of the retreat. To Rauch they were days with purpose:

> Once a man realized that his body is weak and ugly, his nerves destroyed, his soul corrupt, that he bears within him a decayed inheritance, in short, that he is sick and, what is worse, that he is passing his sickness on to his children, what can he desire more deeply than reform? (P. 103)

Another resident tells about his two sons, whom he converted to Christianity when they were still young. He says that he felt morally obliged to do it, that he had no right to imprison them in the "cage called a Jewish Ghetto." He thereby gave them the freedom to choose, "so that they wouldn't come and blame their father for bequeathing them a malignant disease. Their father did what had to be done" (p. 116). As for himself, he does not want to change; nor does he believe in change for its own sake, and he doubts the value of Balaban's experiments. In the case of his sons, he says, the matter is different: he relieved them of fear and shame, the burdens of Judaism. He had not seen them for ten years; his interest is merely therapeutic.

Balaban's own sickness marks the beginning of the end for the retreat. The inner decline echoes the outer decline, as well as the moribund political atmosphere. But for the time being the retreat is a refuge. Balaban's illness meant a return to his mother tongue; his acquired facility with German was destroyed. He blames himself and is stricken with guilt. Time and again Appelfeld draws attention to the undoing of the individual and to the suppressed yearning for authentic selfhood. Yet if this is construed as an intellectual edifice it is repeatedly challenged by the emergence of memory, especially the memory of one's roots. This impasse often leads these characters to contemplate suicide—and this is a major theme in Appelfeld's work. Can we, in a larger sense, interpret the theme of eliminating "Jewish defects" as an attempted suicide? It is, after all, a denial of the self, the very being one is. With his supposedly high-minded intentions, was not Balaban trying to eradicate an entire mode of life?

We have seen, by now, something of the suicide theme in Appelfeld: one suicide is Sophia, another is Isadora. Sophia had written of Isadora: "She courts death with broad, sweeping glances" (p. 132). To Sophia the Jewish religion is tribal, collective, necessarily a religion of the herd, whereas Christianity cherishes the individual and teaches belief in one's personal salvation. To what extent Appelfeld wished to evoke the image of Simone Weil is hard to say; yet in his fiction it is mostly women who are linked to Christianity, as Weil was.

This entire constellation of themes—self-hatred, denial of selfhood and personal identity, suicide (physical and spiritual), Jewishness as death, and so on—must be seen against the background of the eventual *Anschluss* and the doom it portended for Jews in general. An atmosphere of desperation is reflected in the retreat as well: "as if they all agreed that change was impossible and their fate in any case was sealed" (p. 161). A close affinity allowed them to be themselves. The poverty of the place was by now a fact. Summer excursions into the villages became dangerous, and the residents returned beaten when they ventured into the outside world. The provisions brought in were scant, yet their meager meals were eaten in peace. Silence and solemnity settled in on the inhabitants. Coats, jewels, and other valuables were sold to the farmers for food.

"But they helped one another," Appelfeld writes. "If a man fell or was beaten he was not abandoned." That is the novel's last sentence. If any real change took place in the retreat, it was but a temporary respite from a troubled and continuing situation. But as an alarmingly brutal world was encroaching on this community, it managed to gain the heights of humanity, humility, and brotherhood.

17

TO THE LAND OF THE CATTAILS

THE THEME of the return home, a return at any cost, reappears at the heart of *To the Land of the Cattails* (1986).[1] The mother, Toni, and her adolescent son, Rudi, are on a mission which is above history and fact. From the Austria of the *Anschluss*, Toni goes back home to Bukovina, "the land of the cattails," to ask her parents' forgiveness for abandoning them as a young girl and running away with a gentile man. The year is 1938. The environs of Bukovina, where mother and son are traveling, are extremely dangerous. In this novel, as in other late novels by Appelfeld, one event encompasses the mood and serves as a major sign. The cruel and vicious murder of Annamarie, the Jewish innkeeper, a benevolent woman who loved the area and served it well, should have pointed to the danger that mother and son were facing; a carriage with two horses gallops toward the death of its occupants. The return is an attempt to complete an uncompleted circle; at the same time, it is rooted in deep guilt: Toni had to return home in order to come to terms with herself.

One feature that appears and reappears in Appelfeld's fiction is the character who is frozen in time while constantly moving in space. This movement in space often defies common sense and actual circumstances. The overriding principle is the completion of the quest. All signs foretelling disaster are disregarded. The penultimate point in the ceaseless movement of Toni and Rudi will be deportation. This point, depicted in many of Appelfeld's works, is the last station in a character's story. At this stage Appelfeld does not move his characters beyond this point and does not accompany them to the concentration camp.

Toni, in her youth, broke away from Judaism. As a single woman she moved toward a genteel if shady life. She is one of many assimilated Jewish women depicted in Appelfeld's novels. But once she begins her journey back home, this beautiful woman in her late thirties senses her Judaism in a deeper way. True, this mother, like the one depicted in *For Every Sin* (see chap. 19), is a shallow woman whose beauty and coquettishness are emphasized; yet her fatal urge to return home is genuine. Her attempts to teach her son some precepts of Judaism reveal her limited knowledge and intellectual poverty. Unschooled as she is, however, she tries to impart to him her idea of Judaism.

Rudi, who looks like a gentile, never met his father. In his early years, his mother left him with nannies while she was entertained by her numerous lovers. Nevertheless, his love for her is deep, as is his devotion. At a certain point in their wandering toward Dratscincz (Toni's birthplace and the birthplace of Appelfeld's own mother), Rudi's suppressed "other self" emerges. He begins to drink, to act like a Ruthenian peasant, and to neglect the quest to return home. This occurs on the verge of achieving their goal and lasts for months. Rudi awakes from his stupor, however, regains his old self, and rejoins his mother.

One sees another recurring feature of Appelfeld's novels: "romanticization" of an idea or concept. Often it is given shape in a woman who romanticizes reality. The object of romanticization varies from text to text: Christianity in *For Every Sin*, Judaism in *To the Land of the Cattails*. Toni romanticizes Judaism as Rudi has romanticized and idealized his mother. The total devotion of son to mother reflects an uncritical and fatalistic adoption of the mother's idealized, romanticized world. The mother-son relationship, with its obvious Oedipal component, recurs frequently in Appelfeld's fiction, where it serves to portend a symbolic suicide. The absent or rejected father plays no meaningful role in the son's life. In a process of compensation, the son adopts his mother's world and pledges his loyalty to it. The mother, depicted as weak, dependent, and impractical, makes the son the "man" in her life. In his brief attempt to break away from his mother, Rudi expresses anti-Semitic sentiments. For him, Judaism is an act of free choice and a way of placating his mother.

The symbiotic relation between mother and son forms a pattern that recurs in Appelfeld narratives depicting reality before the war and after. Rudi, knowing his mother's weakness and shallowness, does not reject her; instead, in his love for her and in his desire to fill the vacuum left by the weak or absent father, he defers to her wishes and whims.

A mother image is also central in the life of the story's third major character: Arna, the young Jewish girl Rudi finds near the deportation station. Coming close to her hometown, Toni decides to leave Rudi behind and to go face her parents alone. According to her plan, Rudi, on her return, will join her and meet his grandparents. Thus the torn thread will be rewoven symbolically. Toni never returns, however, and it is clear that she has been deported with the rest of the Jews of the village. When Rudi arrives at the village with his horses he discovers that the Jews have been deported because they were Jews. He meets Arna, whose mother sent her for some water and was gone when she returned; the train had left. Arna admires her mother, an Orthodox woman married to a freethinker. Rudi and Arna team up, and the practical girl manages to bring the sick Rudi back to life. They stir resentment wherever they go—a very gentile-looking young man with a very Jewish-looking young girl. A possibility of escape is intimated, or at least it seems this way. Both are motivated, however, by the search for their mothers.

Toward the end of the novel they join other Jews in a forlorn train station waiting for the train that will bring them close to their loved ones. Practical reality or the idea of survival are not part of their considerations. They live in the reality they wish for. The constant wandering on one hand and the *idée fixe* on the other are what motivate their existence. In this respect, Toni, Rudi, and Arna are captivated by their own sense of value and driven on their way to complete their existence.

A mother substitute appears temporarily in *For Every Sin* and *To the Land of the Cattails*. In *For Every Sin*, Theo encounters Mina, a suffering survivor. He is willing to serve her and help her, but his Cain image frightens her away. In the present novel, it seems that Rudi and Arna could create a new kinship family so typical of the early stories, in which people bonded together for the sake of survival. In the later novels, however, the centrality of prewar experience and the rising centrality of the mother shift the emphasis from the surrogate family to the mother-son unit. The bonding in the forests was part of the escape. Neither Toni nor Rudi wish to escape a destined fate. For the sake of satisfying the dead mother, Theo is willing to convert to Christianity; Rudi, though he could blend with the local peasantry and enjoy his love of horses and nature, abandons all other possibilities and joins the other Jews.

Rudi and Arna are close to each other. He admires her knowledge, her practicality, and gives her one of his mother's jewels to wear around her neck. She teaches him Jewish customs and rituals, a thing his mother could not do. Their wandering in the Bukovinian landscape is parallel to Toni and Rudi's endless traveling in the terrain, and wandering as an existential Jewish theme reappears in this novel.

The inevitable question that arises is why we have two sets of characters: the minor characters, who warn Toni and her son to return to Vienna and not go to the heart of trouble, and Toni and Rudi, who are decided in their quest. Looking back with historical hindsight, one knows that the chances for survival, even in Vienna, their place of origin, were slim; that European Jewry was massacred from east to west and north to south. However that might be, one cannot overlook the sense of quiet despair and the feeling that the characters, moored in their private reality/fantasy, are oblivious to the changes that occur in the world around them. Questions that cannot be answered in a clear way present themselves. What is the relation between a feeling of determinism and free will in the life of the characters? Is this question invalid? Must one accept the inevitability of the tragic end? Why didn't Rudi escape his fate? Why did he support his mother to the point of accepting the unknown? There is a serious question about the extent one can take this particular story, as well as others, and apply it to the Holocaust at large.

Appelfeld's pre-Holocaust writings are often devoid of resolution, though their endings vary; occasionally the stories have a conclusive end, where deportation means death. Other stories are open-ended—characters remain moored in the same time, place, and situation. Often the end is intimated yet unstated. The reader is called on to provide the historical framework to complete the story and resolve it. The tragic irony at the end of *To the Land of the Cattails* is chilling. Most of the people waiting at the train station, like Rudi and Arna, have been separated from their loved ones; thus they expect the coming of the train.

> "Where will we be brought together?" a woman asked a man who was leaning against the wall.
> "Not far," answered the man in complete distraction.
> "If so, why aren't they coming to pick us up?"
> "They'll come," said the man. "Don't worry."
> "We haven't been forgotten? Are you sure?"
> The man was about to answer when a long whistle was heard, a festive whistle, and they all stood up and shouted at once, It came. At last it came! The tall man with the noble lineage removed his hat like the Christians, placing it diagonally across his broad chest. The move-

ment, which seemed habitual with him, suddenly inspired them all
with a kind of gravity.

It was an old locomotive, drawing two old cars—the local, apparently. It went from station to station, scrupulously gathering up the
remainder. (P. 146)

The fact that Appelfeld is not a purely realistic writer, that he creates texts that are highly fictive and at the same time relate to historical and personal occurrences, opens his texts to more than one reading. The combination of autobiographical elements and fictional
situations is evident in *To the Land of the Cattails*, and the autobiographical elements are not disguised. As noted, the name of the village
Toni and Rudi are going to is the name of the actual hometown of
Appelfeld's maternal grandparents, the place where his own personal
tragedy began. The description of the destroyed Jewish homes Rudi
and Arna encounter, with torn books strewn on the floor, is identical
to Appelfeld's own description of what he saw on his way to the camp.

18

TONGUE OF FIRE

As we have seen, Appelfeld dedicated several of his later novels to the theme of the assimilated Jew in the years preceding the Second World War. *Rizpat Esh* (Tongue of fire, 1988)[1] takes a new approach and reveals another tragic facet of the penultimate stage in the life of disillusioned, enlightened, assimilated Jews on the eve of the destruction of European Jewry. The looming Holocaust is not a presence in this novel; and yet, through metaphor, symbol, and image, the impending end is forecast. This novel is about erosion: the erosion of the characters' mental states, paralleled by the erosion of the earth beneath their feet. The place depicted is Pracht (literally, "splendor"), a small provincial resort town in Bukovina, where visitors come each summer to gamble, drink, and have a good time. (Most probably Pracht is not unlike Jadova, Appelfeld's birthplace and a prototype of all the resort towns in his fiction.) The preceding year, Pracht drew only four guests, reflecting the uncertainty of the time and giving the guests of the forlorn pension a temporary shelter from external demands.

The characters Rita, Beno, and Zusie carry the brunt of domineering parents who have branded them. Rita Braun, the main character, despises her small-minded parents, who refused to let her go to the big city to pursue her artistic aspirations. She is now a capricious and vulnerable alcoholic; her teen-age son, who accompanies her, is a replica of her parents and of his father, the ex-husband she abhors, in his petty calculation and unimaginative being. As acts of final revenge Rita loses her money gambling and carries on hopeless love affairs with various men. Both her childhood and her married life were prisons to her. The assumed freedom at Pracht attracts her; but in addition to losing money she loses dignity, and yet this is home for her. Beno Shtark, a sensitive young man, has given up a potentially successful career for drink and gambling. His rich mother sends him certified letters containing money. Toward the end she cuts off his allowance completely. Like Rita, Beno has a sweet, compelling personality—childishness tinged by the tragic. Zusie, the beloved daughter of a rich railroad tycoon, is hopelessly in love with her father. Her escort, the intelligent, sensitive Van, follows her wherever she goes, knowing full well that at best he can aspire to being nothing more than her escort. He does not gamble or drink. Son of a Ruthenian mother and a Jewish father, he loves Jews, Jewish traditions, and Hassidism.

The tale is engulfed by water imagery. Early in the narrative, rain ruins the garden and the terrace, leaving the pension suspended over an abyss. The symbol of house over precipice haunts the characters. The flowing water in the river Prut, the rain, and the diluted cognac they all drink point to a flood as a destructive force as well as to the dilution of life. While drink intoxicates the guests and destroys them, the world around them is collapsing—although they remain oblivious. The noble, gentle Beno will eventually dare the Prut and swim to his death in an act of suicide. Despite the shabbiness of the pension, its ersatz quality, the characters have a wholesome dignity about them and about the various modes of self-destruction they adopt in their no-exit lives.

The Hebrew title, *Rizpat Esh*, alludes to a glowing stone (Isaiah 6:6) or, more literally, to a floor of fire. Fire and water undo the weak, lovable, capricious characters. Their rootlessness, their careless existence, and their fickleness portend tragedy. The most solid character in the novel is the old cook, Maria, who mothers the sick and afflicted guests and tries to bring food, comfort, and some insight into their lives. Although a gentile, she is the only one who knows Jewish customs; she insists that the body of Beno be brought to his family estate, to a Jewish grave. Yet Seltzer, the owner of the place, resents Orthodox Jews and decides to bury Beno in the pension yard and to erect a monument in his memory. The heavy monument eventually takes the building down into the abyss.

The assimilated Jews in this novel are mentally bankrupt, unconsciously awaiting their end. Controlled by their past, they are doomed to an existence on the verge of the abyss. Only Maria, who also appeared in Appelfeld's earlier fiction (and whose latest version is depicted in the novel *Katerina*; see chap. 20) believes Jews are the chosen people. Other gentiles working in the pension consider Jews a disease, a contaminative power, an inescapable epidemic. The generosity of the Jews is acknowledged, but they are untrusted and unworthy in the eyes of the simple folk. In *Badenheim 1939* and *The Retreat*, Appelfeld created an insular world, with its own inner fictional space and its own ground rules. *Tongue of Fire* is a psychological novel, with strong realistic elements. The novel is less stylized than the novels of the 1970s, marking a move toward realism in Appelfeld's novels of the 1980s and 1990s.

After the death of Beno, whom she secretly loved, Rita decides to take her fate into her own hands. She leaves the pension at night and tries to get to Vienna, Trieste, and eventually on board a ship to Palestine. The reader is given no indication as to whether she will succeed. (Tzili, in the novel bearing her name, does manage after many a trial to reach Palestine.) In making her escape Rita encounters anti-Semitism, is taken for a prostitute, behaves lewdly, and drinks but manages to find herself on the train to Vienna. Rita, in her nervous fickleness, is constantly on the verge of a hysterical outburst; she is a seismograph for personal and national tragedy, with the inevitability of catastrophe manifesting itself both internally and externally. The historical Enlightenment and emancipation have rendered the Jewish characters in Appelfeld's text rootless and vulnerable. Jewish values, customs, and ceremonies are rejected in an effort to assimilate. Yet despite it all, the Jews continue to feel like strangers and to be regarded as foreigners. In other narratives, the Jewish genius is presented as the artist or self-deluding writer who through excess brings himself/herself to the brink of insanity. In *Tongue of Fire*, the characters are pale copies of earlier tragic figures. Afflicted by a malaise, however, they are pathetic in their escape from reality as they embrace a recklessly dangerous existence.

The characters in this novel endorse their marginality and their failure through a benign self-hate. Seltzer states coolly that one may be of any nationality, just not the Jewish. Is Rita Braun deluding herself? Can the fragile woman possibly be saved by a change? All the characters are preoccupied with the penultimate station in their life. This search, unbeknown to them, replicates the prewar state of Jews in Europe. Earlier characters pursued European culture; in this novel the characters run from success and achievement, choosing alcoholism and gambling as a means of self-forgetfulness. The freedom to be, beyond responsibility and beyond societal expectations, leads to waste, self-forgetfulness, and puerile self-indulgence. Thus the gifted Beno could have been a brilliant scientist, but he preferred to submerge himself in drink.

The shattering of the family is almost complete. The malaise, foreshadowed in *The Pupil of the Eye*, like an illness affects one and all. The utter emotional and intellectual barrenness is tragic. This, in turn brings up another question: can a change be introduced at all? Appelfeld intimates that there is no exit for his mentally exhausted characters in Europe.

The mother-son relationship prevalent in Appelfeld's 1970s and 1980s novels is reaffirmed in *Tongue of Fire*. As noted, Rita Braun's son, Johann, is a replica of his Jewish father. He is critical of his mother's drinking, gambling, and spending habits; yet he clings to her and haunts her existence. In novels that present a mother-son axis, the son is part participant and part observer; his attitude is often negative. Mothers often are portrayed as mentally unstable or intellectually inferior to their sons. All Appelfeld's mothers, with the exception of the mother in *The Age of Wonders*, use borrowed words. Their statements are banal, hackneyed, commonplace. Nevertheless, most of Appelfeld's sons display a deep affection, love, attachment, and devotion toward their mothers. In three of the novels (*For Every Sin, To the Land of the Cattails, Tongue of Fire*) the mothers are at a point of no return, facing an abyss, obviously existing on borrowed time. Like the mother in *The Healer*, female characters either return to their birthplace or to the diametrical opposite, a place which is the farthest away from their small Jewish hamlet, e.g., to some resort or other, for "culture" or for the spurious "togetherness" of gambling and drinking. In *Tongue of Fire*, the mother is committed to gambling and cognac; in *For Every Sin*, the mother is moved by church music; while the mother in *To the Land of the Cattails* is obsessed by coffee and home.

Those obsessions are metonyms for an incapacity to deal with reality. A principle alluded to earlier applies here. Characters are typified by movement: "I move, ergo I exist." The movement can be interpreted as a flight from oneself and from self-realization. Against all odds and changing circumstances, the characters believe that the familiar ground rules will continue to apply. Thus they almost willfully ignore signs that portend a darker reality and interpret them within their own scheme of perception. And here lies the tragic irony—practicality and astuteness in most cases would not have saved the characters from their fate.

A variety of readings can be applied to any literary text. As readers, we activate the text by making it comprehensible to our particular understanding. The combination of autobiographical elements and fictional/imagined situations is evident here and in all novels revolving around the mother-son relationship. One can assume that Appelfeld's loss of his own mother is reflected in this repetitious pattern. These autobiographical elements, interesting as they may be, are of less interest than the interpretation of the complete text. How are we to perceive the image of the mother and the complex, unnaturally compliant relationship between son and mother? An Oedipal reading was suggested earlier where the son replaces a father, who in most cases is rejected by the mother. The reasons vary: he is a gentile and treats her badly; he does not yield to her "artistic" aspirations; he is a Jew and restricts her activities. Regardless of the causes for tension between husband and wife, the son, usually an only son, takes the father's place in trying to follow the mother, and in most cases he defers to her wishes, so that the son fills a void.

An additional reading can be introduced, where the mother allegorically represents a Jewish archetype in courting European culture in a quest for acceptance. There is an intimation of a desire to end a life of incessant wandering. This reading endorses a principle suggested earlier, that wandering is the spatial state of being. This can apply equally to the assimilated Jew, to the acculturated Jew, and to the traditional Jew. This ties in with the idea of vulnerability as a basic feature of the Appelfeldian character. Vulnerability ties the two readings, the psychological and the allegorical. The urge to return home, despite signs that foretell catastrophe, suggests ever so lightly an element of suicide—as if mother and son are on a mission which is above history and fact.

We may therefore point to two basic characteristics that appear and reappear in Appelfeld's fiction: the character is frozen in time, yet is constantly moving in space; and the movement in space suspends laws of common sense or a regard for actual circumstances in the present. The overriding principle is a completion of the quest (whatever its content). All impending signs of disaster are disregarded. This underscores the existence of unique space, time, and logic, and it is within those unique parameters that the characters move.

One can see a recurring feature in Appelfeld's portrayal of the mother and her son: a certain romantic whim captures their lives. Yet it varies from text to text: Christianity in *For Every Sin*, Judaism in *To the Land of the Cattails*. A total devotion of son to mother is translated into adoption of the mother's idealized-romanticized notions uncritically. On a number of occasions we noted that Appelfeld's mother-son relationship has an Oedipal component. The absent or rejected father does not play a meaningful role in the life of the son. As a process of compensation, the son adopts his mother's world and pledges allegiance to it. The mother, depicted as weak, dependent, and unpractical, makes the son the "man" in her life. In *Tongue of Fire*, the pattern is reversed: Rita Braun's Johann despises his mother and sides with his father. This depicts the crack in the wall of self-deception. The mother is deprived of any help or family support.

This pattern of a symbiotic relationship between mother and son was established in Appelfeld's fiction of the 1970s. In *The Age of Wonders*, the family triangle is still intact, and the father has importance. Yet the closeness is between the son and the mother, who becomes the pivotal character in the family. The absence of a mother in the son's life produces a mother substitute, as in *For Every Sin* and *To the Land of the Cattails*. In these novels the centrality of prewar experience is connected to the rising centrality of the mother. In the most extreme cases, the son wishes to become his mother by continuing her desires after her death.

In *Tongue of Fire*, the mother leaves her son behind in her last and final quest for a stronghold. Despondent, alone, at the end of her rope, she begins a journey of unknown yet alarming consequences. Fire and water have eroded her life. Rita Braun is a brave broken woman stranded in a rundown resort hotel. The pressing reality and undaunting self-awareness replace the complacency attributed to women in Appelfeld's earlier novels. Rita tries to reach Palestine. Her heroic-pathetic attempt to break away from herself occurs too late in her life and in the historical era. In *Badenheim 1939*, the encroaching confinement of the vacationers serves as the dramatic movement. In *Tongue of Fire*, it is erosion. Instead of a purported festival we have a process of mental disintegration. The childishness that typifies so many of the mothers in Appelfeld's novels is typical of the few other characters who find refuge in Pracht. Self-hate and self-denial make them Jews devoid of Judaism. Depicting the situation on the eve of the *Anschluss* gives an ironic twist to the whole scene: other powers have already prescribed the fate of these people. The last playground of the Jewish adults in the novel is crumbling under them—they cannot foresee the whirlwind that awaits them. Between suicide and play, between drunkenness and awareness, the characters' last grip on life is marked by disaster. As water erodes their foundations, fire will consume them.

19

FOR EVERY SIN

As we observed, Appelfeld's fiction depicts two movements: the narrative of the assimilated Jewish society before the war, in which excessive cultivation and intellectualism are brought to the point of atrophy, and the narrative of the survivor reduced to an elemental state, with suspended memories and no desire. In the depiction of prewar urbanism, the decline of the family is matched by a Chekhovian rootlessness. Any attempt to leave the cycle of culture and join that of elemental nature proves inevitably tragic. The theme of transformation and change binds the two movements and the various stories that depict the Jew on the verge of the gentile village. Appelfeld is fascinated by the changes in the European Jewish archetype in all its possible variations.

Since the 1970s each of Appelfeld's works of fiction has been centered on a single individual. In his earlier writing, characters reflect off one another in an inarticulate situation. Rarely do we find self-search, confession, or self-laceration. Instead, his typical character is caught up in a process that cannot be evaded, however much it portends change. One can detect a movement toward the center of the experience, toward a more detailed and realistic articulation of situations. Added to the earlier spatial fiction is a temporal, more realistic aspect. Frequently, the actions of his characters can be interpreted as amoral. But that is because Appelfeld has placed his characters beyond the range of accepted structure—as reflected in the truncated dialogue and inane words his characters use, as though Appelfeld were avoiding the presentation of a complete individual. In some of the short stories, it is possible to take a character from one narrative and place him or her in another without upsetting the plot. This enables him to depict hollow men and women in various stages of vulnerability, and in a world beyond ordinary categories of good and evil, so that the reader is asked to suspend ethical judgment.

For Every Sin (1989) relates thematically to times and places depicted in his early collection of short stories, *Smoke*. It echoes stories such as "Three," "Cold Spring," and "Along the Shore." It also has a clear affinity to the later novels *The Age of Wonders*, *The Retreat*, and *The Immortal Bartfuss*. *For Every Sin* is the story of Theo Braun, a refugee, one month after the liberation. His declared purpose is to go back home to Baden-bei-Wien. He shuns the togetherness of the other refugees. The failed or belated return home is a repeated theme in Appelfeld's work and in literature in general. This novel, however, speaks of a different kind of return. Theo's expressed wish is to return home and convert to Christianity. The seeming suspension of the ethical, along with elements of self-denial, self-delusion, and self-hate, appear forcefully. The title is taken from Proverbs: "Hatred stirreth up strife; but love covereth all sins" (10:12).

The love that directs and shapes the personality and deeds of Theo Braun is for his mother, whose wishes he had internalized. The desire to assimilate, to emulate behavioral models of Christian European society, appeared in Appelfeld's earlier work in connection with prewar experiences (as in *Badenheim 1939*, *The Age of Wonders*, *The Retreat*). The desire to go home after the death and torture inflicted upon members of one's own family and after three years in labor camps makes this novel a most incriminating document. The triangle of father-mother-son threatened the continuity of the family in *The Age of Wonders*. In *For Every Sin* it is the erratic behavior of the mother that leads to the demolition of the family. The father, a sincere intellectual, is gradually destroyed by his spoiled, mentally unstable wife, who brings financial and emotional disaster upon the family.

Appelfeld structures the novel carefully, and as the story unfolds, hidden and latent layers are revealed. The slow pace of revelation creates tension and gives us a complete character moving in realistic surroundings. The psychological underpinning and motivation for the actions of the protagonist are slowly and gradually revealed. Characters in earlier stories turned their back to what once was "home." For them it is a nonexistent territory. Early in the novel the reader does not realize the protagonists' motivation. We are slowly made aware that Theo left his friends from the camp and fled without saying a word to them. His animosity to his fellow refugees is clear. He wishes to distance himself from his fellow survivors. Instead of moving south, as most of the displaced persons did, he moves in the opposite direction, north.

The first intimation of the desire to return and convert appears early in the narrative. In his wandering he discovers a chapel which evokes memories of his mother and his childhood. The mother was attracted to chapels, to icons, and the candles lit by local peasant women. Unlike earlier characters who sealed their memories of past and childhood, later Appelfeld characters, more rounded, delve into their earlier being. None of his earlier characters, however, is as complete a captive of his past as Theo Braun. This is one of the most sensitive psychological studies Appelfeld embarked upon; at times it is the most disturbing one.

Theo's movements are centripetal and centrifugal. He tries to break away from the refugees but is inevitably attracted to them, only to feel alienated by them. Almost to the very end of the novel he rejects as repugnant the idea of the bond forged by the horrific ordeal they have undergone. The only people we encounter in this novel are refugees. The Christian world and the village are nonexistent; the places the people move in, the valleys, ravines, and hills, are inhabited only by the refugee population that moves and rests, moves and rests. Some have chosen to stay, like the woman whose legs were frozen by the cold or the woman who lost all her family in the nearby forest; now she has created a tent, and serves hot coffee and food to whoever passes by. None of the refugees refers to Israel, America, or any other destination. They are like mythical creatures, inverted and tragic counterparts of Bialik's mythical giants of "People of the Desert" (Metai Midbar), an elegiac poem dedicated to nature, power, and strength. Nevertheless, despite the seemingly disorganized nature of the survivor population, there is a structure, albeit a loose structure, to their existence. They are a tribe whose family memories maintain its ethos in a fellowship, camaraderie and faithfulness to the tribal code.

In the midst of the wandering masses, Theo is a foreign, alienated element. He is motivated by the memory of his dead mother, who is for him a living presence. In an almost grotesque manner he tries to follow her inspiration and to embody the good qualities of German culture. In his wandering he chances upon a guard's cabin deserted by the Germans. He enjoys the fact that he can still read German, his "mother tongue." (In this novel this term is rife with meanings.) He marvels at the tidiness of the place and approves of the good order of the Germans. This orderliness and cleanliness is indirectly contrasted to the refugees, most of whom still wear their prisoners' clothes and are living in the open spaces without clear order. "An old feeling of pleasure now flowed the length of his legs. 'Everything here is marvelously tidy,' he stated again."[1]

Talking to Mina, a mother figure in distress, he refers to the Germans who inhabited the cabin: "They retreated calmly. They left everything in its place. It seems to me that we should respect that. You have to say a few words in praise of precision and order" (p. 26). At this early phase of his abortive journey, Theo tries to be alone. He believes that being with others weakens the Jew, and the correct idea is "everyone is for himself." Only in this way can an inner order be maintained. Characters appear and disappear in Theo's wandering. Clearly there is something that makes people shun him. It seems that he appears to them as the image of Cain, and the question intimated in the text is: what is his sin?

Does the novel dwell on the negative Jewish stereotype? It is clear that, like Balaban in *The Retreat*, Theo believes in changing the "defective" Jewish archetype. He continues to tell Mina, in her short sojourn in the cabin, about his belief that in order to overcome weakness and fear, what is important is to exercise, to get fresh air and fresh water—and most important, to break the "togetherness." Thus Theo adopts the anti-Jewish stereotypes which were manifested by his mother, and makes them his present credo. What is more, he adopts the Nazi approach to the Jew and repeats it after the Holocaust. This is reiterated by Theo in the contention that a proud person does not live his proud life like an insect. Indirectly he blames the Jews for what befell them. The Jews never taught their children how to fight, to struggle, to come face to face with evil. Theo adopts Mina. He attends to her with compassion, and tries to help her to heal. He changes his own plan on her account and mothers her. But whatever he tries to do for her, she is a partial representation of his feeling toward his mother. Mina avoids him and runs away.

There are two levels in this narrative. The obvious one tells of Theo's adventures as a refugee. The other involves the resurrection of his childhood and youth prior to the deportation. On this second level the image of the mother is the dominant one. In a close reading, the central event in the novel combines the two levels.

Another facet that is tied to Theo is the beating of the traitors and informers, who will be judged by the people's tribunal, despite the absence of formal authority or organization. The cries of the beaten informers serve as a background and a sound track. One collaborator tries to appease the wrath of those who are beating him, but they see themselves as representing justice. Later they will transfer him to a field tribunal. When he pleads, "I lost everyone. . . . I alone remain," somebody tells him, "Don't say 'I.' You lost your 'I.' You're nothing" (p. 49). Theo tries to persuade the informer to get out of the mud; he is disgusted by the man and his fear. The man refuses: "They frighten me more than the Germans. . . . There's no choice" (p. 51). Theo tries to break away from the circle but fails. Self-deceit and self-denial are part of his world.

What happens to Theo in the first part of the novel is like a panto-mime of what will happen to him at the central episode of the tale. His attraction to the informers and their plight adumbrates his sense of guilt. At this early stage his guilt is that of leaving his comrades of the camp, those who stood by him in times of hardship. There is a mission and there is the delay, often attributed to outside factors but in reality having to do with inner forces that preclude a clear and distinct action.

As the novel proceeds the true image of the mother unfolds. To the young child the restless mother, with her enthusiasm for beauty, na-ture, culture, and Bach, seems fresh and delightful. As years pass and Theo grows up, he comes to realize the sickness of the mother, who lived in her own universe and was occasionally committed to an asy-lum. Prior to the deportation, the provincial town suffocated her, and her dreams were of Vienna, Salzburg, and other shrines of culture. The father, crushed by her behavior, asked for a divorce. The rabbis tried to tell him that the time, on the verge of the outbreak of war, was not suitable; but they went through with it all the same. The mother's mental condition deteriorated. Deported before the son and the father, she refused to take a knapsack. "She went to the train dressed care-fully, as she used to go to railroad stations in the past. Her illness was not visible in her. Expressions of pride and softness were mingled in her face" (p. 73).

The sixth chapter is the central one. In one of his numerous en-counters, Theo meets a man and strikes up a conversation with him. Again, Theo repeats his story of going home. The man says he has no home, and offers Theo coffee and rolls. Again Theo voices his credo about togetherness being an illusion. For a moment it seems to Theo that the man is Uncle Salo, his father's elder brother, a pragmatic man who derided idleness. Salo was repulsed by Theo's mother; for him she was the embodiment of sloppiness, idleness, and capriciousness. Whenever he came for a visit, the mother shut herself up in her room and stayed there till he departed. For Salo, the mother was infecting Theo. Theo now feels an affinity with the new acquaintance, who has lost his wife and two daughters and is ashamed of his hoarding habit. But when Theo tries to engage him with the quasi-philosophical question "What do you think will happen?" the man answers, "That strange preoccupation with oneself is a sin which cannot be atoned for." The man's ultimate goal is to free himself of fear, and he repeats, "I'm vermin. Why am I vermin?" (p. 78).

The frankness of the man, his self-assessment, and his torment are pitted against the declared attempt of Theo to return to a place and time that no longer exist. The man offers Theo some hot potatoes he cooked on the open fire. Theo remembers his mother sewing a large yellow Star of David on his jacket, as well as her reveries about future journeys in the spring. On her last days at home she still stood by the window to hear the church choir. After a meal shared with the man, Theo reveals for the first time his intention to go home and convert to Christianity. The man is stunned. Theo says that faith moved him to take this decision. The man is repulsed by graven images, while Theo says that he has only pleasant memories of the church. Theo continues to claim faith and the man is totally perplexed. Theo tries to explain his motives.

> "Bach's cantatas saved me from death. That was my nourishment for two and a half years. . . . I'm going back to the church because Bach dwells there."
> "Your intention gives me the chills." The man couldn't restrain himself any longer.
> "What did I do wrong?"
> "It frightens me more than the gallows square of the camp. Now do you understand?" (P. 82)

The man asks Theo to leave him alone, since his presence drives him out of his senses. The man's anger cannot find words. Theo strikes him with a fear he cannot control. The man offers Theo his place and is ready to leave, giving Theo everything he owns. As the man rises to leave, he grabs Theo's coat, and in an attempt to free himself, Theo pushes the man away. He falls, tumbles over a few times, and dies. The crowd circles around Theo, and Theo realizes that his trial has begun. He is told by one of the people that he should be dealt with as an informer. Theo says, "I'm prepared to stand trial. If I deserve punishment, I'll bear it," and is answered: "What kind of trial are you talking about? You killed him" (p. 88).

One can detect archetypes in this modernistic tale. Theo is Cain, who killed his brother, the one whom the earth cannot contain, the eternal wanderer whose deed is inscribed on his forehead. Another archetype is Oedipal, Theo "kills" the father he did not have. His father was a weak, gentle man who allowed his wife to bring him to a total economic and mental collapse. The strange man, the image of Uncle Salo, is the father he both hated and adored. He hated Salo because he exposed his mother's weakness, and he adored Salo for his strength, which neither he nor his father had. The strange man, the image of Uncle Salo, tells him that he is as idle, unfaithful, and perfidious as his mother. He tries to leave his community and nation in their harshest moment. Theo tries to marry his dead mother by entering the church. Music and Christianity fascinate him and the planned act of conversion is an act of uniting with his mother after her death, in a union to be sanctioned by the church. The spiritual attraction to the church appears in Appelfeld's fiction, but it is mostly connected with women and with a desire for silence, contemplation, and breaking away from mundane reality. It seems as if Theo, through this feminine impulse, is unmanning Judaism.

The phenomenon of self-hate brings to mind Otto Weininger (1880–1903), a Viennese psychologist and philosopher who was born a Jew and converted to Christianity. Weininger received his doctor of philosophy degree in 1902 and committed suicide a year later at the age of twenty-three. His major work is *Geschlecht und Charakter* (Sex and character), a philosophical treatise that justifies male superiority, anti-Semitism, and antifeminism. In his exploration of what he regarded as the fundamental relationship between sex and human character, Weininger saw the Jew as even worse than woman, a force within all people, not just in individual Jews, leading to a belief in nothing, not even in male dominance, as the woman does. That is why, in his view, Jews gravitate toward communism, anarchism, materialism, empiricism, and atheism. Zionism, Weininger claimed, could only come about after the rejection of Judaism itself, since Jews could not grasp the idea of a state in their present circumstances. The Jewish religion he saw as a belief in nothing, in contrast to the positive faith he found in Christianity. Weininger combined elements of romanticism, Wagner, Nietzsche, modern psychology, and biology with many original insights. His anti-Semitism (Jewish self-hate) was taken over by Nazi thinkers as justification for their views. As Sander L. Gilman writes, "Self-hatred arises when the mirages of stereotypes are confused with realities within the world, when the desire for acceptance forces the acknowledgment of one's difference."[2]

Another process can be observed in Theo: the urge to confess, to atone, to face trial, to embrace humanity. Even before killing the man, Theo feels he must atone for sins; he is a traitor, has left his comrades, and has tried to break away from what seems to be his only viable reality. He is a Judas Iscariot. On a deeper level, he is aware of his infatuation with his mother and knows that by adopting his mother's expectations after the Holocaust he is betraying his people. One may wonder: does he also wish to become a woman like his mother? His mother is the only feminine image he plucks from his childhood and young adult life. Will condemnation of the mother mean self-condemnation? Why could he not identify with his father, the self-effacing intellectual? Did he find more strength, determination, and beauty in his mother and her compulsions?

After the killing, Theo believes that it was his deviation from his intended path that brought the dreadful event upon him. Despite his awareness of his father's misery in the failed marriage, Theo hated his father. His father has been progressively erased from his memory. After Theo was separated from his father, his father was shot to death. Yet the father does not have a place in Theo's being. Seemingly, Theo is now on his way home, to complete his declared mission. His pursuers, however, are marching along the horizon, following his advance. He continues to imitate his mother. When asking for coffee he asked for it in her voice; cognac, coffee, and cigarettes were her constant desires. The man Theo killed had cigarettes and cognac in his knapsacks and bags. Theo continues to try to help people he encounters, but he frightens everyone. The only one who never rejected him is his mother. And despite his urge to do penance through help and submission, her prophetic voice continues to be the most meaningful voice in his existence. Her memory continues to possess him; her romantic delusions echo in him: "without wings, my dear, we scuffle about like hens in the farmyard. Mozart will give me wings, and Bach will open the gates of light for us" (p. 115). Theo has translated her aspirations to his own life. The sense of guilt penetrates Theo; he believes in his guilt but not in the fact of his wrongdoing.

The last meaningful personal encounter is with a man he feels is a kindred spirit, a convert who found real radiance in the camp and spirituality in the people who embraced him as a brother. Theo is glad to speak German; the refugees all spoke Yiddish, and Theo expresses an aversion to that language. The man acquired Yiddish in the camps. He is the opposite of Theo, a converted Jew who found his faith in the camps and in the people who made him a believer. The mutual help gave radiance to existence. He discovered humanity in compassion and love. The man is heading for Budapest. His forefathers came from there and he wants to learn how to pray for them. The man is a violinist, a concertmaster in the prewar era. Now he has no desire to go back to music. When Theo asks him if he gave up music, he answers: "Our camp was full of classical music. The commander of the camp was mad about Mozart" (p. 126).

To Theo the man is the embodiment of his father, the incarnation of logic, intellect, and integrity. His father, who was exiled into silence at home by the mad domineering wife, came to life in the image of this man. Theo rejects the images of males who were against his mother: he killed the man who reminded him of his uncle Salo and hated the benevolent man who knew how to embrace reality and the humanity of people. Again and again we see the phenomenon of self-hate and the adoption of stereotypes, mostly anti-Semitic ones adopted against any signs of traditional Jewish behavior. In Theo's case it is the fellowship, the mutual responsibility one Jew feels toward another, that creates within Theo the hostility against the refugees. Simultaneously, however, he is stricken with a sense of guilt, even though he does not feel that he has committed an act of wrongdoing. It seems, as with Joseph K. in *The Trial*, that his very behavior is his indictment. His very attraction to the encircled refugees and his inability to break away from this circle point to his desire to be judged.

The theme of the informer emerges again, and here it ties in with the first story, "Three," in the collection *Smoke*. There too we see a sense of guilt over the desertion of others in the camps. In both *For Every Sin* and "Three," a murder occurs. In *For Every Sin* the "murder" Theo commits and the sin of the informers overlap. The three informers are kept in a trench and food is thrown at them. Like Joseph K., Theo is free to move though kept a prisoner, and he continues to weave the same story of his desire to go back to Baden-bei-Wien. He is told by one man that the company of the refugees is more pleasant to him than that of the murderers. Theo feels he exaggerates, to which the man retorts: "Correct, we exaggerate purposely, to make things visible. Hasn't the time come for things to appear in black and white and in relief?" (p. 151). Ironically, the deep love that Theo appears to seek is to be found among the refugees. A woman tells him that she has learned to love the refugees: "Every refugee is a precious person. I can no longer live in the world of pleasure. Do you understand?" (p. 152). The woman sums up her new reality of the post-Holocaust experience.

Theo imitates his mother, who imitates some romantic notions that have trickled down to the assimilated Jew. It is a rejection of one's own culture and an uncritical acceptance of spurious models, not of the reality of society. Tragically, in this novel, and despite the Holocaust, a lesson is not drawn. Like his mother, Theo cannot understand that in a world that has shattered all normative systems, the model of fellowship and mutual responsibility is the only certainty, as in Camus's *The Plague.* Theo does not realize that he has no home, that Europe is in ruins and so is his home. His mind, like his mother's, is a storehouse of irreality. He never talks about his experience in the camps; he does talk about his mother, and the more he talks about her the more he desires to become a part of her. He knows that he is free to leave, yet something within him does not let him.

A frightful realization besets Theo: he realizes that his German accent has been corrupted. "Then for the first time he felt that something within him had gone awry." Yiddish words cling to him: *Toytn* (the dead), *Lemekh* (simpleton). His mother would not approve of his use of such Yiddish terms. She was sensitive to words and to their correct order. She was concerned also about the sounds; to his father, syntactical precision was important. Gilman writes:

> Yiddish was perceived as a form of pidgin. . . . With the civil emancipation of the Jews, the demonstrable fact that Jews spoke German, but with a marked accent, created the basis for the next level of the perception of the language of the Jews. . . . For even if Jews could speak perfect grammatical, syntactic, and semantic German, their rhetoric revealed them as Jews.[3]

Theo's steps lead him not to his home but to a shed full of refugees. His sin of desertion of his comrades is now fully upon him. His final realization is that he will never go home, and that his fate as a Jew is sealed.

> "Where did you intend to go?"
> "To my hometown, to Baden-bei-Wien."
> "There's no reason to go there. Stay here. We have everything we need. The shed is full of supplies. There's no sense seeking something that can never be attained. We won't bring the dead back to life. You understand that. Here we're together. I won't conceal from you that it

isn't always comfortable, but still, we're together."

Theo gulped down mug after mug. The hot liquid seeped into every part of him and filled him with warmth. Fatigue and helplessness assailed him. He placed his head on a bundle, curled up as if after a big quarrel, a desperate quarrel, closed his eyes and collapsed." (Pp. 167–168)

Here the novel ends.

For Every Sin completes a cycle of Appelfeld's fiction. From the first story, "Three," in his first collection, *Smoke*, to the present novel, almost thirty years have elapsed, and yet themes that appear germinally in his first laconic story are developed, enriched, and articulated in *For Every Sin*. First and foremost, the novel combines two major themes in Appelfeld's fiction: the life of the survivor after liberation and the life of the assimilated Jew in Central Europe, especially in Austria and Romania, prior to the Holocaust. Diametrically opposed to the characters in the early stories, who have eradicated their personal past, the protagonist in *For Every Sin* draws his raison d'être from the past and mostly from the image of his mother.

Second, and of great importance, is the problem set in motion in the earlier stories and early in our discussion: the suspension of the ethical in the fiction of the Holocaust, an approach that seems almost anathema. This leads us to the most complex question—that of guilt. But first the idea of "sin" is to be dealt with. The title of the novel is taken from Proverbs, as we saw: "love covereth all sins." The question is: to what love does the text refer? Does it refer only to earthly love, such as a son's love for his mother, or does it go beyond? The mother's love, as we noted, is the love for the Christian world, a love for Bach, music, the naive identification of culture and civilization. In this respect, the self-hate of the Jew and the Jew's desire to assimilate gain their most grotesque twist after the years of distorted notions about the acceptance of the Jew by the Christian world. Theo wants to go home—to a home that was not a home while he was a young man and clearly no longer exists in the present reality, a month after the liberation.

20

KATERINA

THE PRESENCE of women in Appelfeld's work continues to be central and decisive. As protagonists, autobiographical alter egos, observers, and commentators, women stand for a point of view and are carriers of a realm of equally possible interpretations. In addition, the region of Bukovina continues to fascinate Appelfeld, who places Jews and gentiles, Ruthenian peasants and gypsies, in the typical village, the provincial town, and the capital, Czernowitz.

Katerina (Hebrew, 1989; English, 1992), told in the first person, is a confessional novel. Katerina's voice and her outlook on life are central. At eighty, she is telling her life story, from her parents' hut in a Ruthenian village. Half-blind and physically impaired, she has returned home after sixty years of self-imposed exile. Home was never far away, but she chose not to return. Exile and expulsion are part of the life of this woman, who out of the love for Jews had altered her expected course of life. Through writing and memory she now reconstructs her life, from the latter part of the nineteenth century to the Second World War and after. Silence, semiblindness, respite, and the blurred meadows of Bukovina spreading to the Prut River allow her time and place for her personal testimony. Earlier perceptions of Ruthenian peasantry through Jewish eyes are reversed; it is the Ruthenian view of Jewish life that takes center stage. Yet it is familiar territory in Appelfeld's texts. From his early stories in *Smoke* onward, the village with its Ruthenian-Ukrainian roots is there. As noted, Appelfeld extracts stories, instances, and anecdotes from earlier texts and plants them in later ones, transferring them (typically) from short story to novel. By the same token, marginal characters who played supporting roles in earlier narratives now take center stage. His fiction of the 1980s witnesses the expansion of both plot and character.

Since the autobiographical novel *The Searing Light*, Appelfeld has not returned to depicting the life of survivors in Israel nor attempting to expand the historical map in which his characters act. This move toward a wider historical panorama does not entail a change in perspective or style; it is made possible by continuing to create archetypal characters, themselves unchanged but deeply affected by historical times. (The only breakthrough is in *The Railway*, in which for the first time the Holocaust experience is depicted directly; see chap. 21.) In a strange way, *Katerina* is a modern, inverted picaresque novella. As a maid, Katerina wanders from one Jewish household to another, from the Orthodox to the converted and assimilated Jews, depicting a typology of Jewry in Bukovina. She is on the move, like the Jews she loved in all phases of her early life. Never far from her village or the tavern, she takes upon herself the fate of the people with whom she comes to identify. All her beloved people, the Jews she worked and cared for, die a violent death. She observes the murder of Jews from the pogroms of the late nineteenth century to the era of the Holocaust.

Katerina's own early life is a twisted mirror image of the life of the Jew: from early age she is shunned by her family and by society. She plunges deeper and deeper into identification with the Jewish community. In a grotesque and touching way, she wants to acculturate and assimilate herself into Jewish life, thereby depicting an inverted image of the wish for assimilation on the part of some Jews. Her son, whose father is Jewish, she names Benjamin, and she speaks only Yiddish to him. Her Ruthenian relatives and acquaintances sense that she is affected by her contact with Jews, that she is corrupted in spirit, in speech and mannerism.

Born to a poor gentile family, raised by a harshly domineering mother and a drunken father, Katerina, at age sixteen, moves to the nearest provincial town. There she joins the world of beggars and drunkards hanging around the train station. Pregnant at seventeen, she gives up her child for adoption. Saved by a Jewish woman, she begins an existence that eventually places her in jail for decades.

After the cruel fate of murder and suicide that has befallen some of her beloved Jews, she begins to live with a Jewish man she meets in a tavern. She tries to save him from his drinking but fails. Her desire to create a Jewish home fails as well, although she speaks and reads Yiddish. To the chagrin of her Jewish lover, she becomes pregnant. Her last Jewish employer, a concert pianist, has left her her jewelry, and Katerina lives off it. This is the beginning of her wandering with her child Benjamin, from inns and taverns to Jewish homes, constantly trying to be around Jews, especially on holidays. She never ceases to hear from her relatives and other people of her village, who constantly condemn her frequent moves. One acquaintance attacks her when she refuses his advances. In his rage he takes her baby and smashes him against the wall. With a knife Katerina slashes the man repeatedly and kills him.

The second part of her life is spent in jail. She is sentenced to life imprisonment with hard labor. She sinks into a stupor, avoiding contact with other prisoners. From the loot brought to other women prisoners and later from passing freight trains loaded with Jews, she learns indirectly about their plight. With her liberation from prison at the end of the war, she returns to her village, where she is shunned and feared. Eventually she settles into her old home, to write and contemplate her life.

Katerina believes that all Jews were massacred, and she feels that it is her role to commemorate their existence. She continues to write down some Jewish religious terms, fearing that her own memory will fail her. Y. Ginosar has commented that

> Katerina is the last of the Jews: the Jews are "the Stranger," "The Monster," and so is she. She is convicted of murder; so are they. The mythological Jesus is the son of God, and he is a Jew; her son is half-Jewish/half-Gentile. Her Jesus is her son, the murdered baby. She is depicted carrying her baby around as Mary. . . . As a woman murderer she is beyond forgiveness or atonement in her community. By the same token—Jews are never forgiven. . . . Shaping Katerina as analogous to the Jews, in a detailed fully structured manner, is one of the achievements of the book.[1]

This ties in with the earlier connection established in Appelfeld's work: female characters symbolize Jewishness and the relation to the Jew as woman. The old, bigoted perception of the woman is parallel to that of the Jew. However, Katerina differs in certain respects: despite her self-imposed exile and constant wandering, she takes revenge and has a home to go to. In general, we may say that the Jews are denied revenge. Only in *The Railway* does a Jew, forty years after the Holocaust, perform an act of revenge.

Questions arise pertaining to the autobiographical self and its role in the fictional narrative. Even in the depiction of Katerina we can detect elements that point to the author-character axis. Appelfeld expands the historical parameters of his work and enriches the gallery of characters he presents. The question is to what extent the autobiographical self (embedded in characters such as Kitty, Bertha, Tzili, Theo, and Toni) expands and deepens his later work. A reader, assuming the implied or embedded presence of an autobiographical self in these characters, must pose certain questions: what assertion should take precedence in the reading of the text, the one that claims that every character in a novel bears the autobiographical code of its creator, or should the information in the text lead the reader into creating a connection between character and author?

Appelfeld places his fiction in geographical territories known to him. Many of his characters are combinations of historical characters, characters drawn from texts he read, and people he knew and transformed and transfigured into fiction. The expanded autobiographical self moves in spaces known to Appelfeld. From Bukovina, through the war years, then on to Italy, Israel, and back to Bukovina, his characters are mostly Jews and gentiles who have connections to Jews. One of the most personal, most traumatic experiences, the murder of his mother, is to be found in his early poetry in the late 1950s and in his mature novels after the 1970s. The centrality of Katerina can be a step in expanding the autobiographical dramatis personae in his fiction.

One can detect areas of similarities between the young Appelfeld and the young Katerina. Like Appelfeld, Katerina spent time away from home and still moved in her province. Her most horrendous experiences, and his own, took place on the border of the familiar and the foreign: she chooses to cross the boundary into Jews and Jewishness; he, conversely, had to cross into the Christian world and pretend to be one. Most of his characters choose to break away from their original home, never to return. Tzili, with whom the autobiographical self is most closely identified, chooses to leave her province even though she blends with the time and the place. Appelfeld, as a child left alone, did not have the choices he accords his characters. Like Katerina, Appelfeld was in service to others; but while Appelfeld's experience was cruel, like Tzili's, Katerina is well treated and cherishes the Jews she serves, drawing her mental strength from Judaism.

We referred earlier to the reversed mirror image of the life of the Jew. One can observe the reversed image in the relationship between the author and his protagonist. *Katerina* depicts the desire to be the "other," to absorb a conception of a Jewish way of life. Katerina's simplicity attracts the voice identified with Jewish intellectualism and uprootedness. Her mistake is her venturing into the "Jewish sphere"; this gives her vulnerability as well as eventual power. Her wandering mimics Jewish wandering, and the wandering of Appelfeld himself.

Katerina is a caricature, a tragic character like Tropich, the giant with a huge gentile body and a small Jewish head.

Two maps are presented in the novel; one is of Bukovina, the other of the geography of the self. On one hand the spatial qualities of the map of Bukovina and on the other hand Katerina's psyche and body are at center stage as loci of the true action. Katerina is ravaged like the land; she expands with her pregnancies and gains an equilibrium with the birth of Benjamin. As with the Biblical Benjamin, a reversed image is presented: the Biblical Benjamin caused the death of his mother, Rachel, and it is the murder of Benjamin's murderer that condemns Katerina to life imprisonment. One can assume that through the guise of the old maid recollecting her life, the autobiographical self expresses hidden desires denied it. Could it be that the desire of Katerina, to be adopted by Jews and come close to Jews, is the reversal that occurs in Appelfeldian characters who express a wish to become Christians?

A distinction can be made concerning the use of autobiographical fiction. In Appelfeld's early stories the autobiographical experiences were the basis of the narratives; this trend reaches its apex in *Tzili*. After the 1970s, the autobiographical element appears as a motif in the son-mother axis. This motif can present a mature son, can shift the historical time to a prewar experience; yet at the base is the autobiographical experience of the loss of the mother. The loss of the mother gains momentum once it has left the realm of reality and enters the fictionalized, mythicized state of the expanded autobiographical self of Appelfeld's fiction.

Other reversals occur. On the thematic level, for example, the son loses his mother (in the earlier novels); in *Katerina*, the mother loses her son. Following this logic, it may be noted that for Appelfeld the novel is a reversed mirror image of his autobiographical self.

21

THE RAILWAY

Since the 1980s Appelfeld has ceased to depict the life of Jewish survivors in Israel and has begun to delve deeper into past Jewish intellectual life in Europe, giving it a historical as well as a spatial existence. Forever fascinated with the terminally intellectual Jew of Europe, Appelfeld began to expand on the archetype of the Wandering Jew in the post-Holocaust period. This mode of depiction releases him from historical constraints and allows for movement as the lifeline of Jewish existence. Movement is not only a mode of existence; it is also a state of mind.

Europe after the Holocaust is a Jewish wasteland in Appelfeld's world: there are few Jewish survivors, but they are always on the move. The dynamics, however, does not bring change in Appelfeld's world. It is a repetitious pattern that has left the historical domain and entered the metahistorical. According to Appelfeld the Jew moves but continues to be in the same spot on the map. That is, he continues to be the stranger, "the other," the hovering shadow of an extinct reality. For Appelfeld's characters, Europe of the 1980s is an archaeological site, the largest Jewish cemetery in history. After the expulsion of the Jews from Spain in 1492, the Jews cursed the land and for centuries refused to return to the place where Jewish, Hebrew, and Muslim culture reached amazing heights. In his later novels, Appelfeld's characters remain in Europe and do not look for new opportunities. An almost sick fascination draws them, as the guardians of hell, to return to their hometowns in Europe. This applies not only to *For Every Sin* but also to the protagonist of *Mesilat Barzel* (The railway, 1991). The refusal (or inability) to venture a change is enhanced by the unique nature of those who belong to the tribe of the survivors.

The characters in this short novel have adopted a paradoxically open yet subterranean existence. Ideas of conspiracy and secret cells, taken from the now-defunct Communist movement and the Jewish Bund, still prevail. Spiegelmeister, a mad old ideologue living in Jerusalem in

The Skin and the Gown, continues to adhere to a conspiracy theory. For him the center of the Jewish Empire is Warsaw. The Jewish subterranean existence, in the bunkers and other hiding places, becomes a conceptual underground; using old Communist slogans about underground cells, characters in *The Railway* evoke an old or dead terminology.

How does one come to terms with the post-Holocaust "domestication of the state of exile"? The Hebrew writer Haim Hazaz (1898–1973), in his famous story "The Sermon" (1942), places in the mouth of his protagonist, Yudke, certain issues concerning the major crisis in the spiritual climate in Eretz Israel in the later years of the British Mandate; he does it by creating a clear-cut dichotomy between Judaism and Zionism. In his hesitant and meandering confession/accusation, Yudke reviews Jewish history in the Diaspora. He rejects Jewish history, refusing to recognize it or its claims:

> Now look! Just think . . . what is there in it? Just give me an answer: what is there in it? Oppression, defamation, persecution, martyrdom. . . . I know that we stood up to all that oppression and suffering. . . . But . . . I don't care for that kind of heroism . . . the heroism of despair. Persecution preserves us, keeps us alive. Without it, we couldn't exist.[1]

Hazaz's protagonist continues to talk about a Jewish pyramid, constructed of exile, martyrdom, and the Messiah. "A Jew without suffering is an abnormal creature." Yudke criticizes the nocturnal psychology of the Diaspora. Appelfeld's characters also seek this nocturnal, moonlit mode of existence.

Appelfeld is not the only one to recognize the great intellectual powerhouse of European Jewry. Amos Oz's protagonist in *Touch the Water, Touch the Wind* (1973) is a Jew, a mathematician, who has survived the Holocaust through the exercise of almost superhuman intellectual powers. A man of purified spirituality, he expresses—through Oz's use of the fantastic—what is perhaps the secret of Jewish survival in the Diaspora: spirituality, tenacity, the quest for higher elements, a belief in miracles, and the conviction that the impossible is possible. The protagonist proves to his satisfaction the power of miracle by combining pure mathematics with Hassidic wonders. He then decides to move to Israel, but he no longer performs miracles. Israel is immersed in its practical and concrete concerns. The protagonist moves from Tiberias to the upper Galilee, symbolically rising to a higher sphere. He, his wife, and other characters move in an inexorable cycle of ascent and descent. They must touch reality, must be humiliated and defiled, before their ascent. The protagonist is an alchemist of both matter and spirit who can communicate beyond physical or psychic borders. He is the Wandering Jew as a spiritual *Uebermensch*. The Jew, as one who is thrust beyond borders, is also beyond boundaries. He can touch the water, touch the wind, do the impossible. In his last miraculous act, the earth opens and he and his wife disappear into the chasm.

The glorification of the Jew as an intellectual and miracle worker persists in different combinations in Appelfeld's tales. In *The Railway*, a modern picaresque tale, the first-person narrator is Irwin Zigelbaum, who recounts, in the mid-1980s, his forty years of wandering in Europe. A Holocaust survivor, like a modern land surveyor in the European countryside he continues to move in trains, from south to north and back. Trains make him a free man, unattached. After forty years of wandering, he has his beloved spots, his familiarity with places and people. Haunted by his memory, which dominates him, he nevertheless visits all the stations in his life and in his parents' life. His memory, as he states, has roots in all the members of his body, and constantly emits years and sights. Not unlike Appelfeld's Bartfuss, he has swallowed the Holocaust whole. He maintains a yearly cycle, like the reading of the Torah, in weekly portions, and he has twenty-two stations, parallel to the letters in the Hebrew alphabet. He returns compulsively to a forlorn train station where, during the war, after three days in a sealed car, the people inside were deserted by the Germans.

The life of the narrator is a loose compilation of the post-Holocaust experience of Appelfeld's characters throughout his stories: Italy, smuggling, black marketeering, love of the German language; even the names of characters are repeated, now taking different roles. Haunted by constant nightmares, suffering from an ulcer, the protagonist takes to moderate drinking, fast love affairs, and constant dining in train station canteens. He has his beloved places where he stays, or rather sleeps, in order to regain his strength and to continue his Sisyphian route. On his way, he redeems Jewish holy artifacts in fairs, collects them, and sells them to those who will maintain them and will eventually ship them to Jerusalem.

Beyond this, *The Railway* is a novel about the death of the father and the death of father figures. The protagonist's father and mother were ardent Communists. The mother took part in the assassination of a high official and later became a recluse, addicted to alchohol and cigarettes. The father, who apparently prevented the mother's move to Moscow, was working with the local Ruthenian peasants, trying to convert them to communism. In his zeal he did not hesitate to instigate acts of arson against Jewish businesses and other provocative acts. The mother is seen sitting silently at the window. The father takes young Irwin with him on missions for the party, and does not send the boy to school. The mother, silent and pining, tries to instill in the child a love of learning.

The father-mother-son triangle appears in a new guise in this novel. The mother's silence is reminiscent of *The Age of Wonders*, but her desperation is deeper than the mother's there. The anguish of the son over the mother's agony continues throughout his life. The family is united in the camp, where the parents are shot to death by a German officer. This novel is the last stage in the life of the father figures who survived the Holocaust. They represent Communists on one hand and on the other hand a rabbi, substituting for the Hassidic grandfather. The death of Rollman, an ardent Communist, at the hands of a Jew who resents the havoc the Communists inflicted on the Jewish community, is the death of a father figure. The death of Shtark, a former Communist who returned to ancient Hebrew texts, is another demise of a father figure, and so is the death of Rabbi Ziemmel, the one who collected the lost Jewish religious artifacts.

A personal quest appears as a subtext as well as the surface text in the novel. The information that Nachtigal, the German officer who killed the narrator's parents, is about to return to his hometown, Weinberg, allows the protagonist to fulfill his task: he kills Nachtigal. The novel concludes with the words:

> It was clear to me that my life was ended and consumed in this place, and if I will have another life, it will not be a happy one. Like in a clear continuous nightmare I saw the sea of darkness. I knew that my deeds were devoid of dedication and beauty. I did everything by compulsion, clumsily and always too late.[2]

The combination of a mission and a sense of delay is reminiscent of Agnon's *Book Of Deeds* and Kafka's *The Castle*. The element of concealment, so prevalent in Appelfeld's texts, is lifted here into a mission attached to the protagonist as one embodiment of the Wandering Jew.

This novel marks a departure from earlier Appelfeld narratives. Up to this stage in his work, the domain was that of a Jewish world. *The Railway* relates to the final stages in the narrator's journey and presents, almost for the first time, a direct depiction of the Holocaust. It enters the freight trains and the camp experience, directly relating the anti-Semitism the protagonist senses. Postwar Europe, the Europe of the countryside, had ingested anti-Semitism. The yearly appearance of the itinerant Wandering Jew creates unease at best; at worst there is open hatred. The novel is centered in Austria. In one of the pensions the protagonist sits next to a retired train conductor. After a few drinks the man begins to speak about the good old days when he was a soldier on the Eastern Front. He feels strongly that the Axis brought redemption to the world by killing Jews. It was a disgusting job but a necessary one, he continues to say; at the beginning one was taken aback by the shrieking, but slowly one realized the importance of the job. He feels that they have completed their task; no more Jews are left. Like *Katerina* but from a different point of view, the local population in the countryside and the villages assumes the total demise of the Jews. The appearance of the narrator is like an apparition from a past preferably forgotten.

The belated act of revenge is not accompanied by a sense of mission. Nachtigal, the German officer, is by now a toothless old man, mourning the death of his wife. When the narrator encounters him, Nachtigal is searching for a store to buy milk. The act of killing him has to do with finality as the major thread in the book: the death of father figures; the realization of the mother's silence in being prevented from completing her political mission by her husband. An agent provocateur and a man who despised culture, he was part of the general decline of Jewish intellectualism in Europe. The narrator and other characters are dedicated to one mission: saving the holy artifacts from destruction and shipping them to Jerusalem. The Jew, Hassidic or Communist, has a spiritual dimension. The novel reveals the demise of this dimension after the actual destruction of European Jewry.

It is a novel rich in its numerous characters, minor as well as major, who travel in the insular compartment of their life and never get off. Only their gaze intimates a burned-out existence. The old ideologues, like the narrator, do not enter a historical perspective. Their past is their actual present, and the old message is reiterated by people who are ghosts of themselves.

AFTERWORD

Tʜᴇʀᴇ ɪs an element of concealment in the nonconfessional Appelfeldian story. Yet the conscious concealment evokes the unconscious revelation of things that come up through the reading process despite fictional, symbolic, and other rhetorical devices. We are made aware of a voice behind the fictional characters, the presence of a persona whose sensibility and sensitivity, preference and judgment, moral stance and taste, organize the final text presented to the reader.

The concept of the implied author, a term coined by Wayne C. Booth, concerns "the author's state of mind." For Booth, "the emotions and judgments of the implied author are . . . the very stuff out of which fiction is made."[1] The implied author in the text is an "ideal, literary, created version of the real man." One can add that the fictionality of the implied author, like that of the text, is a result of a conscious process of selection. One assumes that the implied author is a persona and not the real author who wrote the text. Critics often identify characters, themes, and attitudes directly with Appelfeld himself. Thus self-hate, self-denial, and self-rejection are seen to be attitudes of Appelfeld the man. The fact that he confines himself to a particular era, specific events, and characters makes this perception easier. At the heart of the issue is his depiction of the assimilated Jew.

Appelfeld admits that he admires assimilated Jews. Despite their uprootedness, despite the fact that they were cosmopolitan outsiders, they reached the height of sensibility. He often refers to Kafka, Proust, and Joyce (who chose the figure of a converted Jew to portray modern sensibility and displacement). Naiveté, the belief in the possibility of a nonnational, irreligious, cosmopolitan being, blinded the assimilated Jews. Eventually they were condemned by "the blood in their body," as Appelfeld puts it. He told Clive Sinclair that

> the assimilated Jew had a feeling that he should deny his being, his culture, his heritage, his being a Jew. This was a part of it. To become a universalist you should deny yourself. This is of course a tragedy, you can't deny yourself. The moment that you deny yourself, you are punishing yourself. Another danger is that you become a superficial person, because you are an uprooted person without a past. This is a

kind of ambiguity. . . . Being a part of the great world on one side and then you are punished by the world. They do not accept you. They accept you as Jewish. This is the tension that we feel up to our day. Between that deep desire to leave our old heritage, but from the other side, you cannot escape it.[2]

Appelfeld's fiction portrays the attitude of the Germans and the Austrians toward the Jews: an alien element, demons from another world that penetrated their culture and contaminated it. The concept of the implied reader, a term coined by Wolfgang Iser, refers to a reader who, because of a particular moral and cultural attitude toward the text, activates the text to its fullest effect. The implied reader is not the particular reader but rather a composite persona whose reading activates the text and, by filling in the gaps, reconstructs it. One can assume that in the twentieth century, when witnesses and survivors are still with us, conscientious Jews and gentiles are the implied readers of the Appelfeldian text.

But even to the empathic, sympathetic reader, the text presents problems of ambiguity and ambivalence. The ever-present uncertainty, the absence of a satisfactory and determinate single point of view, is what is problematic. This again evokes the complex relation between the Holocaust and its fictional retelling. The distance between reader, writer, and text—and between them and the historical reality—might present a challenge to fictional expression, as if the indeterminacy and ambiguity are morally wrong. Appelfeld had challenged the ethical horizon of expectations of many readers. This is especially true since Appelfeld did not embrace existing motifs and archetypes present in Jewish "destruction literature" but created his own "house of fiction." Even though Appelfeld's fiction does not claim to be a representation of a reality in the mimetic-realistic sense and his fiction creates a reality from shreds of memory and imagination, decoders of his text have criticized him; the absence of a cry for revenge, which does not appear until *The Railway* in 1991, and the nonaccusatory tone toward the assimilated Jew were held against him. Appelfeld found metaphors as the suitable mode of depiction. As we have seen, he creates inverted modern tales where the impossible and the most horrific become possible.

One of Appelfeld's harshest critics is Ruth Wisse, who claims that

Appelfeld knew antisemitism from the inside, from the anti-Jewishness of his own home . . . and it is this initial discovery that has remained the more decisive. The hostility of outsiders appeared to be almost proper retribution for the spiritual meanness of his assimilating family. . . . In his writings, Aharon Appelfeld struggles with a very difficult personal inheritance—the culture of self-rejection in which he was raised and to which, despite everything, he remains attached by strong filial bonds. His desire to confront his past is inhibited by the terrible fate inflicted on the world of his childhood—as well charge your father with parsimony when he has been murdered for his wealth. In trying to achieve the necessary detachment, Appelfeld has cultivated an uninflected style, emotionally neutral, distant, impersonal. But the stifled anger of the son has been transferred onto the parents. Fate sits in judgment on all the ugly, assimilated Jews—fate in the form of the Holocaust. The result is a series of pitiless moral fables, more damning of the victims than the crime committed against them.[3]

Wisse claims that without a straightforward judgment in the tradition of Hebrew-Jewish "destruction literature," and without invoking the language of retribution, the historical verdict has been turned inward upon the Jews. This in turn raises another question already alluded to: once we talk about Holocaust literature, to what extent do we enter a different world that suspends and does away with rhetorical distinctions between author, implied author, and protagonist? To what extent do survivors as artists have a single call: the call of unyielding moral outcry against the victimizer? Is this a discussion beyond the boundaries of literary criticism? To what extent do the honing of aesthetically fine points pale, facing the Holocaust?

In the literary response to catastrophe within the Jewish canon, the medieval poet and historian Ephraim of Bonn (1132–1200) chronicled the persecution of the Jews during the Second and Third Crusades. In his "Sefer Zekhira" (Book of remembrance) he has a *piyut* (liturgical poem) that reads:

> I am stoned, I am struck down and crucified. I am burned, my neck is snapped in shame. I am beheaded and trampled on for my guilt. I am strangled and choked by my enemy. I am beaten, my body is scourged. . . . I am hung, despised, exiled in pain. I am stamped on, ruined, made to pine away. My blood is shed, my skin turned inside out, my home overturned. I am pursued . . . I am raped. All the people that laid me waste have regained their strength . . .

It is a lament for the massacre at Blois (1171) following a blood libel. All the members of the Jewish community were burned at the stake. The single repeated sound in the interlocking rhyme in Hebrew is "Eee," like a moaning or a wail. The concluding line, "This is the law of the burnt offering on the altar hearth" ("Ve'zot Torat ha'olah, he ha'olah al mokdah"), is an ironic reference to the Jews burned at the stake.[4]

Appelfeld's fiction goes beyond this tradition but stays within it at the same time. His is a literature of resignation rather than a literature of indignation. Writing in Hebrew makes him a Hebrew writer who belongs to the wider tradition of response to catastrophe through writing. He does not openly enter into a dialogue with classical Hebraic and Jewish sources. This study has tried to place him as a contemporary Jewish writer within the tradition of Hebrew and Jewish writing as well as to situate him in the heart of modern and postmodern writing. Marginality and passivity are common to his characters, many of whom are portrayed in the penultimate stage of their life. It would be wrong to place him in the margin of Holocaust or catastrophe literature because he does not follow the established convention, the unbroken tradition of literary symbols and archetypes that go back to the Book of Lamentations.

The Holocaust is the most extensive communal catastrophe in Jewish history. To confront it, individual writers have evoked symbols from the canon of Jewish literature. Until the nineteenth century, the Jewish response to catastrophe was mostly within the religious canon —deep piety justifying God's judgment. Modern Hebrew secular writers relate to traditional Jewish motifs and archetypes by incorporating traditional metaphors linked to modern texts. At the heart of many literary works in Hebrew and Yiddish literature are classical allusions and modern ironic perception. Appelfeld introduces irony by facing the unresolvable tension between what seemed and what was, as he probes the psyches of those who perished and those who survived.

Self-criticism has been central to Hebrew and Yiddish literature since the beginning of the nineteenth century. Two giants of Yiddish literature, Mendele Mocher Seforim (Shalom Jacov Abramovitz, 1835–1917) and Isaac Leib Peretz (1851–1915), using local color and colloquial speech, launched a subtle attack upon the ills of contemporary Jewish society, trying to evoke within their readers an awareness of the need for fundamental changes. The same applies to giants of Hebrew literature, such as Joseph Haim Brenner (1881–1921). As early as 1911 Brenner, the moral voice of the era, refused to accept the attempts to beautify reality and make it palatable. He exposes ills, shortcomings, and moral turpitude in the heart of the Jewish community. Like Mendele he was attacked because his literature did not praise Jewish martyrdom and Jewish suffering. Haim Hazaz's story "The Sermon" shows the hesitant protagonist talking about Jewish history as nocturnal history: "The exile, that is our pyramid, and it has martyrdom for a base and Messiah for its peak."[5]

We are in the midst of an argument at the very center of the literature-life axis. On one hand we are faced with the most heinous crime in known history, a crime against our brothers and sisters, a crime whose reverberations we continue to feel to this day. On the other hand, there is a demand for a commitment on the part of an author-survivor to bear witness. Yet, with Alvin Rosenfeld, we must say this in regard to such expectations:

> we lack a phenomenology of reading Holocaust literature, a series of maps that will guide us on our way as we pick up and variously try to comprehend the writing of the victims, the survivors, the survivors-who-become-victims, and the kinds-of-survivors, those who were never there but know more than the outlines of the place. Until we devise such maps, our understanding of Holocaust literature will be only partial, well below that which belongs to full knowledge.[6]

The irrational quality that has dominated human fate in modern life and fiction has forced the fictional characters into unrelieved contradiction. Hegel says that if one approaches the world rationally, the world will respond by presenting a rational image of itself. In the Holocaust, the world approached us with its irrationality, and we respond to it by recasting that world in irrational fiction. Again and again in Holocaust literature, life appears as an unreal game in which the old rules no longer hold. And yet there is the fact of that literature itself to be accounted for: amid the ruins of reason and meaning, the literature has been the most profound attempt in our time to find a meaning for what is otherwise absurd, to find reason in what is otherwise inexplicable.

NOTES

1. Biography

1. Ezra Mendelsohn, *The Jews of East Central Europe between the World Wars* (Bloomington: Indiana University Press, 1983), p. 72.

2. Ibid., p. 175.

3. Quoted from L. A. Easterman, "King Carol, Hitler, and Lupescu" (London, 1942), pp. 229–230.

4. Interview with Shmuel Schneider in *Bitzaron*, Winter–Spring 1982, pp. 5–17.

5. Haim Chertok, *We Are All Close: Conversations with Israeli Writers* (New York: Fordham University Press, 1989), p. 15.

6. Joseph Cohen, *Voices of Israel* (Albany: State University of New York Press, 1990), p. 132.

7. *London Review of Books*, March 17, 1988.

8. A. Appelfeld, "After the Holocaust," in B. Lang, ed., *Writing the Holocaust* (New York: Holmes & Meier, 1988), pp. 84–85.

2. Aesthetics and Narrative

1. Quoted in E. Fuchs, *Encounters With Israeli Authors* (Marblehead, Mass.: Micha, 1983), p.53.

2. Philip Roth, "A Talk with Aharon Appelfeld," *New York Times Book Review*, February 28, 1988.

3. Ibid.

4. Sidra D. Ezrahi, *By Words Alone* (Chicago: Chicago University Press, 1982), p. 366.

5. Ibid., p. 370.

6. A. Mintz, *Hurban* (New York: Columbia University Press, 1984), p. 204.

7. From an interview with Herbert Mitgang in *New York Times Book Review*, November 15, 1986.

8. T. Todorov, *The Fantastic* (Ithaca, N.Y.: Cornell University Press, 1975), p. 25.

9. A. Appelfeld, "Bertha," in G. Ramras-Rauch and J. Michman-Melkman, eds., *Facing the Holocaust: Selected Israeli Fiction* (Philadelphia: Jewish Publication Society, 1985), pp. 157–158.

10. A. Appelfeld, *Massot Be'guf Rishon* (Essays in first person) (Jerusalem: Zionist Library, 1979).

11. A. Appelfeld, "Cold Heights," *In the Wilderness* (Jerusalem: Achshav, 1965), pp. 85–118.

12. *New York Times Book Review*, February 28, 1988.

13. Translated as "Witness" in *Jerusalem Quarterly*, Summer 1980, pp. 91–96. All the quotations are from this source.

14. David G. Roskies, *Against the Apocalypse* (Cambridge, Mass.: Harvard University Press, 1984), p. 9.

3. Smoke

1. The English translation of "Three" appears in Appelfeld, *In the Wilderness;* the excerpt is from p. 5.
2. A. Appelfeld, *Tzili: The Story of a Life* (New York: E. P. Dutton, 1983), p. 1.
3. Fuchs, *Encounters with Israeli Authors*, p. 59.
4. Mintz, *Ḥurban* p. 209.
5. Quoted in Fuchs, *Encounters with Israeli Authors*, pp. 55–56.
6. Appelfeld, "Bertha," in *Facing the Holocaust*, pp. 145, 147.
7. P. Cooke, "They Cried until They Could Not See," *New York Times Magazine*, June 23, 1991, pp. 25, 45–48.

4. In the Fertile Valley

1. A. Appelfeld, "Kitty," in E. Spicehandler, ed., *Modern Hebrew Stories* (New York: Bantam Books, 1971), p. 220.
2. Lilly Rattok, *Bayit Al Blima* (Tel Aviv: Ḥekker, 1989), pp. 74–75.
3. For another view, see N. Aschkenasy, *Eve's Journey* (Philadelphia: University of Pennsylvania Press, 1986), pp. 236–239.
4. Appelfeld, *In the Wilderness*, p. 139.
5. Mintz, *Ḥurban* p. 212.
6. Appelfeld, *In the Wilderness*, p. 85.
7. Mintz, *Ḥurban* p. 211.
8. The English translation appeared in *Jerusalem Quarterly*, Summer 1983; the excerpt is on p. 48.

5. Frost on the Earth

1. Mintz, *Ḥurban* p. 215.
2. Ibid., p. 216.
3. A. Appelfeld, *Kefor Al Ha'aretz* (Jerusalem: Makor/Massada, 1965), p. 124. (Translated by Gila Ramras-Rauch.)

6. On the Ground Floor

1. A. Appelfeld, *Bekomat Ha'karka* (Tel Aviv: Dagga, 1968), p. 7. (Translated by Gila Ramras-Rauch.)
2. A. Appelfeld, "Together," *Jewish Quarterly*, Autumn 1970. (Translated by R. Westbrook.)
3. Mintz, *Ḥurban* p. 221.
4. *Shefa Quarterly* 1, no. 1 (Summer 1977).

7. The Foundations of the River

1. A. Appelfeld, *Adnei Ha'nahar* (Tel Aviv: Hakibbutz Hameuchad, 1971), p. 72. (Translated by Gila Ramras-Rauch).
2. Dan Miron, *Pinkas Patuach* (Current Israeli prose-fiction views and reviews) (Tel Aviv: Sifriat Poalim, 1979), pp. 49–51.

8. *Tzili: The Story of a Life*

1. A. Appelfeld, *Tzili: The Story of a Life* (New York: E. P. Dutton, 1983), p. 21.

2. A different reading is suggested by Esther Fuchs in *Israeli Mythogynies* (Albany: State University of New York Press, 1987): "Bertha, in Aharon Appelfeld's 'Bertha' (1962), and Tzili . . . are both chronically retarded, and because they were born with this mental disease, they are doomed to live and die without the psychological breakthrough which often redeems their male counterparts" (p. 20).

3. Interview with Clive Sinclair in "Writers Talk: Ideas of Our Time" for the series *Writers in Conversation*, Roland Collection, ICA Video.

9. *The Skin and the Gown*

1. A. Appelfeld, *Ha'or Ve'hakutonet* (Tel Aviv: Am Oved, 1971).

10. *The Searing Light*

1. Interview with Avraham Balaban in the Israeli newspaper *Yediot Aharonot*, June 27, 1980.

2. A. Appelfeld, *Michavat Ha'or* (Tel Aviv: Hakibbutz Hameuchad, 1980), p. 107. (Translated by Gila Ramras-Rauch.)

11. *The Immortal Bartfuss*

1. A. Appelfeld, *The Immortal Bartfuss* (New York: Weidenfeld & Nicolson, 1988). This novel appeared in Hebrew in *Ha'kutonet Ve'hapassim* (The shirt and the stripes) (Tel Aviv: Hakibbutz Hameuchad, 1983), which also includes the novel translated as *Tzili*.

12. *The Pupil of the Eye*

1. A. Appelfeld, *Ke' Ishon Ha'ayin* (Tel Aviv: Hakibbutz Hameuchad, 1973). The novel was translated by Hillel Halkin as "Apple of the Eye" but has not been published in book form. Selected chapters appeared in *Forthcoming*, November 1982.

2. Interview with Sinclair for the series *Writers in Conversation*.

13. *Badenheim 1939*

1. "Badenheim, Ir Nofesh" (Badenheim, resort town) appeared as one of two short narratives in A. Appelfeld, *Shanim Ve' shaot* (Tel Aviv: Hakibbutz Hameuchad, 1975). A separate book entitled *Badenheim, Ir Nofesh* appeared in Hebrew in 1980 (same publisher). The English translation, A. Appelfeld, *Badenheim 1939* (Boston: David R. Godine, 1980), altered the title and thus placed this short novel in a historical context. The text has appeared in other English translations, but I prefer this one, by Dalya Bilu. The quotation is from p.1.

2. Ruth R. Wisse, "Aharon Appelfeld, Survivor," *Commentary*, August 1983.

3. M. L. Rozenblit, *The Jews of Vienna 1867–1914* (Albany: State University of New York Press, 1983), p. 195.

14. *The Age of Wonders*

1. A. Appelfeld, *The Age of Wonders*, trans. Dalya Bilu (Boston: David R. Godine, 1981).
2. George Steiner, "Bad Blood," *New Yorker*, March 2, 1992.
3. M. A. Meyer, "The German Jews: Some Perspectives on their History," the B.C. Rudolph Lectures in Judaic Studies, Syracuse University, January 1991, pp. 1, 6–7.
4. Interview with Sinclair for the series *Writers in Conversation*.

15. *The Healer*

1. A. Appelfeld, *The Healer* (New York: Grove Weidenfeld, 1990), pp. 135, 136.

16. *The Retreat*

1. A. Appelfeld, *The Retreat*, trans. Dalya Bilu (New York: E. P. Dutton, 1984). First published in Hebrew under the title "Ha'pisgah" (The summit) in *Bitzaron*, Winter–Spring 1982.

17. *To the Land of the Cattails*

1. A. Appelfeld, *To the Land of the Cattails* (New York: Weidenfeld & Nicolson, 1986). The story has not appeared in book form in Hebrew.

18. *Tongue of Fire*

1. A. Appelfeld, *Rizpat Esh* (Tongue of fire) (Jerusalem: Keter and Hakibbutz Hameuchad, 1988).

19. *For Every Sin*

1. A. Appelfeld, *For Every Sin*, trans. Jeffrey M. Green (New York: Vintage International/Random House, 1989), p. 16.
2. Sander L. Gilman, *Jewish Self-Hate: Anti-Semitism and the Hidden Language of the Jews* (Baltimore: Johns Hopkins University Press, 1986), p. 4.
3. Ibid., p. 18.

20. *Katerina*

1. Y. Ginosar, review of *Katerina*, *Iton* 77, August–September 1989. (Translated by Gila Ramras-Rauch.)

21. *The Railway*

1. H. Hazaz, "The Sermon," in R. Alter, ed., *Modern Hebrew Literature* (New York: Behrman House, 1975), p. 275.
2. A. Appelfeld, *Mesilat Barzel* (Jerusalem: Maxwell-Macmillan-Keter, 1991).

Afterword

1. Wayne C. Booth, *The Rhetoric of Fiction* (Chicago: University of Chicago Press, 1961), pp. 67, 86.

2. Interview with Sinclair for the series *Writers in Conversation.*

3. Wisse, "Aharon Appelfeld, Survivor."

4. T. Carmi, ed. and trans., *The Penguin Book of Hebrew Verse* (New York: Penguin Books, 1981), p. 379.

5. Hazaz, "The Sermon," p. 278.

6. Alvin H. Rosenfeld, *A Double Dying: Reflections on Holocaust Literature* (Bloomington: Indiana University Press, 1980), p. 19.

BIBLIOGRAPHY

Appelfeld's Books in Hebrew

Ashan (Smoke). Jerusalem: Achshav, 1962.
Ba'guy Ha'poreh (In the fertile valley). Jerusalem: Schocken, 1963.
Kefor Al Ha'aretz (Frost on the earth). Ramat Gan: Massada, 1965.
Bekomat Ha'karka (On the ground floor). Tel Aviv: Dagga, 1968.
Adnei Ha'nahar (The foundations of the river). Tel Aviv: Hakibbutz Hameuchad, 1971.
Ha'or Ve'hakutonet (The skin and the gown). Tel Aviv: Am Oved, 1971.
Ke' Ishon Ha'ayin (The pupil of the eye). Tel Aviv: Hakibbutz Hameuchad, 1973.
Shanim Ve'shaot (Years and hours). Tel Aviv: Hakibbutz Hameuchad, 1975. (Includes "Badenheim, Resort Town" and "1946.")
Kemeah Aidim (Like a hundred witnesses). Tel Aviv: Hakibbutz Hameuchad, 1975. (Selected short stories published previously.)
Tor Ha'pelaot (The age of wonders). Tel Aviv: Hakibbutz Hameuchad, 1978.
Massot Be'guf Rishon (Essays in first person). Jerusalem: Zionist Library, 1979.
Michvat Ha'or (The searing light). Tel Aviv: Hakibbutz Hameuchad, 1980.
Badenheim, Ir Nofesh (Badenheim, resort town). Tel Aviv: Hakibbutz Hameuchad, 1980.
Ha'kutonet Vehapassim (The shirt and the stripes). Tel Aviv: Hakibbutz Hameuchad, 1983. (Includes the Hebrew versions of *Tzili: The Story of a Life* and *The Immortal Bartfuss*.)
Be'et Uve'ona Ahat (At one and the same time). Jerusalem and Tel Aviv: Keter and Hakibbutz Hameuchad, 1985. Translated into English as *The Healer*.)
Rizpat Esh (Tongue of fire). Jerusalem and Tel Aviv: Keter and Hakibbutz Hameuchad, 1988.
Katerina. Jerusalem: Keter, 1989.
El Eretz Ha'gomeh (To the land of the cattails). (Chapters 1–3 appeared in *Bitzaron*, April 1990–April 1991. One chapter appeared in *Achshav*, Spring 1984.)
Mesilat Barzel (The railway). Jerusalem: Maxwell-Macmillan-Keter, 1991.

English Translations of Appelfeld's Books

In the Wilderness. Trans. Tirza Sandbank (with the exception of "Three," trans. Sidney Berg, and "Cold Spring," trans. J. Sloane). Jerusalem: Achshav, 1965. (Stories from *Ashan*.)

Badenheim 1939. Trans. Dalya Bilu. Boston: David R. Godine, 1980. (Novelization of earlier story.)

The Age of Wonders. Trans. Dalya Bilu. Boston: David R. Godine, 1981.

Tzili: The Story of a Life. Trans. Dalya Bilu. New York: E. P. Dutton, 1983.

The Retreat. Trans. Dalya Bilu. New York: E. P. Dutton, 1984.

To the Land of the Cattails. Trans. Jeffrey M. Green. New York: Weidenfeld & Nicolson, 1986.

The Immortal Bartfuss. Trans. Jeffrey M. Green. New York: Weidenfeld & Nicolson, 1988.

For Every Sin. Trans. Jeffrey M. Green. New York: Vintage International/Random House, 1989. (Originally published by Weidenfeld & Nicolson.)

The Healer. Trans. Jeffrey M. Green. New York: Grove Weidenfeld, 1990.

Katerina. Trans. Jeffrey M. Green. New York: Random House, 1992.

Appelfeld's Short Stories in English Publications

"1945." Trans. Michael Swirsky. *Present Tense*, New York, 1978, vol. 5, no. 3, pp. 42–45.

"1946." Trans. Dalya Bilu. *Jerusalem Quarterly*, Spring 1978, vol. 26, no. 1.

"A Dream of the Sea." Trans. Yishai Tobin. *Jewish Spectator*, Summer 1978, vol. 43, no. 2, pp. 19–25.

"Apple of the Eye." Trans. Hillel Halkin. Supplement to *Moment*, November 1982, no. 1, pp. 14–16. (Chaps. 11 and 19 of the novel *Ke'Ishon Ha'ayin*.)

"Badenheim 1939." Trans. Betsy Rosenberg. In *Penguin Book of Jewish Short Stories*, Penguin Books, 1979, pp. 141–168.

"Badenheim 1939." Trans. Betsy Rosenberg. *Ariel*, 1974, no. 35, pp. 3–20.

"Bearing Up." *Forum*, Jerusalem, Fall/Winter 1979, no. 36, pp. 185–191.

"Bertha." Trans. Tirza Sandbank. In *Facing the Holocaust: Selected Israeli Fiction*, pp. 143–159.

"Changing the Guard." Trans. Jeffrey M. Green. *Ariel*, 1983, no. 55, pp. 7–11.

"In the Isles of St. George." Trans. Dalya Bilu. *Jerusalem Quarterly*, Summer 1983, no. 28, pp. 48–72.

"In the Wilderness." Trans. Tirza Sandbank. In *Gates to the New City: A Treasury of Modern Jewish Tales*. Avon Books, New York, 1980, pp. 160–164.

"Kitty." Trans. Tirza Sandbank. In *Modern Hebrew Stories*, Bantam Books, New York, 1971 (English and Hebrew).

"Near the Shore." *Hadassah*, New York, January 1966, vol. 47, no. 5, pp. 8–9, 29–30.

"Pilgrimage to Kazansk." *Shefa Quarterly*, Summer 1977, vol. 1, pp. 10–21. Also appeared in *Orot*, August 1970 (English and Hebrew).

"Soul's Friend." Trans. Michael Swirsky. *Moment*, May 1980, vol. 5, no. 5, pp. 51–55.

"The Betrayal." Trans. R. Westbrook. *European Judaism*, London, Summer 1969, vol. 4, no. 1, pp. 10–14.
"The First Night." Trans. Richard Flantz. *Modern Hebrew Literature*, Israel, Winter 1978, vol. 4, no. 4, pp. 22–32.
"The Hunt" (incomplete). Trans. Nicholas De Lang. *Tel Aviv Review*, 1989, vol. 2, pp. 29–37.
"The Journey." Trans. Murray Roston. *Israel Argosy*, 1967, no. 9, pp. 38–62.
"The Messenger." Trans. Barbara S. Benavie. *Present Tense*, Winter 1982, vol. 9, no. 2, pp. 51–55.
"The Road from Drovna to Drovitch." Trans. Edward L. Levenston. *Ariel*, 1966, no. 16., pp. 27–38.
"The Road to Myself." Trans. Arthur C. Jacobs. *Jewish Quarterly*, Autumn 1966, vol. 14, no. 3, pp. 23–24.
"The Woman." Trans. David Strassler. *Present Tense*, 1979, vol. 7, no. 1, pp. 43–45.
"Together." Trans. R. Westbrook. *Jewish Quarterly*, Autumn 1970, vol. 18, no. 3, pp. 45–47.

Selected Secondary Sources

Aschkenasy, Nehama. *Eve's Journey: Feminine Images in Hebraic Literary Tradition*. Philadelphia: University of Pennsylvania Press, 1986.
Bauman, Zygmunt. *Modernity and the Holocaust*. Ithaca, N.Y.: Cornell University Press, 1989.
Berger, Alan L. *Crisis and Covenant: The Holocaust in American Jewish Fiction*. Albany: State University of New York, 1985.
Blanchot, Maurice. *The Writing of Disaster*. Trans. Ann Smock. Lincoln: University of Nebraska Press, 1986.
Chertok, Haim. *We Are All Close: Conversations with Israeli Writers*. New York: Fordham University Press, 1989.
Cohen, Joseph. *Voices of Israel*. Albany: State University of New York Press, 1990. (Chap. 4: Aharon Appelfeld.)
Ezrahi, Sidra Dekoven. *By Words Alone: The Holocaust in Literature*. Chicago: University of Chicago Press, 1980.
Fuchs, Esther. *Encounters With Israeli Authors*. Marblehead, Mass.: Micha, 1982.
———. *Israeli Mythogynies: Women in Contemporary Hebrew Fiction*. Albany: State University of New York Press, 1987.
Gilman, Sander L. *Jewish Self-Hate: Anti-Semitism and the Hidden Language of the Jews*. Baltimore: Johns Hopkins University Press, 1986.
Govrin, Nurit. "To Express the Inexpressible: The Holocaust Literature of Aharon Appelfeld." In *Remembering for the Future: Theme II*, pp. 1580–1594. Oxford: Pergamon, 1988.
Lang, Berel. *Act and Idea in the Nazi Genocide*. Chicago: University of Chicago Press, 1990.
———, ed. *Writing and the Holocaust*. New York: Holmes & Meier, 1988.

Langer, Lawrence. *The Holocaust and the Literary Imagination*. New Haven, Conn.: Yale University Press, 1975.

——. *Versions of Survival: The Holocaust and the Human Spirit*. Albany: State University of New York, 1982

——. *Holocaust Testimonies: The Ruins of Memory*. New Haven, Conn.: Yale University Press, 1991.

——. "Aharon Appelfeld and the Uses of Language and Silence." In *Remembering for the Future: Theme II*, pp. 1602–1609. Oxford: Pergamon, 1988.

Mazor, Yair. "Shirat Ha'sofer, O: Sippuro Ha'nachon Shel Ha'regesh" (The poetry of the author, or: the correct story of the emotion). *Aley Siach* 21, 1986.

McCagg, William O., Jr. *A History of the Habsburg Jews, 1670–1918*. Bloomington: Indiana University Press, 1989.

Mintz, Alan. *Ḥurban:* Responses to Catastrophe in Hebrew Literature. New York: Columbia University Press, 1984.

Miron, Dan. *Pinkas Patuach* (Current Israeli prose-fiction views and reviews). Tel Aviv: Sifriat Poalim, 1979.

Patterson, David. *The Shriek of Silence: A Phenomenology of the Holocaust Novel*. Lexington: University Press of Kentucky, 1992.

Ramras-Rauch, Gila. "The Phenomenology of Time, Space and Silence in Holocaust Literature." In *Remembering for the Future: Theme II*, pp. 1610–1617. Oxford: Pergamon, 1988.

——. "The Holocaust and the Fantastic: A Negative Revelation?" In R. A. Collins and H. D. Pearce, *The Scope of the Fantastic: Culture, Biography, Themes, Children's Literature*. Westport, Conn.: Greenwood Press, 1985.

——. *The Protagonist in Transition: Studies in Modern Fiction*. Berne and Frankfort on Main, 1982.

Ramras-Rauch, Gila, and Joseph Michman-Melkman, eds. *Facing The Holocaust: Selected Israeli Fiction*. Philadelphia: Jewish Publication Society, 1985.

Rattok, Lily. *Bayit al blima* (A precarious hose: The narrative art of A. Appelfeld). Tel Aviv: Ḥekker, 1989.

Rosenfeld, Alvin H. *A Double Dying: Reflections on Holocaust Literature*. Bloomington: Indiana University Press, 1980.

Roskies, David. *Against the Apocalypse: Responses to Catastrophe in Modern Jewish Culture*. Cambridge, Mass.: Harvard University Press, 1984.

Rozenblit, Marsha L. *The Jews of Vienna, 1867–1914: Assimilation and Identity*. Albany: State University of New York Press, 1983.

Schwartz, Yig'al. "Be'ein roeh tavona hatmurot" (Changes come unnoticeably). *Aley Siach* 21, 1986.

Shaked, Gershon. *Gal ḥadash ba'siporet ha'ivrit* (A new wave in Hebrew fiction). Tel Aviv: Sifriat Palim, 1971.

——. *Ein makom aḥer* (No other place: On literature and society). Tel Aviv: Hakibbutz Hameuchad, 1983.

Steiner, George. "Bad Friday" (on Thomas Nevin's *Simone Weil: Portrait of a Self-Exiled Jew*). *New Yorker*, March 2, 1992.

Wisse, Ruth R. "Aharon Appelfeld, Survivor." *Commentary*, August 1983.

Yaoz, Hanna. *Ha'shoah beshirat dor ha'medina*. Tel Aviv: Ekked, 1984.

Yerushalmi, Yosef Hayim. *Zachor: Jewish History and Jewish Memory.* Seattle: University of Washington Press, 1982.

Young, James E. *Writing and Rewriting the Holocaust: Narrative and the Consequences of Interpretation*. Bloomington: Indiana University Press, 1988.

INDEX

DR. GILA RAMRAS-RAUCH is the Lewis H. Weinstein Professor of Jewish Literature at Hebrew College, Boston. Among her books are *The Arab in Israeli Literature* and *The Protagonist in Transition*. She served as chief editor of the anthology *Facing the Holocaust*.

DR. GILA RAMRAS-RAUCH is the Lewis H. Weinstein Professor of Jewish Literature at Hebrew College, Boston. Among her books are *The Arab in Israeli Literature* and *The Protagonist in Transition*. She served as chief editor of the anthology *Facing the Holocaust*.